THE AESTHETICS OF VIOLENCE
IN THE PROPHETS

edited by

Julia M. O'Brien
and
Chris Franke

t & t clark

NEW YORK • LONDON

Published by T & T Clark International
A Continuum imprint
80 Maiden Lane, New York, NY 10038
The Tower Building, 11 York Road, London SE1 7NX

www.continuumbooks.com

Visit the T & T Clark blog at www.tandtclarkblog.com

Library of Congress Cataloging-in-Publication Data
A catalog record for this book is available from the Library of Congress.

ISBN: 978-0-567-54811-5 (hardback)

Typeset and copy-edited by Forthcoming Publications Ltd. (www.forthpub.com)
Printed in the United States of America

CONTENTS

CONTRIBUTORS

Corrine Carvalho, University of Saint Thomas

Cynthia R. Chapman, Oberlin College

Robert D. Haak, Augustana College

Mary Mills, Liverpool Hope University

Julia M. O'Brien, Lancaster Theological Seminary

Kathleen M. O'Connor, Columbia Theological Seminary

Carolyn J. Sharp, Yale Divinity School

Yvonne Sherwood, University of Glasgow

Daniel L. Smith-Christopher, Loyola Marymount University

ABBREVIATIONS

AB	Anchor Bible
BETL	Bibliotheca Ephemeridum Theologicarum Lovaniensium
BibInt	*Biblical Interpretation*
BR	*Biblical Research*
BZAW	Beihefte zur Zeitschrift für die alttestamentliche Wissenschaft
CAD	*The Assyrian Dictionary of the Oriental Institute of the University of Chicago.* Chicago, 1956–
CCS	Continental Commentaries Series
FOTL	Forms of Old Testament Literature
HCOT	Historical Commentary on the Old Testament
HSM	Harvard Semitic Monographs
HUCA	*Hebrew Union College Annual*
Int	*Interpretation*
JAAR	*Journal of the American Academy of Religion*
JANESCU	*Journal of the Ancient Near Eastern Society of Columbia University*
JSOT	*Journal for the Study of the Old Testament*
JSOTSup	Journal for the Study of the Old Testament: Supplement Series
LHBOTS	Library of Hebrew Bible/Old Testament Studies
OTE	*Old Testament Essays*
OTL	Old Testament Library
SBLDS	Society of Biblical Literature Dissertation Series
VT	*Vetus Testamentum*
VTSup	Vetus Testamentum: Supplement Series
WBC	Word Biblical Commentary

INTRODUCTION:
ENGAGING CONVERSATION ABOUT VIOLENCE

Background Discussions

As its name would imply, Prophetic Texts and their Ancient Contexts (PTAC) is a unit of the Society of Biblical Literature devoted to exploring prophets, prophecy, and prophetic literature—all in light of the ancient Near East. The program unit aims to be interdisciplinary and international, bringing together diverse scholars who read and work in different ways. Our interests are not antiquarian, however. We care about the past for its sake and also for its ability to help us think about and respond to the contemporary world.

The events of 9/11/01 spurred the PTAC steering committee to consider the intersecting themes of violence, religious violence, and violent texts. We were aware that earlier academic conferences had taken up these issues from explicitly-religious perspectives. For example, at the 2005 meeting of the Catholic Biblical Society a seminar on Divinity in Ancient Israel was devoted to "Reading the Bible's Violence in a Judaeo-Christian community." That conversation focused on the question of how the truth claims of Jews and Christians complicate their responses to biblical texts that ascribe violence to Israel's deity. Should believers reject violent texts, try to understand them in historical context, and/or justify the violence of God on theological grounds?

The PTAC steering committee pondered how our own field of study—the ancient dimensions of prophetic texts—might offer a distinctive way to approach these and related questions. How might contemporary understandings of violence be enriched, challenged, or redirected by thoughtful analysis of biblical prophetic texts in their ancient Near Eastern contexts? We decided to focus the theme of our 2006 session on The Aesthetics of Violence, the consideration of how the violent imagery and rhetoric of the prophetic texts work, particularly but not exclusively in the past. What do violent images do to readers in the past and present? Do they encourage violent behavior and/or provide an alternative to actual violence? How do depictions of violence define boundaries between and within communities? What can and should readers make of the disturbing rhetoric of violent prophets?

Participants in our 2006 session were invited to explore multiple dimensions of prophetic texts and their violent rhetoric. The results were rich and varied, as some considered the function of violent images in ancient Near Eastern art and in modern film and others advanced our understanding of the poetic skill required for invoking terror through words. The ensuing discussion was lively and engaging, so much so that Andrew Mein, co-editor of the LHBOTS series, invited us to seek additional contributions and shape the whole into the current volume.

The Collection

The essays gathered here go beyond the simplistic question of "is prophetic violence good or bad?" to explore more deeply the complex interactions between rhetoric and behavior and the diverse effects of "beauty" on the reader. Most, to some degree, catalogue the aesthetic literary features of the prophets, but all go far beyond such treatments to explore the complexity of ancient and modern engagement with their violent themes. Some keep their attention focused on the ancient world (Haak and Chapman); some trace comparisons between the language of the prophets and that of contemporary orators (Sharp and Smith-Christopher); some approach our assignment through distinctive theoretical angles (O'Connor, trauma theory; Mills, vampire studies; O'Brien, film criticism); some are explicitly theological (O'Connor and Carvalho). But some common themes emerge. Each essay, in its own way, challenges the assumption that violent images always serve to incite violence. All point to the various ways in which violent rhetoric and images "work"— depending on the social location of the audience. All recognize that defining violence is a subjective task, and many speak autobiographically in response.

Cynthia Chapman places biblical prophetic texts in conversation with Assyrian iconography, particularly the royal palace reliefs. She details the ways in which the violent images of Assyrian art are gendered, how they exalt the king by enhancing his masculinity and demean the enemy through scenes of penetration. She applies these findings to Ezek 23, in which a female-personified Jerusalem gazes at wall images of Chaldeans, finding similar sexual tropes. Her work illumines both the Assyrian reliefs and the motifs of the prophetic text.

Robert Haak uses Zeph 2 as a point of departure for discussing the way in prophetic texts responded to the historical/political situations in which they were produced. Violent rhetoric, he shows, functions differently in times of victory than in times of defeat—differently in the eighth century than in the sixth, He argues that the biblical authors themselves struggled with divine power and violence and urges contemporary scholars do the same. Confronting violence and violent language may help a society to decide against its use.

Kathleen O'Connor applies the insights of Trauma and Disaster studies to the book of Jeremiah, arguing that the prophet's harsh language functions as a survival strategy and instrument of healing. A disaster can overpower the senses and render people unable feel, speak, and take in what has happened to them, dooming them to reenact memories of calamity until they can begin to interpret them. To the communities who experienced the Babylonian attack and exile, the war poems in Jeremiah offer language for naming what has happened to them, reframing their experiences, and rebuilding their lives. Such language is provisional, imperfect, and temporary, and must be interpreted from the perspective of those who experienced violence.

Carolyn Sharp "explores the aesthetics of prophetic diction in the book of Hosea," and compares it with the so-called "Damn America" sermon of the Reverend Jeremiah Wright, made (in)famous during the 2008 U.S. Presidential race. She argues that the book of Hosea and Wright's sermon both are performative rhetoric, shocking hearers not only by what they say but also how they say it. In both cases, the speaker creates a scathing image of the nation's history in order to provoke consent to his conclusion: that the nation is damned. She offers a careful study of Hosea's rhetorical techniques and offers insightful parallels with Wright's address to his own audience.

Daniel Smith-Christopher compares Micah's rhetoric with that of Stokely Carmichael, a "Black Power" activist during the 1960s U. S. Civil Rights movement. He argues that neither "prophet" promoted or celebrated violence. Just as Carmichael's fiery speeches sought to arrest the attention of white listeners and empower black listeners, the threats leveled in Mic 1:6 and 3:12 sought to empower the small farmers who had lost their land in the social upheavals of eighth century Israel.

Yvonne Sherwood demonstrates the problem that violent prophetic rhetoric has posed for the "Liberal Bible" (the view that the Bible teaches hospitality and generosity and makes space for freedom and power) and the "Literary Bible" (the view that the Bible epitomizes high culture and classical rhetoric). The former can cast the prophets as promoting good behaviour—defending the widow and the orphan, promoting equality for all—only by sidelining divine violence. The latter struggles to respond to the prophets' visceral, disjunctive language. Sherwood offers John Donne and Donald Barthelme as fit literary companions for the prophets. All of these authors articulate an antagonistic, violent relationship between author and reader and expose the intersection between violence, aesthetics, and gender. Tracing the political ramifications of accepting biblical thinking on violence, she notes that the very structures that readers condemn in the Bible are often unwittingly adopted in culture.

Julia M. O'Brien considers how the book of Nahum, notorious for its depictions of Yahweh as a warrior and Nineveh as a woman threatened with rape, looks when read in light of contemporary film theory. Devoting special attention to feminist film theory and discussion of the social role of combat film, she concludes that the "realism" of Nahum may not necessarily derive from the book's temporal and psychological proximity to the trauma of Assyrian control. It may also function in other ways—including psycho-sexually and patriotically.

Corrine Carvalho begins her essay with the confession that she likes the prophets' depictions of a bloody God and proceeds to trace the nature of her fascination along personal and scholarly lines. Her study and reflection on the prophetic depictions of God as a bloody warrior range widely: thinking through the appeal of violent movies; carefully studying rhetorical devices in Nahum, Zeph 1, and Isa 63; analyzing ancient Near Eastern depictions of the warrior goddess Anat; and employing theological explorations of the "grotesque." She argues that the questions raised by such texts are hermeneutical and ultimately theological, and she explains that these images of God are satisfying for her because they insist on the otherness and pathos of God.

Mary Mills reads Amos in conversation with the work of Steve Pile, who traces the dynamics of vampire stories and particularly the motif of the vampire as threat to the urban elite. Like the character of the vampire, God and the prophet function in the book of Amos as a semi-sympathetic monster: Amos "pays homage to the monster [God]," without denying the terror the deity inspires. Like Carvalho, Mills sees violent prophetic rhetoric as provoking a profound sense of awe and the Sublime.

Our Hopes

These essays, singly and as a collection, raise important questions about the function of the violent image, in the past and in the present. We present them here hoping that they will continue to generate discussion and, perhaps, to contribute to the creation of a less violent world.

Julia M. O'Brien   Chris Franke
Lancaster Theological Seminary   *College of St. Catherine*

SCULPTED WARRIORS:
SEXUALITY AND THE SACRED IN THE DEPICTION OF WARFARE IN THE ASSYRIAN PALACE RELIEFS AND IN EZEKIEL 23:14–17*

Cynthia R. Chapman

The place of violent images within a definition of visual aesthetic values can never be clearly defined. What one considers violent and how one responds to violent images remains culturally constrained. This study explores the aesthetics of violence in the visual imagination of the ancient Near East, specifically focusing on violent images represented in the Assyrian palace reliefs. While the palace reliefs include depictions of Assyrian kings as builders, worshippers, hunters, and warriors, this study will examine a subset of the reliefs containing scenes of military siege and battle. These siege and battle scenes are examples of state-sponsored art in which violence is depicted with skill and even beauty in order to communicate what the Assyrian kings referred to as the "radiance" and "awe" of their weapons. According to Assyrian royal inscriptions, the radiance of a king's weapons was a gift transferred to him by the gods and a power that brought terror and defeat to the enemy. When we turn to the visual records of warfare depicted on the palace reliefs, we find repeated visual tropes. These tropes depict, on the one hand, the awesome splendor of the Assyrian king's divinely empowered weapons. On the other hand, they show the terrifying violence that left the enemy male sexually exposed, dismembered, and penetrated by Assyrian weapons. The sculptors' choices regarding how to depict military power and violence reveal an indigenous royal vocabulary for the aesthetics of empire that intersected with the power of both the sacred and the sexual.

   The primary sources for this study include the siege and battle scenes of the Assyrian palace reliefs dating from the reign of Ashurnasirpal II in the mid-ninth century through that of Ashurbanipal in the late seventh

   *   An earlier version of this article appeared in *Lectio Difficilior* 1 (2007), online: http://www.lectio.unibe.ch/07_1/chapman_sculpted_warriors.htm (accessed 17 February 2010).

century B.C.E. In addition to the art-historical record, I will also turn to the Assyrian royal inscriptions for textual descriptions of the king, his army, his weaponry, and the violence the king claimed to have inflicted upon the enemy in battle. Finally, I will include one biblical example from Ezek 23:14–17 of what I term "an imagined moment of aesthetic appreciation for Babylonian military state art." This example, despite its focus on Babylonian rather than Assyrian military art, will help us to consider a viewer's response to skillful and ornate depictions of military conquerors and their victims.

Defining the Aesthetics of Violence for the Neo-Assyrian Period

The Assyrian palace reliefs were discovered and excavated in the nineteenth century by European archaeologists. Sculpted on enormous limestone panels and mounted on the palace walls, the reliefs formed a visual narrative asserting the Assyrian kings' legitimately earned power. As state-sponsored art, the reliefs functioned on an ideological level communicating each king's divinely sanctioned rule over what Assyrian inscriptions termed "the four corners of the world."[1] Several types of scenes are present in each of the palaces for which there is a surviving excavated record. These include depictions of the king tending to the sacred tree and worshipping the gods, hunting scenes in which the king defeats lions and bears, images that record the building and decoration of the palaces and temples, and finally, visual records of the king's military campaigns. As a whole, the reliefs formed what art historian Irene Winter has termed a "decorative program" that asserts the king's legitimately earned power.[2] For the present study of the siege and battle reliefs, it is important to note that these battle scenes were often placed within the reception suites of the king's palace.[3] Thus, if one were awaiting an audience with the king, one would be viewing the king's military conquests of foreign lands.

1. For a complete history of the archaeological excavation of Iraq and the concomitant establishment of the museum as a state institution in Europe and America, see Magnus T. Bernhardsson, *Reclaiming a Plundered Past: Archaeology and Nation Building in Modern Iraq* (Austin: University of Texas Press, 2005); Mogens Trolle Larsen, *The Conquest of Assyria: Excavations in an Antique Land, 1840–1860* (London: Routledge, 1994).
2. Irene Winter, "Royal Rhetoric and the Development of Historical Narrative in Neo-Assyrian Reliefs," *Studies in Visual Communication* 7 (1981): 2–38.
3. John Malcolm Russell, *Sennacherib's Palace without Rival in Nineveh* (Chicago: University of Chicago Press, 1991); Pauline Albenda, "Expressions of Kingship in Assyrian Art," *JANESCU* 2 (1969): 41–52.

Defining the aesthetics of violence and the function of the depiction of violence in the Assyrian palace relief siege and battle scenes necessarily involves an exploration of the application of the term "aesthetics" to the ancient world in general and to the palace reliefs in particular. Similarly, because the term aesthetics has always encompassed the "viewer" of a work of art, we will also need to consider the intended audiences of and the hoped for responses to the Assyrian siege and battle scenes. Finally, there has been an unfortunate history of associating all Assyrian art with violence and correlating such violence to crude artistic abilities and a lack of aesthetic judgment. This history requires that we contextualize the siege and battle scenes within the larger repertoire of Assyrian royal art.

Methodologically, I am indebted to the work of Irene Winter who has begun to address the problematic issues related to applying an eight-eenth- and nineteenth-century European term such as "aesthetics" to the ancient Mesopotamian context. Her working definition for ancient Meso-potamian aesthetics will form the starting point for my consideration of the aesthetics of violence in Assyrian military state-sponsored art.[4] The work of Leo Bersani and Ulysse Dutoit entitled *Forms of Violence* and Zainab Bahrani's *The Graven Image* will also inform and interrogate my understanding of the function of violence in the Assyrian palace reliefs.[5]

There is currently no scholarly agreement on the definition and use of the term "aesthetics." There is a modern/postmodern debate over the role of beauty in aesthetic judgments and over the place and attitude of the spectator. Irene Winter begins her discussion of aesthetics by rejecting any universalized notion of "beauty" and any notion of a disinterested spectator.[6] Winter then offers her own working definitions of the terms "art" and "aesthetics" that she argues can appropriately account for and be applied to the art of ancient Mesopotamia. For Winter, "art" includes "works of human agency, for which skill is required and to which stan-dards of correctness have been applied, a portion of the function of which is to be visually and emotionally affective."[7] "Aesthetics" is con-cerned with "the properties of, investment in, and appreciative response

4. Irene Winter, "Defining 'Aesthetics' for Non-Western Studies: The Case of Ancient Mesopotamia," in *Art History, Aesthetics, Visual Studies* (ed. Michael Ann Holly and Keith Moxey; Williamstown, Mass.: Sterling & Francine Clark Art Institute, 2002), 3–19.

5. Leo Bersani and Ulysse Dutoit, *The Forms of Violence: Narrative in Assyrian Art and Modern Culture* (New York: Schocken, 1985); Zainab Bahrani, *The Graven Image: Representation in Babylonia and Assyria* (Philadelphia: University of Pennsylvania Press, 2003), 66–72.

6. Winter, "Defining 'Aesthetics'," 7–8.

7. Ibid., 11.

to works of human agency, for which skill is required and to which standards of correctness have been applied, a *portion* (but not all) of the function of which is to be visually affective and emotionally affecting."[8] The final phrase of this definition contains Winter's alternative to the requirements of beauty and disinterestedness. Rather than be beautiful, a work must be visually affective, and rather than be disinterested, the spectator should be emotionally affected.

In order to determine how people of ancient Mesopotamia might have judged the visual and emotional response elicited by a work of art, Winter seeks to establish an "indigenous vocabulary" for responses to works of art in Mesopotamia. She draws this vocabulary exclusively from written texts of ancient Mesopotamia. Surveying a broad range of Akkadian texts, Winter identifies six terms or qualities that define an ancient Mesopotamian concept of aesthetics. These include: the capacity to elicit a powerful emotional response; the ability for the work to elicit "joy" or "wonder"; the attribute of "light" and/or "radiance"; the value accorded to "ornament"; fitness for the intended task or role to be played; and "beauty" as understood and articulated in its ancient Mesopotamian context. She also adds that, "no sources separate aesthetic experience from experience of the wondrous and/or of the sacred."[9]

Violence and Aesthetics in Assyrian Siege and Battle Reliefs

Visual Tropes of Violence

Turning to an examination of the reliefs themselves, we find that if we compare several siege reliefs we can identify repeated tropes of violence that seem to form necessary components of the battle narrative: a battering ram actively breaking into the walls of the besieged city, speared men falling to their deaths from their city's walls, the beheading and flaying of enemy soldiers, the stripped and dismembered bodies of dead soldiers, and finally the naked, impaled bodies of enemy soldiers. For example, in a siege scene from the palace of Ashurnasirpal II (Fig. 1), we note the battering ram penetrating the walls of the tower, which is physically embodied by the head and upper torso of the enemy soldier emerging from the top of the tower. In the scene of Sennacherib's siege of the Judean city of Lachish (Fig. 2), we see multiple battering rams ascending to the walls of the city in cross-diagonal directions. Impaled men hang just outside their city's gate. A naked enemy male hangs vertically from the city wall.

8. Ibid.
9. Ibid., 12–19.

Figure 1. Ashurnasirpal II's assault of a city. Nimrud, Northwest Palace of Ashurnasirpal II, B.M. 124536 (from E. A. Wallis Budge, ed., *Assyrian Sculptures in the British Museum: Reign of Ashur-Nasir-Pal, 885–860 B.C.*, plate XIII).

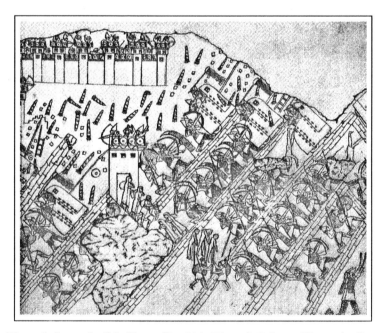

Figure 2. Sennacherib's Siege of Lachish. Nineveh, Palace of Sennacherib (drawing from David Ussishkin).

Finally, in Tiglath-pileser III's siege of an unnamed city (Fig. 3), we note the battering ram, again penetrating the human-headed tower of the city. Three impaled enemy soldiers hang limp in the background, one speared soldier falls to his death, and several naked and dismembered dead are strewn outside their city's walls.[10] A cursory view such as this could lead one to conclude that the violence against the enemy was senseless and indiscriminate, but here is where we must also take note of who and what in the battle reliefs did not become a victim of violence. It is well known, for example, that the Assyrian palace reliefs do not show any casualties on the Assyrian side. The Assyrian king and his army remain clothed, upright, and in charge. What we also find, however, is that enemy women and children are not shown as victims of violence. In fact, many siege scenes take care to show the viewer that enemy women, together with their children, remain clothed and unmolested.[11]

Figure 3. King Tiglath-pileser III leading the storming of a city. Nimrud, Central Palace, B.M. 118903 (from Assyrian Sculptures in the British Museum: From Shalmaneser III to Sennacherib, plate XIV).

10.   The dates for the reigns of these Assyrian kings are 885–859 B.C.E. (Ashur-nasirpal), 744–727 B.C.E. (Tiglath-pileser), and 705–681 B.C.E. (Sennacherib).
11.   For a fuller discussion of the significance of the unmolested presence of women on the palace reliefs, see my *The Gendered Language of Warfare in the Israelite–Assyrian Encounter* (Winona Lake, Ind.: Eisenbrauns, 2004), 46–47.

Decisions about which forms of military violence one depicts and which forms one brackets from view provide clues for developing a preliminary understanding of the role of violence in the aesthetics of the Assyrian siege and battle reliefs. The interest in showing the unmolested state of foreign women and children in deportation lines suggests an Assyrian state aesthetic that would not be served by the depiction of violence against women and children. Similarly, when one looks at the enemy men who become the recipients of violent actions, it is important to note that a limited set of violent actions seems to represent constituent aspects of the Assyrian narrative of military conquest. By "constituent aspects," I mean repeated scenes of violence that appear in the battle and siege scenes of each of the Assyrian kings for whom we have battle and siege reliefs. Each of these stock elements is present within the scene of Tiglath-pileser III's conquest of an unnamed city (Fig. 3): the spearing of the enemy soldier, stripping him, dismembering him, and impaling him.[12]

The Written Record of Royal Boasts

While Winter attempts to articulate a working definition of aesthetics broad enough to encompass the whole range of ancient Mesopotamian art, I would like to use her definition to begin to focus very specifically on the aesthetic values that governed the depiction and bracketing of violence in the military siege and battle scenes of the Assyrian palace reliefs. Keeping in mind Winter's indigenous vocabulary for aesthetics, we can locate several defining traits of ancient Mesopotamian aesthetics within the siege and battle reliefs. One of the first assertions we can make is that these battle and siege scenes with their copious depiction of violent death are indeed appropriately considered works of art governed by aesthetic principles. The palace reliefs are the product of skilled crafts-men, and their construction required an enormous outlay of resources and time. The palace reliefs formed a coherent program of ideologically motivated decoration in each king's palace, and the palace as a whole was thought to embody the wondrous power of the king.[13] We cannot, therefore, separate the depictions of violence from the overall artistic program of the reliefs. To put it another way, we cannot consider a work

12. While Assyrian siege and battle scenes contain a limited set of violent images, Assyrian royal inscriptions are much more detailed and diverse in their descriptions of all manner of violence.

13. Irene Winter, "The Seat of Kingship/A 'Wonder to Behold': The Palace in the Ancient Near East," *Ars Orientalis* 23 (1993): 36–38; Russell, *Sennacherib's Palace without Rival.*

of art apart from its function. Therefore, we must include depictions of violence as part of the desired, projected wonder of the king and his palace.[14]

When we examine the siege and battle scenes in detail, we see that the aesthetic value of ornamentation is clearly visible and ideologically targeted. Returning to the relief of Tiglath-pileser III (Fig. 3), we see that the Assyrian king's uniform, his military machinery, and to some extent his army are all clearly marked through exquisite ornamentation. Likewise, the Assyrian gods are present on the relief as ornamented symbols, or when embodied, as ornamented human figures. The detail accorded the enemy, on the other hand, seems to homogenize enemy soldiers into a single, un-ornamented other.[15] The stripping of the enemy takes this lack of ornamentation to its extreme.[16]

Assyrian royal inscriptions provide a royal accounting of the desired effect of this ornamentation, namely, the qualities of "light" and "radiance," terms Winter identifies as part of the indigenous written vocabulary for aesthetics. In the battle narratives of Assyrian kings, the kings repeatedly refer to the "fear" (*puluḫtu*), "radiance" or "brilliance"

14. I stress here that violence is only a *part* of the overall decorative program of the palaces. I agree with the work of Leo Bersani and Ulysse Dutoit as well as the more recent work of Zainab Bahrani that cautions against equating violence with the Assyrian king and extending that violence descriptively to the Assyrians as a whole. As in all state-sponsored military art, depictions of violence serve the ideological purpose of communicating the power of the ruler. See Bersani and Dutoit, *The Forms of Violence*, 6–7; Bahrani, *The Graven Image*, 66–72. For a summary of early European reactions to the artistic quality of the siege and battle reliefs and the conclusion that they were not "art," see "But is it art?" in Larsen, *The Conquest of Assyria*, 99–107, where the following quotation by Sir Henry Creswicke Rawlinson appears as an early British response to the Assyrian siege and battle reliefs: "Your cases arrived all right and we have been regaling our antiquarian appetites on the contents ever since… The battle pieces, Seiges [*sic*] etc. are curious, but I do not think they rank very highly as art. Ross is altogether disappointed with the specimens and I must confess I think the general style crude and cramped but still the curiosity of the thing is very great, if not a full compensation" (p. 102).

15. For a discussion of clothing vs. nakedness in the palace reliefs of Ashurnasirpal II, see Megan Cifarelli, "Gesture and Alterity in the Art of Aššurnasirpal II of Assyria," *Art Bulletin* 80 (1998): 210–28 (219).

16. Bersani and Dutoit discuss the Assyrian sculptors' use of "the principle of anonymous human alignments as a visual contrast to the isolated individualized king" (Bersani and Dutoit, *Forms of Violence*, 5–6). It is also interesting to note that when enemy men and women are clothed, the details of their clothing mark their ethnicity; when naked, this ethnic distinction is lost.

(*melammu*), and "terror" or "awe" (*šuribtu*) of their weapons.[17] These aesthetically descriptive words communicate a power that was thought to originate from the gods, be transferred to and embodied within the figure of the king, and find expressive power through the king's weapons.[18] It is in the transference of these qualities that we see the ideological alignment of the king, the national deities, and the king's weapons—the sacred, the royal, and the violent. For example, in a standard inscription of Ashurnasirpal II, the king refers to the gods as having "granted to his dominion their fierce weapons (and) made him more marvelous than (any of) the kings of the four quarters with respect to the splendour of his weapons (and) the radiance of his dominion."[19] When Ashurnasirpal II described his first move in a battle, he did so by reporting, "I unleashed against them my lordly radiance (*melam bēlutīya*)."[20] The narrated response to the brilliance of the king and his weapons was fear, as we see in this report from Ashurnasirpal's inscriptions. Describing his attack on the nobles of a conquered king, Ashurnasirpal II claims: "They took fright before the brilliance of my weapons and awe of my dominion" (*namurrat kakkīya šurbat bēlutīya ēdurūma*).[21]

In Sennacherib's third campaign, which included his description of the siege of Jerusalem and his capture of King Hezekiah, his royal inscriptions report, "As for Hezekiah, the terror of the splendor of my lordship (*pulḫi melammē bēlutīya*), overcame him."[22] The same construct chain that combines and thus intensifies the vocabulary of royal radiance and

17. For a fuller discussion of the quality of "radiance" as an aesthetic value in ancient Mesopotamian art, see Irene Winter, "Radiance as an Aesthetic Value in the Art of Mesopotamia (with Some Indian Parallels)," in *Art: The Integral Vision. A Volume of Essays in Felicitation of Kapila Vatsyayan* (ed. B. N. Saraswati, S. C. Malik, and Madhu Khanna; New Delhi: D. K. Printworld, 1994), 123–32; Elena Cassin, *La Splendeur Divine: Introduction à l'étude de la mentalité mésopotamienne* (Civilisations et sociétés 8; Paris: Mouton, 1968).

18. Winter, "Radiance," 124–26.

19. "A.O.101.1," in A. Kirk Grayson, *Assyrian Rulers of the Early First Millennium BC I (1114–859 BC)* (The Royal Inscriptions of Mesopotamia, Assyrian Periods 2; Toronto: University of Toronto Press, 1991), col. i, ll. 26–27.

20. Ibid., col. ii, l. 112a; col. iii, l. 25.

21. Ibid., col. ii, ll. 119–20; See also *CAD*, Š, 344.

22. Translation adapted from Daniel David Luckenbill, *The Annals of Sennacherib* (Chicago: University of Chicago Press, 1924), 31–32, ll. 73–83, 1–49. See also *CAD*, P, 504. A more natural English rendering of the construct chain, "the terror or the splendor of my lordship," is "the terrifying splendor of my lordship." I have opted for the more literal translation to show the effect of piling on vocabulary of royal radiance.

terror is used to describe Sennacherib's encounter with King Lulê of Sidon: "In my third campaign I went against the Hittite-land. Lulê, king of Sidon,—the terror of the splendor of my lordship (*pulḫi melammē bēlutīya*) overcame him and far off into the midst of the sea he fled and died."[23]

While the medium of sculpted stone reliefs may not have been able to capture fully the qualities of the radiance and terror-inducing splendor of the king and his weapons, the selective application of ornamentation may have communicated precisely this radiance.[24] The affective power of the king's radiance became visible through the depiction of violence against the enemy. The violent, humiliating and total death of the enemy testified to the radiant, divinely bestowed power of the king's ornamented weapons.

Sexuality and the Aesthetics of Violence

Penetrating the Enemy

In addition to the indigenous vocabulary for aesthetics that Winter proposes based on written texts, I would argue that repeated images of violence in the siege and battle scenes constitute a visual indigenous vocabulary for aesthetics that communicated the king's power. These scenes, as I have mentioned, include speared, impaled, stripped, and dismembered enemy soldiers. Returning to the royal inscriptions of Ashurnasirpal II, we find numerous examples of his unabashed even boastful description of the violence he has inflicted upon his enemy. One typical example describes his conquest of an enemy city as follows:

> In strife and conflict I besieged (and) conquered the city. I felled 3000 of
> their fighting men with the sword. I carried off prisoners, possessions,
> oxen, (and) cattle from them. I burnt many captives from them. I captured
> many troops alive: from some I cut off their arms (and) hands; from
> others I cut off their noses, ears, (and) extremities. I gouged out the eyes
> of many troops. I made one pile of the living (and) one of heads. I hung
> their heads on trees around the city.[25]

Physical penetration of the enemy with a spear or dagger represents another frequent royal boast. Sennacherib's inscriptions include a lengthy account of his battle against an allied "enormous vassal host" of states

23. Luckenbill, *Annals of Sennacherib*, 29, ll. 37–40.
24. There is evidence that at least some of the reliefs were originally painted. If this is the case, then the radiance of the king, his weapons, and the gods could have been depicted through color as well as ornamentation.
25. "A.O.101.1," col. i, ll. 115–17.

including Babylon.[26] Faced with such an organized and formidable enemy, Sennacherib prayed to his gods for victory and reports that they "speedily gave ear to my prayers and came to my aid." Then, using storm god language, Sennacherib described his divinely bestowed weaponry:

> The mighty bow which Assur had given me, I seized in my hands; the javelin, that pierces lives [lit.: slits throats] (*pāriʾ napšātii*), I grasped... Like Adad I roared... With the weapons of Assur, my lord...I decimated the enemy host with arrow and spear. All of their bodies I bored through (*gimri pagrēšunu upallîša*).[27]

Most acts of violence depicted in the siege and battle scenes have written counterparts in the royal inscriptions. The one repeated visual trope of violence in the palace reliefs that has no clear correlation to a written royal inscription is the image of the stripped enemy soldier. We do not have Assyrian royal inscriptions in which the king reports, "I stripped the enemy and exposed him before my army." It is possible that the image of the stripped soldier corresponds to the royal claim to have "plundered" the enemy. If, however, we examine the trope of nakedness in the depiction of violence against an enemy, it becomes clear that the images are communicating more than simple plundering of the enemy. First, the naked enemy male is almost always positioned such that his genitalia face the viewer, and in many cases are also within the gaze of the Assyrian king. Corresponding to the written boast of having pierced or bored through the enemy, the naked soldier is often depicted visually being penetrated by a weapon, sometimes in a clearly sexual way (Fig. 4 [overleaf]).[28] The idea that the violent depiction of the enemy soldier within a work of art might contain a sexual dimension should not surprise us since the sexual and the erotic are often brought into the service of aesthetics.[29] Bersani and Dutoit noted the erotic element of narrative violence in Assyrian battle reliefs and argued that the visual narrative was deliberately paced such that the object of desire, the city or the enemy male, was isolated. The narrative then moved toward the desired object in a series of what they termed "explosive climaxes."[30]

---

26. Luckenbill, *Annals of Sennacherib*, 44–45, ll. 63–88.

27. Ibid., 44–45, ll. 71–81.

28. Chapman, *The Gendered Language of Warfare*, 159–63.

29. See, e.g., Elisabeth Bronfen, *Over Her Dead Body: Death, Femininity, and the Aesthetic* (New York: Routledge, 1992); Graham L. Hammill, *Sexuality and Form: Caravaggio, Marlowe, and Bacon* (Chicago: University of Chicago Press, 2000), 1–40.

30. Bersani and Dutoit. *The Forms of Violence*, 40–41. Bersani and Dutoit, however, did not see the element of the erotic in the sexualized exposure and penetration

Figure 4. Sexually exposed soldier falling from his city's wall with weaponry aimed at his exposed buttocks. Nimrud, Northwest Palace of Ashurnasirpal II, B.M. 124553 (from Assyrian Sculptures in the British Museum: From Shalmaneser III to Sennacherib, plate XIII).

The Iconic Capture and Feminization of the Enemy

In an article entitled, "Violence and Vision: The Prosthetics and Aesthetics of Terror," Allen Feldman discusses the sexual power of the gaze in what he terms a "scopic regime."[31] While he is referring to the camera lens and the rifle scope of the modern world, much of what he asserts concerning the "militarized gaze" is helpful in understanding the dynamic of power that is operative within the depictions of sexual exposure and violent penetration of the enemy male in the palace reliefs. First, Allen argues that visual appropriation becomes a metonym for dominance over others.[32] In this sense, the simple depiction of an enemy city appropriates it into the empire. Sculpting into rock the figure of the

of the enemy male. Instead, they located "aesthetic pleasure" in the geometrically shaped spaces formed by the interlocking bodies and weaponry, shapes which created, in their words, "interstitial sensuality" (p. 108). In light of the naked, penetrated, and dismembered body of the enemy male, I find Bersani and Dutoit's emphasis on erotic geometry forced.

31. Allen Feldman, "Violence and Vision: The Prosthetics and Aesthetics of Terror," in *Violence and Subjectivity* (ed. Veena Das, Arthur Kleinman, Mamphela Ramphele, and Pamela Reynolds; Berkeley: University of California Press, 2000), 46–78.

32. Ibid., 49.

Assyrian king gazing over the conquest of a city secures his dominance of that city eternally. The placement of the sculpted relief in the reception suites of the royal palace serves as a secondary level of symbolic appropriation of a foreign city into the boundaries of the king's empire. A "scopic regime" for Feldman involves "the agendas and techniques of political visualization."[33] Proscribed modes of visualization allow one to establish truth claims. For the Assyrian kings, there was a repeated vocabulary of visual conquest that established the "truth" of the Assyrian king's dominance and control over the known world. The violent decimation of the enemy and the undisturbed ornamented presence of the king communicated the radiant and divinely endowed power of the king's weapons.

Feldman also discusses the way that the militarized gaze is linked to if not identical to the male gaze. By male gaze, he means the gaze that is active, appropriating, defining, and controlling a field of vision. It is also a gaze that often penetrates into the private space of the enemy. The "iconic capture" of an image by whatever means often involved the depicted person, whether male or female, receiving what he terms the "veneer of iconic femininity."[34] In other words, the very act of depiction feminizes the subject insofar as femininity has been correlated ideologically to passivity and immobility.[35] When we look at the siege scenes such as this one of Tiglath-pileser III (Fig. 3), the one problem is that the king himself is iconically captured and visually appropriated into the image of battle. This is why it is so significant that the king stands outside of the battle scene, gazing over it. The depicted image operates on two levels. First, it is an image of a king who gazes over the image of a decimated city, which he has militarily and visually appropriated. The king's eyes become the sculptor's eyes, and therefore he is not feminized through depiction. Second, when we turn to the enemy soldiers, their sexually exposed and violently penetrated bodies seem clearly feminized through their total passivity and immobility. The averted gaze of the enemy male also marks him as iconically captured. Repeated images of identical forms of violence represent an additional, non-verbal set of indigenous royal Assyrian vocabulary depicting conquest. Exposure,

33. Ibid.
34. Ibid., 61.
35. Ann Kessler Guinan has demonstrated the ideological social status reduction of males through sexual penetration with reference to Mesopotamian sex omens in "Auguries of Hegemony: The Sex Omens of Mesopotamia," *Gender and History* 9 (1997): 462–73; see also my discussion of the feminization of the enemy soldier in Neo-Assyrian curses, *The Gendered Language of Warfare*, 48–58.

penetration, and dismemberment form part of the Assyrian aesthetic of violence that communicates the wonder and radiance of the king's divinely endowed power. Violence, sexuality, and the sacred power of divine weapons were brought into the service of royal truth claims.

The Role of the Spectator:
Ezekiel's Use of Sexuality, Violence and the Sacred

As mentioned above, the response of the spectator to a work of art con-stitutes a foundational element of any definition of aesthetics. With that in mind, I would like to turn to a recorded moment of aesthetic appre-ciation of military violence found in the book of Ezekiel. It would be especially tidy from a historical perspective if I could turn to the account of Judean emissary X who had viewed this panel of Tiglath-pileser III's conquest of a city (Fig. 3) and had recorded his response to the image in a diary. Unfortunately, when we are dealing with ancient history, we rarely have that kind of neat correlation. In Ezek 23, however, the prophet remembers the Assyrian conquest of Samaria and anticipates the later Babylonian conquest of Jerusalem.[36] He then captures that memory in the form of a narrative vision. His vision of two sisters, personified capital cities, whoring after foreign lovers and ultimately being maimed and killed by them, combines the prophet's obvious relishing in images of violence, the feminine, and the erotic. Within this vision-encapsulated memory, the prophet also captures a secondary layer of aesthetic appre-ciation. In this case, his imagined Jerusalem, a woman he names "Oholi-bah," gazes upon the sculpted reliefs of Babylonian warriors and responds with unabashed lust. The text reads:

> And she [Oholibah/Jerusalem] continued her whoring, looking at men sculpted upon the wall, images of the Chaldeans sculpted in red. Belted waistcloths upon their loins, flowing turbans upon their heads, all of them looking like elite officers, a picture of the Babylonians whose birthplace is Chaldea. She lusted after them with a look in her eyes, and conse-quently sent messengers to them in Chaldea. So the Babylonians came to

36. This chapter of the book of Ezekiel has been dated anywhere from the mid-seventh century B.C.E. to the period just prior to the destruction of Jerusalem in 587 B.C.E. based on the language that suggests Judah as an independent kingdom engaging in serial alliances with Assyria, Babylonia, and Egypt. For a discussion of the dating of this chapter, see Julie Galambush, *Jerusalem in the Book of Ezekiel: The City as Yahweh's Wife* (Atlanta: Scholars Press, 1992), 112–15; and Walther Zimmerli, *Ezekiel 1: A Commentary on the Book of the Prophet Ezekiel, Chapters 1–24* (Philadelphia: Fortress, 1979), 482–83.

her, to the bed of love, and they defiled her with their whoring. And after
she became unclean through them, she turned away from them in disgust.
(Ezek 23:14–17)

This is the only reference in the Hebrew Bible to the viewing and appreciation of some form of military art. Whether Ezekiel himself had
actually seen carved Babylonian or Assyrian reliefs we can never know,
but he had at least heard of them and could imagine a feminized
Jerusalem being sexually aroused by the sculpted and brightly painted
images of Babylonian military officers.[37] The name "Oholibah" means
"my tent is within her," a reference to the wilderness tabernacle and to
the holy of holies in the Jerusalem temple. In this sense, Ezekiel understood the military threat against his city to involve not only the sexual
allure of foreign military officers, but also the sexually defiling presence
of those same officers in the sacred space of his god. Vision, the gaze,
violence, the sacred, and the sexual are all present in this multi-layered
narrative of conquest.

In Tiglath-pileser III's siege of an unnamed city, it is his actively
penetrating gaze that iconically captures the city and its inhabitants. His
power and dominance as a male warrior-king is confirmed and enhanced
through the sculpted representation of his conquering gaze. In Ezekiel's
vision, it is the gaze of the female-gendered Jerusalem that iconically
captures the passive and immobile images of Babylonian military

37. Several scholars have conjectured what Ezekiel might have been referring to
when he mentioned men "sculpted upon the wall," but there is simply not enough
evidence from the text or from the scant archaeological records of Babylonian art to
know what Ezekiel's referent might have been. Ezekiel is, however, assuming that
his audience is aware of sculpted and painted images of Babylonian military officers.
The various explanations for Ezekiel's sculpted men include: Walther Zimmerli's
conclusion that the reference to sculpted men remains "obscure" (Zimmerli, *Ezekiel
1*, 486); Eichrodt's suggestion that the Judean penchant for all things foreign may
have indicated that Babylonian-style military frescoes were in the houses of the
Judean elite (Walther Eichrodt, *Ezekiel: A Commentary* [Philadelphia: Westminster,
1970], 325); Silvia Schroer's investigation of the specific vocabulary of the text
demonstrating its links to texts on the Solomonic temple and to features found on
painted reliefs of both Mesopotamia and Egypt (Schroer, *In Israel gab es Bilder:
Nachrichten von darstellender Kunst im Alten Testament* [Göttingen: Vandenhoeck
& Ruprecht, 1987], 179–83); Moshe Greenberg's attempt to identify archaeological
finds that exhibit various aspects of the described soldier's uniforms (Greenberg,
Ezekiel 21–37: A New Translation with Introduction and Commentary [New York:
Doubleday, 1997], 478–79); and Margaret Odell's suggestion that Assyrians may
have had a practice of showing foreign emissaries, including those from Judah, their
palace reliefs of defeated Chaldeans as an object lesson aimed at deterring rebellion
(Odell, *Ezekiel* [Macon: Smyth & Helwys, 2005], 302).

officers. The affective power of her gaze is demonstrated when it results in the physical delivery of those same officers into the confines of her kingdom, her capital city. The importation of the Babylonian military officers onto Jerusalem's "bed of love" parallels the secondary level of appropriation in the Assyrian palace reliefs. Namely, the Assyrian king captures and kills actual enemy soldiers on a physical battlefield and then permanently appropriates them into his empire by having their limp, penetrated forms sculpted in permanent immobility on the walls of his capital, the heart of his empire. The female-gendered Jerusalem's active and sexually appropriating gaze upon sculpted Babylonian warriors results in actual physical specimens of those warriors being brought into the confines of her kingdom. It is here, however, that the parallels between the two images cease. For what we find is that the active and sexually appropriating gaze of a female-gendered Jerusalem renders her sexually transgressive and prefigures her ultimate demise.[38] To discover whose gaze actually controls this vision, we need only to look at the chapter as a whole to realize that it is Ezekiel's gaze, his divinely channeled vision, that appropriates and iconically captures both Jerusalem and her Babylonian lovers. Whereas in the siege scenes of the Assyrian kings the gaze of the gods is aligned with that of the king, the gaze of the Israelite god is aligned with the prophet visionary against Jerusalem.

Ezekiel describes the conquest that his god, Jerusalem's forsaken husband, will bring upon the overly forward female Jerusalem. First, he uses surprisingly literal military language describing how the Israelite god will bring the Assyrians and the Babylonians against her. The text reads: "And they shall come against you from the north with chariots and wagons and a host of peoples; they shall set themselves against you on every side with buckler, shield, and helmet" (Ezek 23:24). Ezekiel clearly emphasizes that the Assyrians and Babylonians who are brought in as conquerors are the same "desirable young men" whose sculpted bodies

38. Galambush discusses the role of the active gaze of the woman Jerusalem as a reversal of her being a passive object of the gaze in Ezek 16 (Galambush, *Jerusalem in the Book of Ezekiel*, 116). Odell characterizes Ezekiel's use of military, sexual, and bestial imagery as Oholibah's "crossing the boundary from order into chaos" (Odell, *Ezekiel*, 303). I would add that one of the ways that Ezekiel characterizes chaos is through the transgressively active gaze of his female-gendered Jerusalem. Cf. S. Tamar Kamionkowski, who sees gender reversal in Ezekiel as a whole as a symbol of "cosmic chaos." Specifically with regard to Oholibah, Kamionkowski emphasizes the passivity of Jerusalem in this chapter in contrast to the female-gendered Jerusalem of Ezek 16 (*Gender Reversal and Cosmic Chaos: A Study of Book of Ezekiel* (JSOTSup 368; Sheffield: Sheffield Academic, 2003], 140–46).

had aroused her (Ezek 23:23). After using literal military language to describe the set-up of the attack, Ezekiel reverts to metaphorical language that sexualizes violence in order to describe the conquest: "They shall cut off your nose and your ears, and your survivors shall fall by the sword. They shall seize your sons and your daughters, and your survivors shall be devoured by fire. They shall also strip you of your clothes and take away your fine jewels" (Ezek 23:25–26).

Dismembered, stripped, and bereft of her children, Ezekiel's imagined Jerusalem stands in sharp contrast to the conquered women depicted on the Assyrian palace reliefs who together with their children remain clothed and unmolested. Instead, Ezekiel's female-gendered sacred city resembles the feminized conquered male soldiers of the reliefs who are likewise dismembered, stripped, and shamed before their families. What both sets of images share is an aesthetic sense that the sculpted male warrior is radiantly alluring in his divinely empowered masculinity while victims of violence are feminized through sexual exposure and penetration. Repeated images of sexualized violence constitute an indigenous vocabulary for an aesthetic depiction of earned power.

MAPPING VIOLENCE IN THE PROPHETS: ZEPHANIAH 2

Robert D. Haak

Zephaniah 2:4–15 reads:

2:4 Since Gaza will become deserted, and Ashkelon a desolation;
Ashdod, at noon they will drive her out, and Ekron will be uprooted,

2:5 Woe to the inhabitants of the district of the sea, the nation of Kerethites.
The word of YHWH is against you, Canaan, land of the Philistines.
Indeed, I will exterminate you so that there is no inhabitant.

2:6 The district of the sea, "the pastures of Keret,"
indeed will become shepherds and enclosers of flocks.[1]

2:7 And it will become a district for the remnant of the house of Judah,
upon them they will graze,
in the houses of Ashkelon, in the evening they will lie down,
for YHWH their god will give heed to them and restore their fortunes.

2:8 I have heard the taunt of Moab and the insults of the sons of Ammon
with which they taunted my people and boasted against their border.

2:9 Therefore, as I live—oracle of YHWH of hosts, the god of Israel—
indeed, Moab like Sodom will become and the sons of Ammon like Gomorrah,

---

1. The structure of this (and the previous verse) hinges on the treatment of *krt* in the difficult phrase *khbl khym nwt krt*. Most recent attempts have understood this term as related to the root *krh*, "to dig." Others understand the term as related to the root *kr*, "pasture." Earlier understandings (based on the reading of the LXX) that connect the term directly to Crete have met with little success. The phrase here is understood to refer to part of the area inhabited by the Kerethites (cf. v. 5) or to be a poetic designation of the entire area (cf. Lam 2:2). This understanding, coupled with the recognition of the double designation of the objects of the Woe in vv. 5–6, reveals a relatively regular poetic structure and clears up the grammatical difficulties. The verb, *whyt*, is in agreement with the second term (*nwt*). The distribution of the nominal forms shows a balance of gender (*khbl* m. // *nwt* f. //*rʾym* m. // *wgdrwt* f.). The word *wgdrwt* is understood here as a feminine plural participle of the root *gdr* rather than the more common nominal form. The feminine form was chosen to provide gender balance.

a possession of thorns and pit of salt and a desolation forever.
The remnant of my people will plunder them and the rest of my nation will take possession of them.

2:10 This belongs to them instead of their majesty for they taunted and boasted against the people of YHWH of hosts.

2:11 Awe-full is YHWH against them for he lays waste[2] all the gods of the land
and they bow down to him, each in his place, all the "jackals" of the nations.

2:12 Even you, Cushim… pierced by the sword are they.

2:13 And his hand will stretch out over the north, and he will exterminate Asshur,
and he will make Nineveh a desolation, a desert in the wilderness,

2:14 and flocks will lie down in her midst, all the "beasts" of the nation.
Both "owl" and "bustard"[3] in her capitals will spend the night;
the sound of the "Watcher"[4] (will be) in the window,
"Ruin" on the sill, for I will lay waste her cities.

2:15 This is the exultant city, the one dwelling in security,
the one saying in her heart, "I am and no one besides!'"?
Indeed, she has become a desolation, a lair for beasts,
everyone passing over will whistle and shake his hand.

(author's translation)

In many ways this essay is an experiment. In the first place, the ideas are an experiment in my own thinking. I am essentially an historian of the religion of ancient Israel and Judah. I have concentrated my work primarily on the end of the seventh century in Judah, trying to understand

---

2. It seems likely that this is one of a number of words which have "polar" nuances—"to lay waste"/"to be heavy." No single English word will pick up both nuances which were probably apparent to the ancient reader.

3. The identification of the animals is uncertain.

4. The comments of J. J. M. Roberts, *Nahum, Habakkuk, and Zephaniah* (OTL: Louisville: Westminster John Knox, 1991), 203, indicate the difficulty of this part of the verse. "The last line of this verse is a crux and is probably corrupt. Both the text and translation are uncertain." The suggestion here is that the consonantal text be kept intact. The letters of this phrase are redivided as *qwly swrr*. The second word is related to the root *swr*, "to behold," often in the Psalms related to the watching of an enemy. It may be that this word should be connected to the Ugaritic *mt-w-šr*, which some have interpreted as a divine name, "Death-and-Evil." The first word, *qwly*, is formed in an unusual manner (but cf. Ps 116:1) and may have given rise to the misunderstanding of the MT and Versions. The terms "Watcher" and "Ruin" are seen as epithets of personified evil forces/gods that have taken residence in the devastated cities. While this "solution" is not without problems, it does keep the consonantal text intact and obviates the need felt by many to emend the rest of the line more drastically.

the context and writings of prophets such as Habakkuk and Zephaniah. While work on these prophets is the basis for the following thoughts, I will use this opportunity to try to paint a "big picture" against which Zephaniah and Habakkuk (and Jeremiah and the others) can be seen.

The second "experimental" part of this project is that it is not strictly historical but more likely theological. I am not so much asking "What happened?" as I am "What were the authors of the biblical texts thinking and how did their agenda change?" This change, I believe, is reflected in the texts in ways that may also reflect historical development, but of this I am not so sure. It is the development within the texts that I will be tracing. That this has historical implications has yet to be shown.

A third unusual aspect of this study is that it is much more personal than most of my work…and more personal than most of the work done in our profession.[5] Actually, I am not so sure that this is a true statement. The post-modern world has taught us that much of what we do is personal, no matter how "objective" we try to be. In the end, that which gets our attention, the problems with which we struggle, the issues we explore, the approaches we take are all reflections of our own struggles and explorations.

What may be different is that I want to be explicit about this at the beginning. I am asking questions about "violence" and "power" and how these relate to the religious ideologies of the community to which I belong. I did start thinking about these issues before 9/11, but there can be no denial of the fact that these issues took on a new intensity after those events, including the events of "violence" and "power" that Americans are experiencing (and participating in) to this very day. If we ever thought we could, it is now clear that we can't sit back and examine these issues from the standpoint of a non-participant. We are involved, in ways that go to the center of who we are and who we wish to be. When I ask about the prophetic understanding of violence and power and its relationship to the political systems of that day, I am as much asking how I understand those relationships today.

This topic is experimental in another way. I believe the prophets (or at least the prophetic literature) are experimenting with these issues. I believe there is a change in the way that prophets related to the power and violence of their day. It is this development that I hope to trace.[6]

5. Note the same confession made in the present volume by Corrine Carvalho, "The Beauty of the Bloody God: The Divine Warrior in Prophetic Literature," 131–32.
6. The comments here do not examine the complex issue of violence in the Psalms. David G. Firth in *Surrendering Retribution in the Psalms: Response to*

Violence in the Prophetic Texts

There can be little doubt that we live in a world marked by violence in both the private and public spheres. We ourselves fear becoming the objects of violent actions. A friend gets stabbed on her way to work… and we look over our shoulder a bit more fearfully. A bomb goes off—in a crowded market in Jerusalem or at an office building in Oklahoma City—and we wonder if we might be next. What we used to take for granted, we now notice. A plane flies unexpectedly low overheard. We look up and wonder why.

Does this experience of violence inform and change our reading of the ancient texts? On one level, the answer to this question is simple. Modern understandings of the role of the reader in the process of communication make clear that what we bring to the text is a vital element in the process of communication. As we change because of our experience, what the text communicates also changes. On another level, the issue is not so clear. What responsibility do we bear as those who read (and who encourage others to read) these texts? Do we perpetuate violence in our own day by our very act of reading these ancient accounts of violence?[7]

Most of us pay taxes and vote in a country that projects its military might throughout the world. Our aircraft carriers ply the waters of the Persian Gulf. Our tax dollars buy land mines and rubber bullets that continue and extend the violence. We send our sons and daughters with guns to find weapons of mass destruction. Violence is a fact of our lives whether we seek it or not.

We seem to share this experience of violence with the authors of the biblical texts. They too feared and at times perpetuated violence. We read of their agony as victims of war. We also hear of their jubilation as the victors. At other times their violence was surely more private. Feminist scholars have highlighted violence against women[8] in the

Violence in the Individual Complaints (Paternoster Biblical Monographs; Waynesboro, Ga.: Paternoster, 2005), has exposed a strand in the Psalms that sees all forms of human-initiated violence as inappropriate. This certainly is not the only biblical view (or even the only view in the Psalms).

7. Joseph A. Marchal, "To What End(s)? Biblical Studies and Critical Rhetorical Engagement(s) for a 'Safer' World," *SBL Forum* (August 14, 2006). Online: http://www.sbl-site.org/Article.aspx?Articled=550.

8. Drorah Setel, "Prophets and Pornography: Female Sexual Imagery in Hosea," in *Feminist Interpretation of the Bible* (ed. L. Russell; Philadelphia: Westminster, 1985), 86–95; Renita J. Weems, *Battered Love: Marriage, Sex and Violence in the Hebrew Prophets* (Overtures to Biblical Theology; Minneapolis: Fortress, 1995).

biblical world and our own. One wonders how many voices of the victims we will never hear. At times, the biblical texts speak of violence in ways that shock us and make us extremely uncomfortable. At times it even speaks words which we may not be able to share, words to which we respond "No!"[9] However, Corrine Carvalho suggests that violent language may be employed at times in a "rhetoric of resistance."[10]

Some of the most violent prophetic texts can be found in the units that scholars have called the Oracles Against the Nations (OANs).[11] The primary method by which these violent texts have been handled in "public" contexts of which I am aware is to ignore them. I don't recall ever hearing a sermon preached on these texts (although I suspect such sermons have been preached). Ignoring the texts and the violence they portray may be an option for some. We can just hope that they go away. But this doesn't seem to be an option for the scholar. The texts are there. They confront us with their claims. How will we respond as readers and scholars?

An example of violence in the OANs can be found in Zeph 2:4–15. The violence of the text is evident: "I will exterminate you so that there is no inhabitant" (Zeph 2:5); Moab will become a "desolation forever" (2:9); Cush will be "pierced by my sword" (2:12); Asshur will be "exterminated" and Nineveh will become a "desolation" (2:13).

How do we read such texts in light of our own experience? Does it matter that we have seen the "desolation" of Hiroshima and Nagasaki? That we have seen the "extermination" of the victims of the Holocaust? That we have seen the "devastation" of Rwanda? That we have seen the sky over Baghdad lit up on CNN? That we have seen the casualties of war in our own communities? It is likely the author of this text had seen horrifying violence in his own day. We share this experience. But how should we respond to Zephaniah's use of this experience? How much can or should we share in the violence of this text?

When confronted with the violence of this text, and others like it, my first reaction is to try to bring the text under control and thereby also to control the violence it expresses. It may be that the first realization we must have is that this is an impossible task. We can't ultimately control the reading of this text. The violence it expresses has been and will be used for many purposes, including perpetuating the "extermination" of

9. Athalya Brenner, "On Prophetic Propaganda and the Politics of 'Love': The Case of Jeremiah," in *The Feminist Companion to the Latter Prophets* (ed. Athalya Brenner; The Feminist Companion to the Bible; Sheffield: Sheffield Academic, 1995), 256–75.

10. See, in the present volume, Carvalho, "The Beauty of the Bloody God," 132.

11. Robert D. Haak, "Zephaniah's Oracles Against the Nations" (paper presented at the Chicago Society of Biblical Research, Chicago, 1991).

peoples and the "devastation" of lands. These are dangerous and effective texts. As J. Harold Ellens reminds us, "Religious metaphors can kill."[12] What we may be able to shape is our own participation in the world created by the texts. As scholars, we can and must influence the reading of these texts, first by coming to our own understanding of them and then by speaking of this understanding in our own contexts.[13]

There are two primary and related dangers when reading such texts. The first of these is the danger created by our failure to insist on the metaphorical nature of (all?) biblical language. When pressed, most of us would admit that our "god" language is metaphor (note, I did not say "only" metaphor). Athalya Brenner, among others, has examined in very productive ways the violence connected to the biblical metaphor of god as "husband."[14] But God is not "husband," not "shepherd," not even "mother." In monotheistic traditions, at least, there is a recognition that all language about God is metaphor. Even accounts of "direct" experience of "God" can only be indirectly communicated in languages that are by their very nature metaphoric.

When a reader takes a metaphor (any metaphor) literally, there is a danger. The misogynistic use of the "husband" metaphor is a case in point. The danger is particularly great for texts that at first glance seem to be non-metaphorical, texts such as the OANs. After all, Nineveh did become a "desolation" in some sort of reality. Summers spent digging in the dirt of Ekron have shown that it was indeed "uprooted." Because of these "facts," the temptation is to forget the metaphorical nature of Zephaniah's OANs. As scholars studying these ancient texts, we must continually insist on the recognition of their metaphorical nature or we inadvertently contribute to their danger.

This is not to say they are "just" metaphorical. I suspect that we all have had the experience of a student saying, "Well then, it's just a

12. Daniel J. Gaztambide, "Is God Bipolar or Are We Just Crazy? A Psychology and Biblical Studies Section Report: Personality, Aggression, and the Destructive Power of Religion," *SBL Forum* (December 19, 2005). Online: http://www.sbl-site.org/Article.aspx?Articled=466; cf. J. Harold Ellens, ed., *The Destructive Power of Religion: Violence in Judaism, Christianity, and Islam* (4 vols.: Westport, Conn..: Praeger, 2003); Marchal, "To What End(s)."

13. Anyone following the conversations of the academic world in the past few decades recognizes the importance of the topic of "violence" within the field. The significance of this topic is reinforced by the work of Eugen Drewermann, which may be accessed conveniently in Matthias Beier's *A Violent God Image: An Introduction to the Work of Eugen Drewermann* (New York: Continuum, 2004).

14. Athalya Brenner, "Pornoprophetics Revisited: Some Additional Reflections," *JSOT* 70 (1996): 63–86; Weems, *Battered Love*.

story?" At this point, I often go off on a rather long and impassioned speech about the power that words, metaphors, can and do have—all the while hoping that my words have the power to change something in the students' understanding of the world and of the texts. So, I think we as biblical scholars have the responsibility to insist on the metaphoric nature of these texts.

A second danger, I believe, is allowing these texts to be read without an understanding and appreciation of their context. I would suggest that the context (and our understanding of it) determines our understanding of the violence of a text. A possibly simplistic example might be the word "Fire!" In the context of a burning building, it may be a word of warning and hope for those who hear it. In context of someone facing a squad of soldiers, the same word may be a word of death.

Let us now turn to the context of the OANs specifically. There has been a considerable debate concerning the nature of these units, particularly about the origin of this form.[15] Some have argued that it originated within the cult. Others have claimed that it developed within actual war settings. While there is some value in this debate, for our purposes the question of the origin of the form may not be very important. The more important question is the usage of the form within the prophetic writings.

Mapping Violence

The chart opposite may provide a starting point for discussion of the contexts of violence within the biblical texts, to help categorize violent material within scripture, especially in OANs. The purpose is to be suggestive rather than exhaustive.

Within the political sphere, there are three general experiences of violence: (1) violent situations resulting in national victory, (2) situations in which violence is threatened but has not yet occurred, and (3) situations where the violence and loss have been experienced. Each of these experiences demands a response.

A variety of responses is available. If "we[16] win," it may be explained that "we" deserve the victory because of some quality that we possess.

15. Cf. Helmer Ringgren, "Enthronement Festival or Covenant Renewal," *BR* 7 (1962): 45–58.

16. Eleanor Beach continually reminds me that the definition of the "we" in these contexts is crucial. "We" might win as a nation—but those out of power in the nation may not experience this in the same way as those in power. Note Smith-Christopher's caution about the power of violent language in a different context. See, in the present volume, Daniel Smith-Christopher, "On the Pleasures of Prophetic Judgment: Reading Micah 1:6 and 3:12 with Stokely Carmichael," 72–77.

The Experience of Violence[17]

Experience	Explanation	Theology		Example
We Win	we deserve	God is for us		David and enemies
	we don't deserve	it's a gift of God		Joshua
Threat (OAN)	enemy wrong	our God will win		Rabshakeh
	warning to us	God wins when we repent		Nineveh–Jonah
	impending loss	God punishes us		Jeremiah
We Lose	we deserve	God punishes/divine justice	→ future restoration	Ezekiel[18]
		but parents do		"sour grapes"
		God testing	→ we pass test	Maccabees—refiner's fire—Revelation
	we don't deserve	God allows	→ we are martyrs	Maccabees and New Testament
		God made mistake	→ divine injustice	Job
		means of redemption	→ God rewards	some New Testament
	we were 'unlucky'	God not controlling		Ecclesiastes
		God absent		God wakes—Psalms

17. I would like to acknowledge the contribution of my partner, Eleanor Beach, in discussions about the details of this chart, which developed from her teaching. She is very interested in the question of violence both within the biblical world and our own world.

18. An interesting example of a "modern day prophecy" might be seen in by Roland Cap Ehlke's "Ode to America," *Concordian* (Fall 2006): 13. This poem calls on America to return to its true values in worship of God and associates a range of current problems with the eroding religious landscape.

Alternatively, it may be that the victory is understood as a gift of the deity, with no particular basis in our own contribution. When under threat of violence, we may conclude that the enemy is deluded, since God will surely give us the victory. Alternatively, it may be that God is in control and the (possible or actual) defeat is a warning to us to change our ways. Once a defeat is experienced, a wider range of possibilities exists—from explanations that assume that God is still in control to those that assume Gods inability or unwillingness to prevail.

In each of these situations violent language in prophetic oracles may have been used in ways that either tended to decrease or to increase the actual violence. For example, in the situation where "we" win, the violent images may justify our own use of power and tend to increase our use of violence, or they may be a reminder that the power does not essentially belong to us—but rather to God. God is in control, we are not. While this distinction may make little difference to the recipients of the violence, it does offer options for the perpetrators' attitude toward the violence. If "we" don't experience victory because of our own merits, it might result in a more benevolent use of power (if such a thing exists). The power may be seen as something that we don't own and control, but rather as something that belongs to God. There is no doubt that the danger is great here. The "benevolent victor" is not the only possible outcome of this theology. If the victor is identified with the deity, the actual violence may increase. The conqueror might say, "We are not doing the violence, it is God. We are just the ones carrying it out."

Where do the OANs fit into this scheme? Most (if not all) of the OANs begin within a situation of threatened violence. The development of this form may well be a response to the use of terror as a tool of propaganda in the eighth and seventh centuries, particularly by the Assyrian empire. Recent studies have examined the use of terror by the Assyrians, both in texts and in pictorial representations.[19] While we cannot be sure of the means by which this terror was conveyed to areas such as Judah, we can be quite certain that by the end of the seventh century (and

19. Erika Bleibtreu, "Grizzly Assyrian Record of Torture and Death," *BAR* 17, no. 1 (1991): 52–61, 75; Leo Bersani and Ulysse Dutoit, *The Forms of Violence: Narrative in Assyrian Art and Modern Culture* (New York: Schocken, 1985); cf. Rachel Magdalene, "Ancient Near Eastern Treaty-Curses and the Ultimate Texts of Terror: A Study of the Language of Divine Sexual Abuse in the Prophetic Corpus," in *The Feminist Companion to the Latter Prophets* (ed. Athalya Brenner; The Feminist Companion to the Bible; Sheffield: Sheffield Academic, 1995). See, in the present volume, Cynthia R. Chapman, "Sculpted Warriors: Sexuality and the Sacred in the Depiction of Warfare in the Assyrian Palace Reliefs and in Ezekiel 23:14–17," 1–17.

possibly quite a bit earlier) Judahites were aware of this propaganda. An example of the knowledge of this terror may be the story in 2 Kgs 10 of the beheading of the sons of Ahab during Jehu's coup in Israel. The image of heads piled at the city-gate evidently reflects the terror tactics of the Assyrians in their conquests. Even if this text does not depict historical reality in Jehu's time, it is recognized as a terror tactic by the time of the Deuteronomistic History, probably within the seventh century.[20] As the level of rhetorical violence is increased by the propaganda of the Assyrians, there seems to be a parallel increase in the use of violence within the prophetic materials, particularly in the development and extension of the OANs.[21]

The earlier comment about the importance of context means that one shouldn't generalize about all OANs. Each metaphor and each context must be examined. There are no OANs in general, all are specific. In the case of the oracle in Zephaniah, what is the context?

First, I would contend that the use of this form in Zephaniah must be understood as a metaphor. The oracles are designed to announce and influence the foreign policy of the Judahite monarchy. They are propaganda. In understanding propaganda, the "audience" plays a crucial role. The audience of these oracles was not Cush or Moab or Philistia—the literary objects of the violence. The audience was instead the elite in the capital, Jerusalem (and possibly the allies who were stationed there).[22] Had they the means, it may be that the political leadership would have attempted to effect the devastation that is described. But these specific oracles, which I believe were set originally within late seventh-century Judah, were spoken at a time when these means were not available.[23] Judah was in no position to carry out literally the violence spoken of literarily. Within a brief time, Judah itself would be devastated. In spite of the violent words of this text, Judah found itself in the position of being under the threat of violence at the hand of the superpowers of the day. The question was that of the "proper response."

The OANs in Zephaniah seem to contend that, although the threat of violence is present, the ultimate result will be Judah's victory. The "proper response" to the threat of violence is to change foreign policy by shifting alliances away from the old pro-Assyrian policies that had

20. Mordechai Cogan and Hayim Tadmor, *II Kings* (AB 11; New York: Doubleday, 1988), 113, 117–22.
21. Eleanor Beach points out a similar increase of the use of violent sexual imagery as the power of the elite diminishes in the context of international superpowers Assyria and Babylon (personal communication).
22. Cf., in the present volume, Chapman, "Sculpted Warriors," 2.
23. Haak, "Zephaniah's Oracles."

worked for so long. This change will not only lead to the devastation of the enemy, but it will also ensure that Judah will benefit from this situation. The words become words of hope and promise to the audience, the elite of Jerusalem. It announces that the changed foreign policy will result in the takeover of territory by Judah (Philistia, 2:7; Ammon, 2:9; etc.).

The specific OANs in Zephaniah fall within the first explanation under threat—the enemy is deluded. They have threatened us with violence, but our God will turn this violence back on them. And Judah (and especially the elite), because of their changed foreign policy, will benefit from God's victory on their behalf. These oracles function as words of hope to the Judahites in a violent situation. Theologically, they are a statement of belief that Yahweh is still in control.

In fact, this seems to be the basic assumption throughout the prophetic texts—Yahweh is in control. Whether we win, lose, or are threatened, the prophets contend that ultimate control is in the hand of Yahweh. As long as this assumption is granted, there is hope. No matter how great the threat, Yahweh may be directing this violence. The punishment may end, or our suffering will be reversed. Yahweh remains in control.

In prophetic texts using the OANs in other contexts, we can see this position shift. In some texts, the prophet has turned the OAN into an oracle against Judah itself. Here the oracle becomes a warning to us.

In other texts, after the experience of loss, the OANs directed against others become an announcement of our political restoration. It seems quite possible, and maybe even necessary, that an oracle that was composed for one context was able to shift usage into another context—for example, from a context of responding to a threat to a context of experiencing loss. This adaptability led to the preservation of these oracles.

What all of these contexts have in common is the ancient prophetic assumption of Yahweh's continued control. In our own day, some have questioned the validity of this assumption. Events such as the Holocaust have raised the possibility, maybe even the necessity, of reconsidering the assumption of God's control.[24] Our society has experienced violence of a type that may not have been conceivable to the authors of the

---

24. Hans Jonas, "The Concept of God After Auschwitz: A Jewish Voice,'" in *Jewish Theology and Process Thought* (ed. Sandra B. Lubarsky and David Ray Griffin; SUNY Series in Constructive Postmodern Thought; New York: State University of New York Press, 1996), 143–57; reprinted from *Journal of Religion* 67 (1987): 1–13; Levi A. Olan, "The Prophetic Faith in a Secular Age," in Lubarsky and Griffin, eds., *Jewish Theology and Process Thought*, 25–34; reprinted from *Journal of Reform Judaism* (Spring 1979): 1–9.

prophetic texts. And this experience may change our assumptions. We may well conclude that God is not in control, in fact, must not be in control of such violence. Within the biblical literature, this questioning also occurs, but outside the prophetic literature.

Violent Language Today

But, if it is the case that God is not in control, this may raise the most dangerous prospect of all. If violence is not under the control of anyone but us, the danger of the metaphor seems to be increased. We alone are responsible for controlling this violence. We have to play the role that the prophetic texts gave to God—a dangerous role for humans if the biblical witness is taken seriously.

So, what is the solution to our dilemma? Where do we go from here? I suspect that I am not the only one who will avoid proposing "the answer" to this question.

Some would argue that we must reject this language of violence in all cases in our day. They would argue that the use of this language on any level merely perpetuates a system that takes violence as the norm and that ultimately keeps in place a system in which unacceptable violence is bound to occur. Only by refusing to participate can we avoid responsibility for the violence that this type of language models and reinforces.[25]

While I understand this position, my own intuition is that we cannot find a position in the human realm which does not deal with violence. Ignoring violence or even only condemning these texts in fact increases the danger. Violence and violent language must be acknowledged as a part of human existence. They cannot be ignored.

In order to be taken seriously I believe that we have to recognize the value this language may have in a given context. In a time of victory, it can temper our tendency to claim total control of power. In a time of threat it can provide hope and direction for a suitable outcome. In a time of defeat, it can provide a matrix of meaning from which a new life can be built. We, as scholars, must recognize the potentially positive uses of this type of language (while recognizing its danger).[26]

But we must also insist that the context be taken seriously. We must be in the forefront in pointing out the misuse of violent language within our own contexts. If our society allows this type of language to continue,

25. A. P. Goldstein, "Aggression," in *Encyclopedia of Psychology*, vol. 1 (ed. R. J. Corsini; Oxford: John Wiley & Sons, 1994), 39–43, and, in the present volume, Carvalho, "The Beauty of the Bloody God," 131–52.

26. Cf. Carvalho, "The Beauty of the Bloody God."

if we continue to participate in this language, we must do so with an understanding of the danger and a willingness to accept the responsibility of its use.

It may be that the use of violent language needs to continue precisely because the threat of actual violence is so dangerous. Before violent action is taken, we need to express the words which describe the action. This may act as a reality check to the contemplated action. For example, as long as we continue to live in a society which sees war as one option for settling disputes, we must use the words of war clearly to make real the destruction of war to those sitting safely at home, far from the violence they only see on the nightly news. It may be ironic that the best way to decrease the amount of actual violence in our world is to increase the vitality of the metaphors of violence which are used to the point that the actual violence becomes "real" to the society. Only when the reality of violence is understood and felt in a society can responsible use of violence be claimed. It may be that in a given case, when confronted with the reality of violence, a society may decide against its actual use. And if the decision is taken for violent action, responsibility for the consequences may also be recognized.

Power in the Prophetic Texts

Given all that has just been said, I wonder if this concentration on "violence" in the prophetic texts gives us a foreshortened view. Can we speak of violence and violent language without also speaking of a larger issue? It may be that "violence" is really just a subcategory of the broader category of "power." I would like to explore at this point the thesis that we see within the prophetic literature as an experiment concerning the relationship of the divine to "power," specifically political power as found in the monarchy. Although I am going to start at the "other end" of this question—that is, the relationship of the monarchy to power in the monarchical period of Judah's history—the issue came to the forefront of my thinking as I was trying to set the Exilic prophetic writings into a context that my undergraduate students at Augustana could understand. In talking about the Zion traditions as they were later reflected in the writings associated with Ezekiel and Second Isaiah, they raised the question of what had happened to the "David"-part of what we call the David–Zion story. This set us looking for the powerful Davidic ruler, a figure who isn't there in these prophetic books.

There can be little doubt that during the time of the monarchy, power of all sorts found its home in the person of the king and the institutions which surrounded the kingship. Much of the literature found in the Bible either is trying directly or indirectly to come to terms with this reality. Well-known texts are found that are critical of the power of kingship. Other texts are equally adamant that royal power comes directly from god.

What is the view of the prophets concerning political power, particularly the power of the king? As usual, there is no monolithic answer to this question. On one end of a spectrum we have stories in which prophetic figures clearly challenge the power of a monarchy. The stories of the relationship of Elijah and Elisha to the Omride dynasty of Israel are illustrative. The story of Naboth's vineyard seems to be a clear critique of the power of the monarchy, especially the monarchy in the guise of the Omride dynasty. It is tempting to see these texts as critiques of the notion of political power itself. Isn't this text saying that political power is inherently evil and that only God should be the locus of power?

The work of Robert Wilson more than a decade ago should make us leery of this conclusion.[27] Based on the anthropological work of I. M. Lewis,[28] Wilson drew the distinction between "central" and "peripheral" prophecy. Elijah and Elisha were parade examples of peripheral prophets. However, the significant thing to realize is that for Lewis both central and peripheral prophets are concerned with the maintenance and extension of power. Neither type of prophet is promoting a policy that moved away from power. The question was not power/no power. The question always was *whose* power. The stories of Elijah and Elisha make it clear that peripheral prophecy participated in violent power in dramatic fashion. One only has to think of the slaughter of 450 priests at the foot of Mt. Carmel or the ravaging of forty-two boys for comments about Elisha's lack of hair. It is not that the peripheral prophets despised power or violence. They simply were located on the margins of political power looking in.

The other end of the spectrum is also illustrated in stories of the prophets. Here we find prophets who are part of the power structures of the day. Nathan, the advisor of one king and arguably the creator of a second, moves in and out of the halls of power. Whether the stories of Nathan have any historical referent or not, we find other prophets such as Isaiah of Jerusalem who are quite certainly historical figures and who advise kings closely, not only on what we would consider "religious"

27. Robert R. Wilson, *Prophecy and Society in Ancient Israel* (Philadelphia: Fortress, 1980).

28. I. M. Lewis, *Ecstatic Religion: An Anthropological Study of Spirit Possession and Shamanism* (Harmondsworth: Penguin, 1971).

matters but also about matters of foreign policy and war tactics. In these stories there does not seem to be any question of the relationship of Yahweh to political power. These prophets knew that the God of Israel was the power behind the throne. The only question was whether the king and the country would recognize this fact and act accordingly.

This assumption of connection between monarchy and deity continues into the seventh century. The real question for them was to define what a "true, pious" king would look like. That the king would be an extension of the power of the deity was not really in question. Habakkuk, Zephaniah, even Jeremiah and the rest do not question that God acts through the king. The only question is *which* king and *which* policies were truly the will of the deity. Was Yahweh pro-Babylonian or pro-Egyptian? What was the deity-approved foreign policy? What wars did Yahweh want the nation to engage in? Whose vision of God was correct? Kings (and everyone else) had to pick—Hananiah or Jeremiah? And the power-brokers of the country were pushed to pick the "right" king. "If only we could pick the proper king, he would implement God's will and all would be right with the country...and with the world. We just need a proper king."

This consensus attitude begins to break down with the reign, and subsequent death, of the consensus "proper" king—Josiah. Finally, the king comes to the throne who meets the requirements of the definition of the "proper" king—at least the demands of those authors whose texts remain in the Bible. Twice, at the beginning and at the end of the account of Josiah's reign in the book of Kings, we hear the author's evaluation: "He did what was right in the sight of the Lord, and walked in all the way of his father David; he did not turn aside to the right or to the left" (2 Kgs 22:2). Later we read: "Before him there was no king like him, who turned to the Lord with all his heart, with all his soul, and with all his might, according to all the law of Moses" (2 Kgs 23:25). The power of this king and the power of God are the same. The program and propaganda surrounding this king have been the focus of many studies over the years. The complexity of the material surrounding the rule of Josiah is caused, I think, by one thing: Josiah finally fulfilled (or created?) the role of the perfect king, the one through whom Yahweh's power would be manifest.

And then...and then... Josiah headed out to Megiddo and came back dead. And the author of Kings concludes his second evaluation with the ominous words, "nor did any like him arise after him" (2 Kgs 23:25). The experiment was over. The longed-for candidate had arisen. He had done all the right things. And the results were his death and the failure of his program and the looming destruction of the nation. The identification of the royal power with the power of the deity had finally been achieved. And yet, rather than leading to the "Messianic" golden age, it led toward the defeat and destruction of the nation. What was the response?

At least some within the nation continued to look for the "more perfect" king, the Messiah who would inaugurate the paradisical kingdom. But for others, especially within the prophetic materials within the Hebrew Bible, there is a remarkable shift. It seems as if someone said, "Hey, this is not going to happen. We have tried to find, and did find, the best possible king. And he failed. We need to look elsewhere." They do not come to the conclusion that Yahweh is not a god of power, but rather they conclude that God's power will be manifest in ways beyond the national monarchy. Their gaze becomes international. They look to empire.

Ezekiel, a prophet who saw the power of God in magnificent ways, insists in one place that only God will be the ruler over the people: "As I live, says the Lord God, Surely with a mighty hand and an outstretched arm, and with wrath poured out, I will be king over you" (Ezek 20:33). This god is surely a god of power and even violence, but he acts on his own, not through a local political leader, a monarch—even an ideal one. It is interesting to note that, although the term "king" is used by the author of Ezekiel for the kings of Babylon, Egypt, and Tyre, there is only one reference to the ruler of Judah as "king." In that place, Ezekiel seems to be on the verge of the old idealism, resting his hope in the Davidic king: "My servant David shall be king over them; and they shall have one shepherd. They shall follow my ordinances and be careful to observe my statutes. They shall live in the land that I gave to my servant Jacob in which your ancestors lived, they and their children and their children's children shall live there forever, and my servant David shall be their prince forever" (37:24–25). For Ezekiel, the ruler of the New Jerusalem is now demoted to "prince." There may well have been good, practical political reasons for Ezekiel to downplay the power of any coming ruler, but it is clear that his vision of the new Jerusalem is not dependent on the national monarchy.

The same can be said of the vision of the return and the new land found in Second Isaiah. In Second Isaiah, it is God himself who progresses down the royal highway. Only twice is the term "king" mentioned in the writings of Second Isaiah. In 41:21 the author reports the oracles of God to those who think there is another god: "Set forth your case, *says Yahweh*; bring your proofs, *says the king of Jacob*." As with Ezekiel, the all-powerful god, the one who can tell the "former things" and who can stir up "the one from the East" is the true king of the nation. We see this echoed in 44:6: "Thus says Yahweh, the king of Israel…"

This rejection of the national kingship as the possible carrier of the manifestation of the power of God can also be seen in other biblical stories with an anti-monarchical slant. I have recently been using *A Brief History of Ancient Israel* by my friend Victor Matthews as a text for a course. At one point he highlights the anti-monarchical stories which are found in the book of Judges and Samuel, stories such as the report of Samuel's warnings to the people who want to trust in the power of the king in 1 Sam 8.[29] He, along with many others, sees these stories as remnants of some egalitarian past that is remembered down into the days of the monarchy and beyond. I have always found it incredible that people living before the time of the monarchy would have been so critical of the institution of monarchy itself. This is especially the case since the stories themselves admit that the monarchy was what these people (or at least some of them) wanted and expected. Even if there was some sort of anti-monarchical sentiment in the pre-monarchic times, how could these stories have survived the 400+ years of the monarchy in Israel and Judah? People and stories which are critical of the powerful do not tend to survive so well.

One should ask, "When would these stories have rung true?" They seem to me to be the stories of a people with long experience of the monarchy, people who at one time had not only known but created the arguments to invest the very power of God in the person of the king, people who now, after the failure of the ideal king, warned against the temptation of this option. Even the ideal Josiah could not be the locus of God's power.[30]

The prophets, and others, who had come to place their hope and confidence in the power of the righteous king now seem to be searching for a new candidate. In some cases, the intuition to place this power in a royal figure continues—even if the royal figure is beyond the borders of Judah. For example, Second Isaiah morphs his messiah into "the one called from the East," Cyrus. It seems likely that these changes to the way of thinking about the relationship between power and the monarch often had real-life political motivations and ramifications. Is it an accident that this move away from dependence on national royal expressions of power comes just at the time when the prophets (and the rest of the people of

29. Victor Harold Matthews, *A Brief History of Ancient Israel* (Louisville: Westminster John Knox, 2002), 34, 40, et passim.
30. The disillusionment of some of the biblical writers with the hope for a "perfect king" seems to be eerily echoed in our day. Cf. the recent work of David Kuo, *Tempting Faith: An Inside Story of Political Seduction* (New York: Free Press, 2006).

the nation) were faced with the reality of the overwhelming power of the Babylonian and then the Persian Empires? Does it serve Ezekiel's purpose to not be perceived by the Babylonians as expecting a world-dominating king for the people of Judah? Does it work to the advantage of Second Isaiah to have it be known that he and his followers are supporters of the new "super-king" on the block? These speculations could be the start of a whole new exploration.

Power, Politics and Biblical Scholars

While some biblical authors continue to hope for the national "messianic" ruler, there is another trajectory that follows the lead of Ezekiel and Second Isaiah. It is drawn to the identification of the power of God with the superpowers of the day. We might ask, "What happens if and when the connection between the power of God and the power of the super-power empire become identified, not only on the part of the author but by the superpower itself?" The attempt of Second Isaiah to identify Cyrus' rule with the will and power of the god of Judah may have had some effect within the exilic community. But we have no indication that Cyrus himself accepted or exploited this connection.

This trajectory seems to me to reach one of its natural extensions in the developments of Christianity, which at the time of Constantine and after entwines its identity with the rulers of the Empire. For many Christians from that time forward, the power of God and the power of the empire became entwined in ways that we still have not unraveled. The experiment, begun in the prophetic texts in which the power of God and the power of the empire are identified, may find its ultimate conclusion in experiences of the community that go well beyond the time of the texts.

How should we as scholars who live in the shadow of the results of this experiment judge these results? I would suggest that, just as the historical experience of the failure of the "perfect king" Josiah led to a re-evaluation of the idea of the identity of God's power with the rule of the national king, so the historical experience of the identification of Christianity with the power of the empire also needs to be re-evaluated. This wedding of religious ideology with real political power led down a path that resulted in such events as the Inquisition and the Holocaust. These results must lead us to a re-evaluation of the identification of God's power with the power of any superpower. This identification must be questioned especially by those of us in the academy who are in conversation with the authors of these earlier texts.

What conclusions can be drawn from this study? I will suggest three conclusions for consideration:

1. Violence and power are part and parcel of the biblical texts, maybe especially the prophetic texts. This fact cannot and should not be ignored. At the same time, we should insist that these texts were created and existed in a political and historical context. Indeed, to read these texts outside these contexts falsifies them in significant ways. To read them as if they have no political implications and no implications for the understanding of power today is also a mistake.

2. The prophetic texts are not univocal on these issues any more than they are on many other issues. This recognition should keep us from reading and interpreting the texts in simplistic ways. There were a variety of views about kingship, about power, and about violence and the relationship between them in ancient times. If we pick and choose the texts we want to hear, we will be misrepresenting the texts.

3. The failure, in prophetic terms, of even the best of Judah's monarchs was a challenge to the prophets of ancient Judah—and continues to be a challenge to anyone tying religious power and political structures closely together. We as teachers and leaders have the responsibility to make it clear that those making this identification today are extending their theology into an area of the prophetic experiment which has been shown to be dangerous and the results of which are already known and unacceptable.

The identification of a political candidate or policy with the will of God is particularly tempting in these political days. Stories that pointed out the "triumph" of the religious right in the person and policies of the Bush administration became a commonplace. On the other side, many a Democrat felt that if only the "right" and "just" and "true" candidate would prevail, that candidate (Obama or another) would surely save the nation from destruction, and lead us truly to the Promised Land. This comes at a time when some of the "prophets" who saw the triumph of George W. Bush as the beginning of the golden age have reconsidered their position.

I would contend that it is our job as those who have seen the failed results of the previous prophetic attempts to tie God's identity to a particular king or a powerful empire to speak out forcefully about the failed results of these experiments. This is hard to do, no doubt. The paths taken in these experiments are tempting. But we know the disasters waiting at the end of both these paths—and have a responsibility to warn others and to call them to take some other way.

RECLAIMING JEREMIAH'S VIOLENCE[*]

Kathleen M. O'Connor

Introduction

Here is what I know about biblical violence:

The Bible portrays God as violent, punishing, and abusive—not always, not consistently, but clearly, broadly, and indisputably. Believing communities often ignore these and other violent texts, or use them as validations of harsh religious strictures, or assume they contain a definitive insight into God's character.[1]

Here is how I came to my personal impasse on texts of divine violence:

I was teaching a Doctor of Ministry course on the book of Jeremiah at Columbia Seminary about ten years ago. Before the class got more than five or six chapters into the book, students rebelled. The book of Jeremiah, they said, is unacceptable in the world today because it is fraught with the violence of God. Page after page of poetry and prose overflows with divine anger against the people. God appears in them as an abusive, battering husband, an angry and offended covenant partner,

    * This essay arises from research begun with the help of a Henry Luce III Fellowship in Theology. An earlier version was first presented as a keynote address at the Academy of Homiletics Annual Meeting in Boston, 2008.

    1. In his book, *Facing The Abusing God: A Theology of Protest* (Louisville: Westminster John Knox, 1991), David Blumenthal maintains that God is abusive in the ways humans are abusive. Walter Brueggemann in *Theology of the Old Testament: Testimony, Dispute, Advocacy* (Minneapolis: Augsburg Fortress, 1997) claims something similar. For him, one stream of the biblical testimony, what he calls "counter testimony," reveals an abusive, angry God. See also the recent discussions of the problem of divine violence in David A. Bernat and Jonathan Klawans, eds., *Religion and Violence: The Biblical Heritage* (Sheffield: Sheffield Phoenix, 2007), and Jeremy Young, *The Violence of God and the War on Terror* (New York: Seabury, 2007). And see the eloquent article by Catherine Madsen, "Notes on God's Violence," *CrossCurrents* 51 (2001): 220–56. Thanks to Walter Brueggemann for this reference and for years of comradely arguments about God.

an executor of battle against God's own people, a violent male, abuser of female Judah, and, on top of that, God blames the victims for historical catastrophe. From within the ranks of Judaism, David Blumenthal underscores what is at stake for these students: "Reason and common sense tell us that a loving God does not kill innocent children, or exterminate loyal followers, or punish the righteous."[2]

Because of such divine violence some feminists and psychologically informed readers have abandoned both the Bible and the churches that endorse them. And of course, divine violence provides ammunition to anti-religious thinkers such as David Hawkins and Christopher Hitchens, not to mention Bill Maher. My vocational problem as professor of Old Testament in a seminary is that I agree with all these people.

What is left of poor old Jeremiah after this? Marcion was right. Cut out the prophet, and while we are at it, the whole Old Testament and large portions of the New, because they do not portray the God of Love. For several years, I could go no further and I let Jeremiah lie fallow, at least in the classroom, because I had no refutation. But Marcion was declared a heretic in 144 C.E.

Here is what I think about violence in Jeremiah now:

Jeremiah's fire and brimstone is a survival strategy, an instrument of healing, a way to make meaning and rebuild life in a world destroyed. To excise the book's violence, to ignore it, to fly from it, not only violates an ancient text arising from its own cultural world; it is also deprives us of insight into theological and pastoral creativity in the healing of wounds after disaster.

Here is how I was led to reconsider violence in Jeremiah:

I came upon the work of Old Testament scholar Daniel Smith-Christopher, who uses both trauma and refugee studies to interpret violence in the book of Ezekiel.[3] This led me to an interdisciplinary field called Trauma and Disaster Studies. These investigations overturned everything. Drawn from anthropology, sociology, cognitive psychology, and literary criticism, trauma and disaster studies investigate the impact of violence upon individuals and communities. They serve as an "heuristic" or "finding" device. They offer spectacles to "find" what is hidden beneath the opaque surfaces of human suffering; they explain why so

2. David Blumenthal, "Theodicy: Dissonance in Theory and Praxis," in *The Fascination of Evil* (eds. David Tracy and Hermann Härring; vol.1 of *Concilium*; Maryknoll: Orbis, 1998), 95–106; or http://www.js.emory.edu/BLUMENTHAL/ Theodicy.html.

3. Daniel L. Smith-Christopher, *A Biblical Theology of Exile* (Overtures to Biblical Theology; Minneapolis: Fortress, 2002).

much of Jeremiah's vision is harsh and troubling, and they show how Jeremiah's violence helps.

The disaster that gives birth to Jeremiah is the Babylonian assault on Judah in the sixth century B.C.E., including three invasions, three deportations and fifty years of military occupation. Every passage in Jeremiah addresses this disaster—announcing, enacting, or explaining it. For the book's audience, the disaster has already happened. I am trying to read with them.

When traumatic violence afflicts a whole society,[4] trauma becomes a public disaster. Disasters interrupt life on a vast scale. Smith-Christopher describes a disaster as "disastrous only when events exceed the ability of the group to cope, to redefine and reconstruct" their world.[5] The community is rendered inert in an enormity of devastation.

Disasters overwhelm everything. They overwhelm human capacities and resources. They inflict injury on human bodies and spirits, on their social world, on the environment, and on everything that gives meaning to life.[6] In a disaster, death and physical destruction is only part of what happens. When victims regain a certain level of physical safety, when some "new normal" appears, less visible consequences of disaster can endure indefinitely and vastly inhibit a society's chances of survival.

Here are some these consequences of disaster that underlie the book of Jeremiah:

Fractured Memories
People cannot fully experience traumatic violence it as it occurs. They cannot absorb it into consciousness as it is happening because violence overpowers the senses. At the same time the violent events are imprinted on the brain in fragmented pieces, in fractured memories of the events. In the aftermath of violence, memory fragments stomp around in the mind like menacing ghosts, as if they were alive with a will of their own. We know about this from soldiers returning from Iraq, from survivors of child abuse, even from people who know more limited trauma such as medical operations or automobile accidents.

---

4. For studies of disasters and their social impacts, see E. L. Quarantelli, ed., *What is a Disaster? Perspectives on the Question* (London: Routledge, 1998), and on responses to trauma from various cultural perspectives, see John P. Wilson and Catherine So-Kum Tang, eds., *Cross-Cultural Assessment of Psychological Trauma and PTSD* (New York: Springer, 2007).

5. Smith-Christopher, *A Biblical Theology*, 79.

6. Elaine Scarry, *The Body in Pain* (New York: Oxford University Press, 1985), 61.

Wordlessness

A second related effect is that traumatic violence also takes away speech. It overwhelms victim's ability to talk about what happened. According to Elaine Scarry, severe physical and emotional pain[7] unmakes speech, reducing sufferers' expressions to groans and screams disconnected from meaning, in a kind of pre-language state.[8] German writer, W. G. Sebald, documents the enveloping silence that followed the Dresden Fire bombings for more than half a century after World War II.[9]

Numbness

A third impact of traumatic violence follows from the first two. Violence shatters emotional responsiveness; it makes victims' hearts turn to stone.[10] Trauma and disaster make people numb and make grief unreachable because feelings disappear, and they cannot grieve their many losses. I do not address this here except to mention that the book of Jeremiah is not filled with weeping and lamentation for nothing.

Loss of Faith

Perhaps disaster's most important consequence for understanding divine violence in Jeremiah is that disasters destroy faith in God, the world, and other people. Traditions and institutions that once firmly anchored life before the catastrophe collapse with the physical world. Doubt of even the most basic sense of safety leaves people God-forsaken and betrayed.[11] As a solar eclipse blots out the sun, calamity blots out God. That means that God's own life is at stake in the wake of disaster.

How can a community survive such anchorlessness? How can it recover? How can God survive such boundless devastation?

Psychologists Paul Antze and Michael Lambek report that trauma sufferers are condemned to reenact memories of violence until they begin the work of interpretation.[12] Others insist that victims must re-experience,

   7. Ibid.
   8. Ibid., 4–21.
   9. W. G. Sebald, *On the Natural History of Destruction* (New York: Random House, 2003), 3–32.
   10. Bessel A. van der Kolk, "The Black Hole of Trauma," in *Traumatic Stress: The Effects of Overwhelming Experience on Mind, Body, and Society* (ed. Bessel A. van der Kolk, Alexander C. McFarlane, and Lars Weisaeth; New York: Guilford, 1996), 3–23 (12).
   11. Kai Erikson, "Notes on Trauma and Community," in *Trauma: Explorations in Memory* (ed. Cathy Carruth; Baltimore: The Johns Hopkins University Press, 1995), 183–99 (198).
   12. Paul Antze and Michael Lambek, *Tense Past: Cultural Essays in Trauma and Memory* (New York: Routledge, 1996), xix; Bessell A. van der Kolk, Alexander C.

retell, and reframe the violence until it is no longer fire-breathing horror that engulfs everything. But how can this happen when to remember is to be re-traumatized, to re-experience the original violence as if it were still happening? And there are no words for it. And the God of promise, the God of Zion, the God of the Temple, of covenant, of kingship, of priest-hood, of worship, the God of Judah is *in absentia*.

Jeremiah

Here's how trauma and disaster studies help me reclaim Jeremiah's violence:

Jeremiah[13] does the life-saving work of a preacher–poet–theologian. He looks at his people's situation, he lives among them and sees their world; he names it, and re-frames it by imaginatively re-inventing tradi-tions they share. This interpretive work rebuilds them into a people.

Jeremiah's violence enables Judah's survival. It brings up memories of invasions, but—and this is key—it does so "at a slant," in poetry and symbol. Borrowing words of Emily Dickinson about poetry in general: "Tell all truth but tell it slant."[14] To tell the truth slant means to put it at a distance, slightly outside life, as if on a screen, in a poetic world, so the violence does not come back to strangle and re-traumatize readers.

The War Poems

The poems in Jer 4:5–6:30 cluster around scenes of battle, so I call them "war poems." They gather up all the kinds of violence I mention above. Three other passages outside these chapters continue the military imagery found here (8:16–17; 10:17–22; 13:20–27). Of these, ch. 13's poem tells of the rape of Zion, and that is where I am headed.

War in Jeremiah's poetry is no ordinary war, no news report. It is mythic battle cast in a cosmic realm.[15] Mythic warfare takes place in

McFarlane, and Onno Van der Hart, "A General Approach to Treatment of PTSD," in *Traumatic Stress: The Effects of Overwhelming Experience on Mind, Body, and Society* (ed. van der Kolk et al.; New York: Guilford, 1996), 417–40.

13. By Jeremiah, I refer to the book and the presentation of the prophetic figure within it. I make no claims here about the historical person of Jeremiah.

14. Dickinson's can be found online at http://www.americanpoets.com/poems/emilydickinson.

15. This is what Calvin might call "dramatic theater," according to Serene Jones "'Soul Anatomy': Calvin's Commentary on the Psalms," in *Psalms in Community: Jewish and Christian Textual, Liturgical, and Artistic Traditions* (ed. Harold W. Attridge and Margot E. Fassler; Atlanta: Society of Biblical Literature, 2004), 265–84. For Calvin, the psalms are "textual theater wherein traumatized persons can

another frame of reference than the literal. Rather than showing Babylon attacking Judah, one army against another, the poems depict an ethereal enemy, called "the foe from the north," who threatens and finally attacks a woman, the Daughter of Zion. She is, of course, the personified city of Jerusalem and YHWH's cast off wife from the broken marriage metaphor in chs. 2–3.[16] Across these poems, language of siege creates a loose, arcing coherence, an implied narrative that culminates in the rape of this city-woman (13:20–27). This poetry creates language, defends God, and helps the people. The three elements intertwine. Divine violence is essential to its purposes.

The War Begins (4:5–7). A voice announces impending attack and urges the people to run for shelter:

> Blow the trumpet through the land;
>   Shout aloud and say,
> "Gather together, and let us go
>   Into the fortified cities!"
> Raise a standard toward Zion,
>   Flee for safety, do not delay,
> For I am bringing evil from the north,
>   And a great destruction. (4:5–6)[17]

The sights and sounds of this poem carry readers smack into middle of terrifying memories of approaching war; by metonym, small details of battle evoke the whole thing. The audience knows the sound of the

---

adopt identity scripts that strengthen their faith, even in the midst of the harm they are experiencing" (p. 269).

16. Walter Brueggemann, *Exile and Homecoming: A Commentary on Jeremiah* (Grand Rapids; Eerdmans, 1988), 56. Judah and Jerusalem are nearly interchangeable figures across Jeremiah. She has many names: Jerusalem, Judah, Daughter of Zion, daughter of my people. When God addresses Jerusalem as a woman, an ancient Near Eastern tradition of cities as feminine comes into play. Cities and nations are feminine in the ancient Near East, and often personified as female figures, evoking goddesses charged with protecting cities among Israel's neighbors. See Michael H. Floyd, "Welcome Back, Daughter of Zion!," *CBQ* 70 (2008): 484–504; Elizabeth Boase, *The Fulfilment of Doom? The Dialogic Interaction between the Book of Lamentations and the Pre-Exilic/Early Exilic Prophetic Literature* (LHBOTS 437; New York: T&T Clark International, 2006), 53–54; Julie Galambush, *Jerusalem in the Book of Ezekiel: The City as Yahweh's Wife* (SBLDS 130; Atlanta: Scholars Press, 1992); Kathleen M. O'Connor, *Lamentations and the Tears of the Word* (Maryknoll: Orbis, 2001), 14; Christl M. Maier, *Daughter Zion, Mother Zion: Gender, Space, and the Sacred in Ancient Israel* (Minneapolis: Fortress, 2008).

17. Translations are from the NRSV unless otherwise indicated.

trumpet musters troops and raising the standard gathers horses and riders to strike. But memories of violence come to the fore in glimpses, only glimpses. As the poem continues, the foe turns into a lion stalking his prey:

> A lion goes up from its thicket,
>   A destroyer of nations has set out;
> He has gone from his place
>   To make your land a waste;
> Your cities will be ruins
>   Without inhabitant. (4:7)

This poem portrays what has already happened to readers. Though the poem sets the assault in the future, it has already happened. The bleak landscape of war, the place where readers live mentally and spiritually, is "told at a slant," as a macabre dance among human and super-human parties. The foe from the north is a bestial enemy who plans "to make your[18] land a waste" (4:7).[19] The foe, sent by God's "fierce anger," joins God in a gravely uneven match against the Daughter of Zion, expressed by second feminine singular forms, "your land, your cities."[20]

Even as the war poems stir up the whole emotional world of terror, they set memories of war in a symbolic world, as if it were happening to someone else. The violence can be faced but slowly, fragment by fragment.

War Against a Woman (6:1–30). An overwhelming sense of powerlessness is a typical response to traumatic violence. One is helpless, watching the violence happen. By depicting the war as an attack on a woman, the poems capture the powerlessness of victims and their humiliation as a defeated people. There are really two wars in these poems, cosmic and domestic. The two poetic spheres illuminate each other and offer two languages to tell about the violence. They provide words for the speechless. As the poems jump from battlefield to household, they limit exposure to terrible memories. Here is one example in poetic speeches about the approaching invasion among God, the enemy and the people (6:1–6):

---

18. Second feminine singular forms in Hebrew.

19. See John Hill, *Friend or Foe? The Figure of Babylon in the Book of Jeremiah MT* (Leiden: Brill, 1999).

20. For theological analysis of God as warrior against Judah, see Louis Stulman, *Jeremiah* (Abingdon Old Testament Commentaries; Nashville: Abingdon, 2005), 81–85.

The war:

> "Flee for safety, blow a trumpet,
> raise a signal for evil looms from the north and a great destruction." (6:1)

The marriage:

> "I have likened Daughter Zion to the loveliest of pastures,"
> says God, longing for his once lovely wife. (6:2)

The war and the marriage:

> Shepherds with their flocks shall come against her.
> "Prepare war against her; up, and let us attack at noon!"
> "Woe to us for the day declines and the shadows of evening lengthen!"
> "Up, and let us attack by night, and destroy her palaces!" (6:4–5)

This subtle inter-mixing of war and marriage imagery not only brings up violent memories in short doses, but it also reframes the cataclysm as a result of the people's failed relationship with God. That means, no matter how angry, God has not died.

God controls both the martial and marital spheres. Husband God, "The Lord of Hosts," orders his wife's destruction and even designs the military strategy to do it:

> "Cut down her trees; cast up a siege ramp against Jerusalem."

Then God pumps up the troops to justify the attack:

> "This is the city that must be punished;
> there is nothing but oppression within her." (6:6)

An oddly intimate affair, the war is a personal vendetta by a disgruntled, violent husband. He pours his wrath over the land, destroying everything: "the children in the street," young men, husbands and wives, the old and the ill, houses, and fields (6:11–12). Divine fury sweeps away everything and everyone that make life worth living.

This is the plight of readers; this is the violence of their world, and it is their experience of God. Things get worse; the army approaches on the horizon:

> "See, a people is coming from the land of the north,
> a great nation is stirring from the farthest parts of the earth.
> They grasp the bow and the javelin,
> They are cruel and have no mercy,
> and their sound is like the roaring of the sea;
> against you, O Daughter of Zion!" (6:22–23)

Their target is unmistakable. She is the one whom God loves.

The Rape Poem (13:20–27)

God's anger at the Daughter of Zion explains, elucidates, and interprets the war. It offers vivid language to name the violence, and paradoxically, it defends God. God's anger means that God is in relationship with them and that cause and effect are at work in the world.

In the rape poem, any remnants of married love turn to horror. God commands the Daughter of Zion: "Lift up your eyes and see those who come from the north" (13:20). And when she wants to know, "Why have these things come upon me?," the answer is clear. It is all her fault. "It is for the greatness of your iniquity that your skirts are lifted up and you are violated" (13:22). The "lifting of skirts" may be a euphemism for rape, but the second clause makes rape certain: "you are violated."[21] The violator, unnamed in v. 22, becomes her husband God in v. 26: "I myself will strip off your skirts over your face" (13:25–26, my translation).[22]

Jeremiah's language world shrinks vast assaults by an army into an attack upon one woman. The rape imagery reduces the scope of the violence for a destroyed people. Female rape is a familiar metaphor for war in the Old Testament and a common weapon of war throughout history unto this very day. It is an apt metaphor for invasion. Rape brutalizes in the most intimate of ways; a stronger one subdues a weaker one, hurts her (or him), shames and humiliates her,[23] and turns her into a bleeding victim, gasping for life.[24] God's rape of Zion is appalling and unbearable theology. It is horrendous because it translates military attack into the violence against a woman, because it makes God the agent of sexual assault, because it makes women scapegoats for the nation's fall,

21. The Hebrew reads, "your heels undergo violence," heels being "private parts" according to Jack Lundbom, *Jeremiah 1–20* (AB 21A; New York: Doubleday, 1999), 686. It is well known that rape is a persistent weapon of warfare. Pamela Gordon and Harold C. Washington, "Rape as Military Metaphor in the Hebrew Bible," in *Feminist Companion to the Latter Prophets* (ed. Athalya Brenner; Sheffield: Sheffield Academic, 1995), 308–25. Throughout history unto this very day women are assaulted and sexually penetrated in violence that not only harms them horribly, if they survive, but also shames their men who cannot protect them.

22. Lundbom, *Jeremiah*, 686, discusses the Hebrew of these verses and understands the assault as public shaming by exposure, though he also connects the verses to the sexual assaults against women common in war (Amos 1:13; Isa 3:17; Ezek 16:39–40).

23. On shame in Jeremiah, see Amy Kalmanofsky, *Terror All Around: The Rhetoric of Horror in the Book of Jeremiah* (LHBOTS 390; New York: T&T Clark International, 2008), 65–68.

24. See Susan Bryson, *Aftermath: Violence and the Remaking of a Self* (Princeton: Princeton University Press, 2002).

because it sees sexual assault as suitable punishment, and because it locates hideous actions within God. It is utterly unacceptable speech about God.

But trauma and disaster studies suggest a different way to understand. The fact that the rape is appalling and unbearable, unspeakable and unacceptable is surely the point! To be victims of invasion *is* appalling, unbearable, unspeakable, and unacceptable, a ripping apart, an intimate destruction of life. This poem of God's violent rape of Zion gives the people back their story and brings to speech the profound terror and harm of Babylonian assaults. The rape shows the people the reality of their suffering, as if in a mirror. To see and name this reality as what they have suffered is the first step toward healing.

War is rape on a national scale. The rape poem—in the language of James Boyd Wright speaking about Homer's *Iliad*—"reproduce(s) the difficulty of the world itself."[25] Through it, Jeremiah conveys life-destroying violence, painful physical penetration, traumatic powerlessness, and shameful humiliation, and the victim survives the assault to live with its consequences.[26] The rape of Zion revisits memories of frightful violence and painful history through a narrowed window, as a drama of violence against one vulnerable figure who stands in for the whole people. Rape is what happened to them; it is their lives rendered symbolically, their fragmented memories drawn into a narrative, into new speech for a speech-destroying disaster. Jeremiah's war poems restore the capacity to speak the unspeakable.

Violent God as Survival Strategy

That God does this seems beyond the theological pale, beyond the possibility of redemption as God-talk. To the contrary, Jeremiah's war poems keep God alive. That God's rape is a "text of terror"[27] is central to its purpose and to its capacity to defend God. For Judean victims, defeat by Babylon means that Judah lost the war to superior deities, to Marduk and his pantheon. It means that Judah's God is ineffectual, effete, and has "been disappeared." But if God is the author of Zion's rape, God is not disappeared, not a defeated lesser being, not diminished, but powerful,

25. James Boyd White, *When Words Lose Their Meaning: Constitutions and Reconstitutions of Language, Character, and Community* (Chicago: University of Chicago Press, 1984), 87.

26. See Bryson, *Aftermath*.

27. A term made part of the interpretive lexicon by Phyllis Trible in her book by the same name, *Texts of Terror: Literary-Feminist Reading of Biblical Narratives* (Philadelphia: Fortress, 1984).

active, and present. The Babylonian deities have not triumphed, nor has ungoverned Fate propelled events. For victims of disaster, this is a life raft.

For many of us this theology is a leaky raft, at best. Modern Western thinkers do not believe that either divine anger or human sinfulness fully explain disaster. We understand both national and personal catastrophes to come from complex webs of cause and effect.

But what I see in this shocking violent imagery is a provisional effort to make sense of the disaster, to hold onto God, to cling mightily to the Creator in the midst of destruction all around. I see engagement in life-giving, world-altering interpretation. I see in God's violence a potent stammering toward meaning, a poetic offering that begins the work of interpretation, of making sense of the senseless. God's punishing violence gives the disaster predictable causes. It provides orderly structure, direction, and purpose that extend beyond the visible world. And, that God is Punisher offers one way, among many in Jeremiah, to integrate the disaster into the long stream of the nation's existence, its long narrative memory.[28] The disaster thus begins to be assimilated into the larger story of their relationship with God from the time of Abraham, Sarah, and Hagar. They are still connected to their past identity as God's people,

To tell of the fall of the nation as a result of God's punishment reframes the disaster. It defends God from charges of injustice and arbitrariness. It strives to persuade readers that God is innocent of cruelty, reluctant to punish, and required to do so because of Judah's sin.

God's violence is not the book's only word about God. Like the rest of the book, the war poetry characterizes God in complex, conflicting ways. God is both fierce military commander who sends the foe from the north and also troubled husband, reluctant and heart-broken at having to punish his wife so terribly. And Jeremiah himself further complicates God's character by blaming God for deceiving the nation about the disaster (4:10). The rest of the book will confuse and obscure the divine character even more. And yet, the fact that God is a multi-faceted character, something much more than violent, does not reduce the difficulties created by that violence.

And God's violent character is only one side of the theological difficulty. Another is its rhetoric of human responsibility. If God is the enraged punisher, then the people bring on the punishment and force God to act. We moderns know, of course, that even if rulers are corrupt, priests fail, and people contribute to their downfall in any number of

28. Kalí Tal, *Worlds of Hurt: Reading Literatures of Trauma* (Cambridge: Cambridge University Press, 1996), 6.

foolish, sinful ways, other historical factors contribute to the cataclysm. But this rhetoric of human responsibility is also a partial, provisional explanation of catastrophe.

To seek out responsible parties in the face of disaster is an inevitable human activity; it is a strategy of survival. Assigning responsibility makes events understandable, reins them into a palatable size, finds cause and effect in unmanageable disorder. Blaming someone or something for disaster is a search for justice and order in the universe when all evidence of justice and order has vanished from view. Like a ball tossed about in a game, blame for the disaster changes hands frequently in Jeremiah, just as it did after the ruinous floods in New Orleans, 2005. "Why did this happen to us? "Whose fault is it?" To these questions, wrong answers, partial explanations are better for victims than no explanation. That it is our fault is a provisional answer.

When people take responsibility themselves for traumatic violence, they also claim agency. By laying responsibility for toppling the land upon the people, Jeremiah transforms passive victims into actors in their own lives. "If you got yourself into it, you can get yourself out of it." If the people's behavior caused the collapse of their world, a change in behavior can give them a different future.

Psychologists insist that taking responsibility for experiences of violence can be helpful, even when the thinking is wrong. Romie Janoff Bulman[29] writes that when people blame themselves for their life-threatening illnesses—I ate too much meat, I should have stopped smoking sooner, I should have exercised more—they do better emotionally than those who do not; so also with rape victims and survivors of child abuse. Self-blaming projects order onto the universe and creates a wall of mental protection from fear of repetition of the same violence. Self-blaming individually or within a community is a temporary survival strategy, and markedly different than an outsider blaming the people of New Orleans for the city's destruction.[30]

Jeremiah's war poetry gives survivors a way forward because they insist that Judah has been unfaithful, not God. God has tried in every way to possible to intimidate or coax Judah to return. This means that, no matter how inadequate an explanation of historical events this may be to Western sensibilities, the divine violence proclaims that life is not utterly

29. Romie Janoff Bulman, *Shattered Assumptions: Towards a New Psychology of Trauma* (New York: Free Press, 1992), 125–29.

30. Even when outsiders accuse inhabitants of sin as the cause of tragedy—for example, when certain evangelists blamed New York and New Orleans for the fate of their cities—the speakers themselves are seeking order in the world to keep fear at bay.

random, that God is not powerless, and that people have some control as actors in their life. They are the punished ones, but the system itself has meaning. For survivors of cultural collapse, this is a word of salvation.

Jeremiah's violent poetry creates a vocabulary of experience, builds a common language among survivors to name what happened, gives shape to disaster, and helps Judeans face it in small portions. The poetry mythologizes disastrous events to reduce them to "a set of standardized narratives" that turn disaster from something frightening and uncontrollable into something contained and predictable.[31] The book's violent language makes collective experience become conscious and public and articulates an imaginative alternative universe that slowly, episodically, brings readers into their own unhinged world, invites them to relive their experiences and, perhaps, begin come to terms with them. The violence of these poems expresses pain and marches into its center.

Jeremiah's violent poetic worlds of marriage and warfare and his God of punitive anger are what Brueggemann calls "an open ended poetic reading of reality."[32] They are not incitements to violence among readers, at least not originally. They may become that when read uncritically without regard to the violent world that gave them birth. Maybe we read them that way because our culture encourages violence to solve problems, to entertain us, and because as a nation we are largely not victims of disaster at present. Viewed from the perspectives of trauma and disaster studies, these poems express the violence inflicted on the nation; they do not create it. If this is so, Jeremiah's violent worlds need not be excused, nor wished away, nor accepted at face value as the way God is.

In our present world of cascading disasters, both natural and human made, of war upon war in the Middle East, of economic collapse and personal trauma, we need Jeremiah's violence, understood critically as the fiery danger that it can be, and the balm of Gilead that it is. Preachers and teachers need caution and love in facing the violence already experienced by individuals in their communities and in viewing the world outside. They need neither shrink from the violence of Jeremiah's God nor take it as the last word about God. Perhaps, instead, Jeremiah's Violent One is best viewed in terms Robert Frost proposes for poetry in general, as "a momentary stay against confusion."[33] Maybe that is what all theology is, a momentary glimpse of the unsayable.

31. Tal, *Worlds of Hurt*, 6.
32. Brueggemann, *Exile and Homecoming*, 52.
33. Robert Frost, "The Figure a Poem Makes" (1939), quoted by Christopher Benfey, "The Storm over Robert Frost," *The New York Review of Books* (December 4, 2008): 49.

HEWN BY THE PROPHET:
AN ANALYSIS OF VIOLENCE AND SEXUAL TRANSGRESSION IN HOSEA WITH REFERENCE TO THE HOMILETICAL AESTHETIC OF JEREMIAH WRIGHT

Carolyn J. Sharp

Aesthetics is never "simply" representation. Every cultural act is a complex expression of power relations received by an interpretive community. This is obviously true of paintings, photography, and other enduring visual representations. It is also true of transient aural media such as musical and preaching performances. Because aesthetic acts mediate power, they are inevitably implicated in politics and ethics. Studying a painting, watching a film, or hearing a speech, the audience encounters power enacted on multiple levels, including that of the content being represented; the overt or veiled position of the artist/writer/speaker; the constructed position of the implied audience (which the real audience may accept, refuse, or reframe); and the means by which representation is enacted and received (the gaze, the voice, hearing). Each act of representation has the potential to purvey truth or to distort, to invite assent or engender resistance, to constrain or expand the cultural imagination of its audience.

The present essay explores the aesthetics of prophetic diction in the book of Hosea, paying particular attention to violence and sexual transgression as subtexts of Hosea's rhetoric. Francis Andersen and David Noel Freedman write in their Hosea commentary in the Anchor Bible series,

> There is certainly turbulence in Hosea's thought that would seem to interfere with the composure of mind needed for composition in classical forms; this circumstance could, however, make for a flow of lyrical expression as sublime as more formal work. Without claiming too much for the perfection of his art, we feel at least that Hosea's abilities should not be restricted in advance of studying his work, whether by the constraints of such conventional forms as genre, or by the supposed primitive stage of prophetic discourse in his time.[1]

---

1. Francis I. Andersen and David Noel Freedman, *Hosea* (AB 24; New York: Doubleday 1980), 71.

The confused and disturbing qualities of Hosea's rhetoric have long challenged interpreters. Hosea presents a high incidence of garbled grammar, instances of impossible syntax, and a marked lack of clarity about historical referents. The book of Hosea began to take shape during the tumultuous decades after the death of Jeroboam II, a time during which no fewer than six kings sat on the throne of Samaria. According to the standard historicist reading, Hosea's oracles are difficult in large part because of their originally oral delivery in chaotic political circumstances. On this sort of reading, the book's turbulent aesthetic reflects the theopolitical upheavals of the latter part of the eighth century; opaque references to Gilgal, Bethel, Mizpah, and so forth may be understood as belonging to Hosea's polemic against Yahwistic syncretism or idolatry at those cultic sites;[2] and so on.

While such historicist observations are commonplace in Hosea scholarship and may be accurate in part, my reading moves away from the presumption that eighth-century sociopolitical history is the obvious or only conceptual framework in which to interpret the utterances of the prophet. I agree with Ehud Ben Zvi that the book of Hosea does not cue its readers to read its oracles as relating only to specific contemporary situations in the time of Hosea.[3] Rather, the "history" created by the text may itself be a metaphor for insider/outsider tension around boundaries having to do with the identity of Israel as a people writ larger, throughout the sweep of Israel's history early and late. While some grammatical and conceptual issues in Hosea may fairly be considered to be the products of unintended errors in the composition, redaction, or transmission of the text, other aspects of the inaccessibility of Hosea's rhetoric may be due to traditio-historical challenges that the prophet intends to present to his implied audience. That is to say, the tumultuous aesthetic of Hosea may be a meaningful feature of the book. If it is, it may be analyzed in its own right, not merely as an unfortunate by-product of historical accident, but as a performative quality of the prophet's discourse.

---

2. The assumption that there was an active Canaanite fertility cult in the eighth century has come under criticism from Gale Yee and Alice A. Keefe, among others. Yee and Keefe focus on a historical-contextual explanation of Hos 1–2 that takes seriously socioeconomic issues prevailing in the time of Hosea and particularly the movement toward monarchically controlled "agribusiness" trade that exploited local farmers. See Gale A. Yee, " 'She Is Not My Wife and I Am Not Her Husband': A Materialist Analysis of Hosea 1–2," *BibInt* 9 (2001): 345–83; Alice A. Keefe, *Woman's Body and the Social Body in Hosea* (JSOTSup 338; Sheffield: Sheffield Academic, 2001).

3. See Ehud Ben Zvi, *Hosea* (FOTL 21A/1; Grand Rapids: Eerdmans, 2005).

That disjuncture, ambiguity, and fragmentation in texts can signify rather than simply flag the absence of meaningful signification has become virtually axiomatic in poststructuralist literary analysis. The hermeneutical possibilities attendant upon that insight from the world of theory have, however, been only tentatively explored in the prophetic corpus to this point, with the notable exception of James R. Linville's work on Amos.[4] Interpreters interested in the breakdown of coherent signifying do not tend to be historical critics invested in recovery of an original and definitive textual meaning. The more agile postmodernist readers in Hebrew Bible scholarship generally focus on aporias and tensions that enliven the reception of biblical texts at the level of cultural metanarrative,[5] although sustained attention has been paid to ambiguity and irony in Esther by Timothy K. Beal and some others.[6] But incoherence and opacity may be explored with an eye to aesthetic effect as well, and this project is compelling to me. Disjuncture in biblical words and imagery may be construed as a rhetorical strategy employed by the ancient author in order to destabilize discourse and violate the expectations of the implied audience. The biblical prophetic books act powerfully on the imagination of their implied audiences by means of dramatic metaphors that generate conflict, sharp ironies that undermine interpretive mastery, and unexpected shifts of tone that entrap the audience. Ambiguity can confuse the implied audience until escape becomes impossible. Disjuncture and violence in prophetic rhetoric may be part of a purposive communication strategy.

To explore this possibility, the present essay will bring an analysis of violence and sexual transgression in Hosea into conversation with a highly visible 2003 sermon of Jeremiah A. Wright, senior pastor emeritus of Trinity United Church of Christ in Chicago. The content of what has come to be called Wright's "God Damn America" sermon has been deplored by some critics as inflammatory and applauded by others as prophetic. Reference to Wright's homiletic can provide a contemporary framework for understanding the rhetoric of Hosea, whose witness

4. James R. Linville, "What Does 'It' Mean? Interpretation at the Point of No Return in Amos 1–2," *BibInt* 8 (2000): 400–24.

5. Tod Linafelt, *Surviving Lamentations: Catastrophe, Lament, and Protest in the Afterlife of a Biblical Book* (Chicago: University of Chicago Press, 2000); Yvonne Sherwood, *A Biblical Text and Its Afterlives: The Survival of Jonah in Western Culture* (Cambridge: Cambridge University Press, 2000).

6. See, for example, Timothy K. Beal, *The Book of Hiding: Gender, Ethnicity, Annihilation, and Esther* (Biblical Limits; New York: Routledge, 1997); Sherwood's deft examination of the reception history of Jonah in *A Biblical Text and Its Afterlives*; and Linafelt's *Surviving Lamentations*.

likewise has been deplored by some critics as inflammatory and celebrated as prophetic by others. For convenience, my own unofficial
transcript of the relevant part of the sermon is attached at the end of this
essay. A video clip of this part of the sermon may be viewed at http://
www.youtube.com/watch?v=RvMbeVQj6Lw.[7] Also engaged at key
points in this endeavor will be the homiletical theory of John S. McClure
as expounded in his 2001 book, *Other-Wise Preaching: A Postmodern
Ethic for Homiletics*, and particularly his chapter entitled "Exiting the
House of Tradition." McClure wrestles with the identity-forming and
decentering aspects of Scripture-based homiletics in the late modern and
postmodern eras. His interest in the deconstructive agenda of the preacher
holds significant promise for a contemporary analysis of Hosea's rhetoric.

Some preliminary observations about form and content in Hosea are in
order. The rhetoric of Hosea seems to be heavily historically contex-
tualized: place names and references to tradition are abundant in its
fourteen chapters. Yet Hosea remains elliptical as to the explicit significance of its historicizing referents, including the many geographical
names. Further, Hosea exhorts its audience to understand the prophetic
word by means of a shocking metaphor—actually a complex of motifs
concerning whore, mother, and offspring—that changes so mercurially
that apprehension can be only momentary and unstable at best. The
diction of Hosea continually frustrates the one seeking to master its full
significance. We might say that the incoherence of Hosea repeatedly
violates the (assumed) competence of the audience.

In what follows, I will consider two fronts on which the performative
rhetoric of Hosea signifies by means of confusion and shock. First, I will
explore the ambiguity of Hosea's elliptical allusions to tradition via place
names. My argument is that Hosea's ambiguity requires the implied
audience to reconstruct a subtext uniting these disparate references into a
damning history of Israel's faithlessness. Hosea's people are schooled
about who they have been historically (and per Hosea, it is a grim picture) as they struggle to understand what the prophet is saying. My
second line of inquiry will suggest that the incoherence with which the
metaphor complex of whore/mother/offspring is deployed functions to
reconstruct the implied audience as a new subject resistant to their own
theological and ethical errors of the past.

7. Sermon, "Confusing God and Government," delivered by Jeremiah A. Wright
on April 13 2003 at Trinity United Church of Christ, Chicago, Illinois. Online:
http://odeo.com/espisodes/17890793, published March 21 2008 and accessed February 14 2009.

Underlying my approach is the conviction that content ought not be considered as a "message" constructed apart from the unstable acts of communication in the book of Hosea. The way in which Hosea prophesies is inseparable from what he is saying; content is embodied aesthetically by Hosea's ambiguous and unstable ways of communicating. Two examples from other parts of the biblical corpus may be adduced briefly here to illustrate the point, relevant to both hermeneutics and aesthetics, that form and content can interact in significant ways.

First, consider the elegant binary form of sapiential aphorisms in wisdom literature such as Proverbs. In this sort of didactic instruction, the alternatives are spelled out with superb clarity and straightforward definition. Pellucid simplicity is characteristic not only of the content of the material but also the way in which the material is structured and formally presented. This kind of sapiential material is constituted by a predominance of short declarative sentences that describe two options. Simple similes abound. Notably infrequent are the elusive metaphor, the ambiguous characterization, the ironic aside that risks being misunderstood. This is not to say that sapiential forms do not present complexity. They certainly do, at the level of syntagmatic relationships between verses and juxtaposition of larger blocks of material, and also, as Carol Newsom has shown, in the way in which genre functions to activate and reframe cultural norms.[8] But with wisdom maxims, the apparent simplicity of diction reinforces the apparent simplicity of content, toward the didactic end of persuading the hearer that there is a breathtakingly simple choice to make between an excellent option and a disastrous option.

A second example of the semantically significant interplay between diction and content may be seen in Ezekiel's pornographic metaphorization of Israel as nymphomaniacal whore, something explicit in Ezek 16 and 23 and characteristic of the diction of the prophet in other passages as well. The florid tone and sexually graphic diction of Ezekiel convey compulsiveness on the part of the text about sexual practices, whether real or metaphorical.[9] Ezekiel's hyperbolically passionate reflections on

8. Carol A. Newsom, *The Book of Job: A Contest of Moral Imaginations* (New York: Oxford, 2003), 11–31.

9. See Fokkelien van Dijk-Hemmes, "The Imagination of Power and the Power of Imagination: An Intertextual Analysis of Two Biblical Love Songs: The Song of Songs and Hosea 2," *JSOT* 44 (1989): 75–88. The original catalyst for my consideration of this issue was an observation made years ago by one of my students, Michael S. Thomas, who remarked to me, "Ezekiel's very description of the rabid sexual exploits of this unfaithful woman is, in itself, shameless."

metaphorical sex represent, in a seemingly uncontrolled and voyeuristic aesthetic, precisely that which his metaphors are being employed to indict. The intensity of the prophet's obsession drives home the urgency of the matter at stake—namely, the way in which Israel's flagrant unfaithfulness threatens to defile the very holiness of God.

We could muster other examples of ways in which diction shapes and contributes to meaning, not only at macrostructural levels such as that of genre, but also at microstructural levels as in the case of onomatopoeia.[10] In the above examples, I have focused on mimetic relationships. Each of these forms of diction seems to represent and perform the subject around which its discourse has been structured. My contention regarding Hosea is that two aspects of the diction of Hosea—the elusive historicizing references and the unpredictably shifting whore/mother/offspring metaphor complex—host a complicated interaction of form and content that is mimetically significant for the meaning of the book. Harold Fisch has observed that shifts in the aesthetics of Hosea create a meaningful incoherence: this "is a poetry of love and estrangement, [and] neither can be entertained without the other... It is this oscillation of love and hate, nearness and distance...that shatters continuities. Images of love carry with them their dark antithesis. Images of anger are menaced and arrested by memories of devotion."[11] Here I contend that aesthetic antithesis creates incoherence at the level of construction of audience. The obscurity of Hosea's citations of Israel's history and the turbulence of Hosea's shifting metaphors are intended both to imitate the implied audience's lack of comprehension and to remedy it, to destabilize the implied audience and compel the (real) audience to reconstruct themselves as faithful worshippers of the true God.

First, then, I consider Hosea's elusive and ambiguous references to Israel's tradition history. My focus will be clarified by considering the "history" of American government-sponsored oppression that Jeremiah Wright retails to his audience in his so-called "God Damn America" sermon.

10. For just one example, consider the "Sword Song" of Ezek 21. Interpreters have noticed that the violent play of guttural sounds in the Hebrew here may evoke the flashing attack of the sword being described.

11. Harold Fisch, "Hosea: A Poetics of Violence," in *Poetry With a Purpose: Biblical Poetics and Interpretation* (Bloomington: Indiana University Press, 1988), 136–57 (140).

Tradition History in Hosea

> Preaching is, in part, a living practice of memory that negotiates the rela-
> tionship between an ancient canon and the lived experience of succeeding
> generations.[12]

To prepare to consider Hosea's homiletics as a "living practice of
memory," we may turn to the preacherly pyrotechnics of Jeremiah
Wright. Wright is a skilled negotiator of intersections between biblical
texts deemed authoritative by his religious tradition, on the one hand, and
the memories and contemporary experience of his congregation, on the
other. In his 2003 sermon, he paints a history of North American governmental power founded on systematic oppression of racial minorities and
indigenous peoples:

> Prior to Abraham Lincoln, the government in this country said it was legal
> to hold Africans in slavery in perpetuity... The Supreme Court... said in
> its *Dred Scott* decision in the 1850s, no African anywhere in this country
> has any rights that any person has to respect at any place, any time... When
> it came to treating her citizens of Indian descent fairly, she [America]
> failed. She put them on reservations. When it came to treating her citizens
> of Japanese descent fairly, she failed. She put them in internment prison
> camps. When it came to treating the citizens of Africa fairly, America
> failed. She put them in chains... Put them on auction blocks. Put them in
> cotton fields. Put them in substandard housing. Put them in scientific
> experiments. Put them in the lowest-paying jobs. Put them outside equal
> protection of the law. Kept them out of their racist bastions of higher
> education.[13]

In his rhetoric, Wright evokes a metanarrative of United States governmental marginalization and abuse of people of color. At a rapid-fire pace,
he piles up example after egregious example of discrimination, to
prepare his audience to assent to the climax of his oratory, something
that could shock patriots and traditional biblical exegetes alike: "'God
damn America'—that's in the Bible!" Wright clearly is reading his
current audience, the congregation at Trinity United Church of Christ, as
(potential) descendants and allies of those who have been exploited and
harmed by the United States government for many generations. The
history of American racism is presented as defining for those who hear it
now—those who are addressed by the sermon—and this history is set

---

12.   John S. McClure, *Other-Wise Preaching: A Postmodern Ethic for Homiletics*
(St. Louis: Chalice, 2001), 28.
13.   All quotations of Jeremiah Wright are from the 2003 sermon whose partial
transcript is supplied at the end of this essay.

over against the purposes of God. So, too, we will see Hosea create a
"history" of his people, invite his audience to identify with it, and set it
over against the purposes of God.

Wright subtly creates two audiences, speaking throughout his sermon
in a first-person plural voice of inclusion. There is the "we" who have
been powerless to stop slavery and other forms of racial discrimination in
the United States from the 1800s to the present moment. There is also the
"we" who can now stand up to governmental exploitation, those who
dare to join Wright in saying "God damn America!" as a form of godly
resistance to racism. We will see that Hosea also creates two audiences.
His first audience is comprised of those who were complicit in the
history of transgression that the prophet maps. The prophet speaks of this
sinful Israel in the third person and also employs confrontational direct
address, as for example, "O Ephraim, you have played the whore" (5:3)
and "Since the days of Gibeah you have sinned, O Israel" (10:9). Hosea
also implicitly creates a space for another audience, one that can see
Israel's sin for what it was and move beyond it. In what follows, it is my
contention that Hosea metaphorically destroys that first audience (that is,
sinful ancient Israel and those who continue to identify with it) through
his rhetoric, so as to clear a cultural space for the constitution of a new
Israel made up of those who understand God's purposes aright.

Hosea draws the attention of the audience back to the dark tradition
history of ancient Israel—ancient already in the time of Hosea's audience, whether that be construed as eighth-century Israelites or Ben Zvi's
post-exilic Yehud *literati*.[14] To draw again on the words of McClure,
Hosea is negotiating the relationship between an ancient canon and the
lived experience of his community. Hosea's audience is compelled to
reconstruct historical events and their significance for their own present
through Hosea's repeated references to earlier places and traditions.
These references are signaled by Hosea by an extraordinary density of
cartographic references: the Valley of Jezreel, the Valley of Achor,
Gilgal, Beth-Aven, Mizpah, Tabor, Shittim, Gibeah, Ramah, Adam,
Gilead, Shechem, Baal-Peor, Beth-Arbel, Bethel, Admah and Zeboiim.
Places elicit stories, and in the dark shadows around these narratives of
cultural identity, we find violent reversals. Drastic, unexpected eviscera-
tions take place with every mention of a geographical metonym.

How are the implied audience's traditions eviscerated? Each of the
place names in Hosea evokes an instance of sexualized or gustatory
rebellion in Israel's history, peculiarly embodied kinds of unfaithfulness
involving desire and consumption, illegitimate sex and illegitimate food.

14. See Ben Zvi, *Hosea*.

The traditio-historical references to place in Hosea are saturated with allusions to boundaries, unbounded desire, and death. These historical references create a complex intertext within the discourse of Hosea. At the nexus of these linked traditions, we find insiders' and outsiders' transgression of cultic and cultural boundaries by means of sexuality and eating. With virtually no exceptions, each of the geographical references has to do with Israelite insiders transgressing boundaries scripted by the law of *herem* or exacting vengeance for infractions of covenant.

Dinah, Achan, Jael, the Levite's concubine, Phinehas, Jonathan, Agag of the Amalekites: they are all here. Their stories have to do with rending individuals and community limb from limb, with sexual and social penetration that leaves the community (and occasionally outsiders) hewn in pieces. The allusions are multivalent, to be sure. But each of them involves illicit desire and the breaking of an explicit or implicit ban that had kept Israel intact from the LORD's wrath.

The narrative of origins in Hos 1–2 is determinative for all that follows in the book—both for the metaphors Hosea employs and for the theopolitical issues he engages. Hosea 1 suggests that the punishment to be wreaked on Israel is due to the bloodshed of Jezreel. Even the words of promise that Hosea speaks highlight the role of Jezreel: the restoration of a single leader over the united people of Israel and Judah will show that "great will be the day of Jezreel" (2:2).[15] But Jezreel comes up only once more in the book of Hosea and would not seem, on the surface, to provide the key motivation either for Hosea's rhetoric of judgment or for his words of promise. A consensus among interpreters would have it that Hos 1 simply condemns the "blood of Jezreel" as metonym for politically motivated violence, understood with reference to the dynasty of Jehu a century earlier. But consider where else we read "blood" and "Jezreel" together: 1 Kgs 21. Jezebel's plan to secure the vineyard of Naboth the Jezreelite is the beginning of the bloodshed: falsely accused of cursing God and king, Naboth is stoned to death. The sulking Ahab brightens and helps himself to Naboth's vineyard. Then the word of God comes to Elijah: "Say to [Ahab]... In the place where the dogs licked up the blood of Naboth, dogs will lick up your own blood" (1 Kgs 21:19), and so it happens. The blood of Jezreel runs faster and deeper with the coup of Jehu, who murders Joram, has Jezebel killed, has the seventy sons of Ahab butchered, and executes "all of [Ahab's] leaders, close friends, and priests" in Jezreel (2 Kgs 10:11). He has forty-two kin of

15. All biblical references will be to the Hebrew text, which in some instances in Hosea is numbered differently from versions in English translation.

Ahaziah of Judah murdered, and he exterminates all of the relatives left to Ahab in Samaria and the prophets, priests, and worshippers of Baal in Samaria.

What can it mean in Hos 1, then, that God will repay for the blood of Jezreel? The tradition reference begins with Ahab's obsessive desire for Naboth's vineyard and Jezebel's misuse of power to appropriate that vineyard; it ends in a bloodbath as Jehu slaughters his way to the throne. We have here a collocation of motifs of illegitimate desire, eating, and dismemberment. Ahab wants Naboth's vineyard for a vegetable garden, and will not eat when his aim is initially frustrated (1 Kgs 21:1–4); the oracle of punishment against Ahab and Jezebel involves animals licking the blood and eating the flesh of the miscreants; after Jezebel is thrown to her death, Jehu goes in to eat and drink (2 Kgs 9:34), and after his meal, he finds she too has been gorged on by the dogs; Jehu has the seventy sons of Ahab decapitated. Illegitimate desire rends the body of Israel as a people, leaving it dismembered in pools of blood. To think that this is the way of God is Israel's idol. This is Israel's unfaithfulness. So begins the dark traditio-historical subtext of Hosea's prophesying, anchored at the very outset in this story of the first "child" whom Gomer/Israel bears.

The next place name, "Valley of Achor" in 2:17, may be readily connected to Hosea's cartography of faithlessness by way of Josh 7. The Valley of Achor serves as a cultural reference point for a people that has itself become spoil because of the greed of Achan in keeping spoil for himself. After the lots yield the guilty Achan, Joshua interrogates him in what is one of the more chilling scenes in the Hebrew Bible: "My son, give glory to the LORD God of Israel and make confession to him; tell me now what you have done; do not hide it from me" (Josh 7:19). What tortures lie unexpressed between Joshua's whispered threat and Achan's confession in the next verse? Achan is summarily executed, but the problem is more persistent: Israel's unfolding history in Judges and onward will show that "the Israelites are unable to stand before their enemies…because they have become a thing devoted for destruction themselves" (Josh 7:12).

Next, in Hos 4, are Gilgal and Beth-Aven. Gilgal is certainly an important regional cult shrine, but also the place of desire and dismemberment where Samuel hews Agag in pieces. The enemy king Agag and the riches of his army are taken as illegitimate spoil by Saul, from whom the kingdom of Israel will be torn as a consequence (1 Sam 15). It falls to the mighty Samuel to make the situation right. As he raises his blade, Samuel taunts Agag with the threat that his mother will be made childless (1 Sam 15:33), anticipating a major motif in the violent diction of Hosea.

Beth-Aven is a pejorative name for Bethel, but more concretely a place of desire and consumption in the Saul narratives. In the heat of battle, troops having just passed beyond Beth-Aven, the golden Jonathan partakes of illicit honey and speaks a dangerous word that weakens the boundaries keeping Israel safe from God's glory: "How much better today if the troops had eaten freely of the spoil taken from their enemies!" (1 Sam 14:30). God will not, then, answer the priest of Saul until the sin has been blotted out from their midst. The fate of Achan looms in the shadows of memory as the lots point to Jonathan. He is interrogated by Saul as Achan had been by Joshua before him. Jonathan confesses, stands ready to die, and is redeemed. A noble reprieve—but later, when we see whom else Saul leaves alive (Agag), it dawns on us that perhaps the better part of valor might have been zeal.

The place names come fast and furious in the middle chapters of Hosea, with multiple traditio-historical linkages among them. Mizpah, Gibeah, and Gilead: all these sites are implicated in the horrendous story of desire, sexual violence, dismemberment, and internecine butchery in Judg 19–21.[16] The Levite's desire for his alienated concubine creates the circumstance of a dangerous journey back from her father's house at Bethlehem. Eating and drinking are featured prominently—excessively—as the cause of a five-day delay that leaves the Levite eager to press on during the evening. Illegitimate desire and appalling violence become inseparable in the gang-rape of the concubine by the men of Gibeah. "All the Israelites," including Gileadites (Judg 20:1), convene at Mizpah and cry out for vengeance. The wholesale slaughter that follows leaves the ground soaked in the blood of many thousands of Israelites and many thousands of Benjaminites. Yet more blood is spilled when the men and the sexually experienced women of Jabesh-gilead are butchered so that their virgin daughters may be given to the surviving Benjaminites. The entire book of Judges ends with the hyperbolically excessive capture and implied rape of more virgins from among the dancers at Shiloh. The moral disintegration of Israel is complete.

Tabor (Hos 5) is the site of agonistic struggle and death in Judg 4–5. The routed Canaanite commander Sisera flees to Jael's tent, exhausted by his desire for security and urgently in need of the water/milk that she

16. Francis Landy notes also that Mizpah is the home of the notorious judge Jephthah, who must sacrifice his beloved daughter due to an imprudent vow (Judg 11). On Landy's reading, "Mizpah recalls the paradigmatic case of a person trapped by a word," which may be relevant to the cartographic operations of Hosea's map-making writ larger. Francis Landy, *Hosea* (Sheffield: Sheffield Academic, 1995), 67.

offers. The sexualized positioning of the commander in the tent alone with a woman, and between Jael's feet in the poetic version, has often been remarked by interpreters. Drinking and sex and death bleed into one another as Sisera is butchered by Jael through violent penetration. Her tent peg is pounded through his skull in a reversal of the implicit rape threat that he had posed to her and thus to the social "body" made up of Israel and its allies.

With Baal-Peor and Shittim (Hos 5) we are drawn back to Num 25 for the story of apostasy constructed around Israel's illicit sex with Moabite women. Here we see excessive double penetration, the hapless Israelite Zimri and his Midianite lover Cozbi impaled during coitus by Phinehas's single spear thrust. Plague further decimates the communal body that had been pierced by illegitimate desire. When it is over, 24,000 Israelites lie dead on the ground.

Shechem (Hos 6) is the site of a pre-monarchic shrine, but also the unforgettable cultural site of the rape of Dinah the daughter of Jacob by Shechem, the son of Hamor, and the subsequent slaughter of the unsuspecting Shechemites by Simeon and Levi. We may see a veiled gesture toward metonymic dismemberment in the circumcision performed on Shechemite males by Israelites who turn out to have been hostile all along—how gentle is the hand that wields the flint? The overall point of the story is debated. Perhaps the misguided desire here is Shechem's, and his violence against Dinah shows us an Israel vulnerable to the predations of unexpected enemies. Alternatively, the misguided desire may belong to Simeon and Levi, who punish the initiative taken by Dinah to establish an exogamous relationship with the Shechemites by overcompensatory butchery that leaves Israel more politically vulnerable than ever, as the rebuke of Jacob makes clear.[17] Either way, illegitimate desire and hyperbolic slaughter are collocated once again in the grim subtext of Hosea.

Admah and Zeboiim (Hos 11) are cities of the Plain obliterated in the destruction of Sodom and Gomorrah.[18] Allusion to these cities evokes a story of desire, violence, and death at the heart of Israel's identity. Illegitimate desire after the destruction of Sodom yields Israel's most intractable local enemies, Ammon and Moab, because of Lot's excessive drinking of wine and the incestuous sex that Lot's misguided daughters

17. Gen 34:30; see Lyn M. Bechtel, "What if Dinah is Not Raped? (Genesis 34)," *JSOT* 62 (1994): 19–36.
18. Admah and Zevoiim are mentioned not in Gen 19, but in Gen 10:19; 14:2, 8; Deut 29:23.

subsequently perform with their father (Gen 19). Even at the level of Abraham's own kin, Israel's body is riven from within by sexual transgression and from without by the enemies that Israel's misdeeds have begotten.

Two geographical references remain unclear in the traditio-historical cartography of desire and death that Hosea maps out: Adam and Beth-Arbel. The latter (Hos 10:14) remains obscure as regards tradition-historical freight, although its fall to Shalmaneser V in the time of Hosea's prophesying would make it a vivid contemporary reference point for the prophet.[19] In any case, we do know what Hosea chooses to signify by the reference. He says that it was the site of atrocities committed against mothers and children dashed in pieces, and he identifies it as an appropriate analogy for the Israelites' future because they have "eaten the fruit of lies" and trusted in their own power rather than God's might (10:13). Hosea again links images of death, dismemberment, and illicit consumption as a means of attacking Israel's social body.

"Adam" in 6:7 remains perplexing. Scholarly debates continue about Adam as a relatively insignificant geographical location vs. Adam as the primeval man in the Garden of Eden. Ambiguity in the grammar of the relevant phrase troubles both readings, although not fatally.[20] Marvin Sweeney argues that we should take Adam as the location where the waters stood in a heap while Israel crossed the Jordan into Canaan (Josh 3:16); by these lights, Adam would serve as marker of a crucial liminal moment in the Conquest narrative.[21] But the pressure of the collocation of sex, eating, and death in the subtext of Hosea's geography may point instead to Adam as eater of forbidden fruit, the one who brings fruitless toil and death upon himself through his desire. The allusion may well be polyvalent. If Adam is a place, it is a place resonant with implicit connections to the transgression of the ancient one after whom it was named.

The traditio-historical references of Hosea present stories of sexualized desire, eating, penetration across boundaries, and dismemberment that have deadly implications for the community of Israel as a whole. The elliptical nature of Hosea's references compels his audience to reconstruct that damning subtext, story by story, as they try to figure out

19. Marvin A. Sweeney, *The Twelve Prophets*. Vol. 1, *Hosea, Joel, Amos, Obadiah, Jonah* (Collegeville: Liturgical, 2000), 4.

20. If Adam is taken as a place, the expected preposition *bĕt* is missing, although the phrase can still work syntactically. If it is read as the person Adam, the expected definite article used in Genesis is missing, although that need not be determinative either. See the balanced discussion of Andersen and Freedman in *Hosea*, 438–39.

21. Sweeney, *The Twelve Prophets*, 74–75.

what he means. Other kinds of prophetic entrapment have long been recognized. Reading the oracles against the nations in Amos, we imagine the ancient audience's eyes widening in horror at their entrapment as Amos suddenly turns his invective against Judah and Israel. So too we may imagine Hosea's audience growing more and more shocked as they realize what his cartography has been mapping out: their own ignominious heritage of transgression.

I turn my attention now to a related aspect of the violent diction of Hosea: his governing metaphor of whore/mother/offspring.

Reconfiguring the Audience as Resistant Subject

> What "really happened" is unavailable. The canonical words suggest that this scene of representation exists as a result of an encounter of some sort, experienced by an ancestor or a group of ancestors in relation to a sacred object, event, location, utterance, or epiphany... [P]reachers transport themselves and their hearers (back?) to this originary scene. Even though we know that the words on the page barely scratch the surface of it, in an act of memory we gather at this scene... We hesitate there, knowing that others past and present have been and are at that same imaginary scene, in a similar situation of desire and deferred fulfillment.[22]

Just as "Jezreel" controls the historicizing subtext of the prophesying of Hosea as a representation of the identity of Israel, so too the related metaphor complex of whore/mother/offspring starts the book with a tight grasp not only on Hosea's speech but on Israel's identity. Hosea's calling as a prophet to Israel is inextricably tied to his deferred desire for the figure of Gomer, which mirrors God's deferred desire for a faithful people. The whore/mother/offspring complex is the focus of the metaphorization that governs Hos 1–3 and, as a central part of that narrative of origins, arguably is meant to guide interpretation of the rest of the book. We read those stories first, before plunging into the fractured and confusing oracles of chs. 4–14: the reader may experience Hos 1–3 as the anchoring discourse, the discourse that makes the most sense in the book. The implied audience of Hosea gathers, as it were, at Hos 1–3 as an originary textual site of memory and metaphor construction. But the governing metaphor seems to lose control of its own signifying as the unstable discourse of Hosea unfolds. The audience's desire for understanding—for semantic mastery—is continually frustrated due to the instability and slippage of Hosea's discourse.

---

22. McClure, *Other-Wise Preaching*, 30.

Pregnancy, miscarriage, stillbirth, the evisceration of pregnant women, and the death of beloved offspring permeate the latter chapters of Hosea. Hosea portrays Israel as mother to threatened or butchered children and also as children watching their mother be threatened by a rageful husband-God. "Contend with your mother, contend!" the prophet exhorts Lo-ruhamah and Lo-ammi, "else I will strip her bare…and make her like a wilderness" (2:4–5). Thus Israel is pressed inexorably into division against itself. The audience has to be willing to undergo deconstruction: if it heeds the prophet, its fractured identity will become the marker of faithfulness rather than a by-product of disobedience. The "children," representing Israel, must contest the faithless choices of the mother, who is also Israel. The audience is configured now as both target of violence and horrified spectator.

And so the deconstruction begins. As the book of Hosea unfolds, the images of carnage are unrelenting: "They have born illegitimate children; now the new moon shall devour them along with their fields" (5:7). "Ephraim's glory shall fly away like a bird—no birth, no pregnancy, no conception! Even if they bring up children, I will bereave them until no one is left" (9:11–12). "Now Ephraim must lead out his children for slaughter" (9:13). "Give them a miscarrying womb and dry breasts!" (9:14). The God of this faithless people snarls, "Even though they give birth, I will kill the cherished offspring of their womb" (9:16), and "the tumult of war shall rise against your people…as Shalman destroyed Beth-Arbel on the day of battle when mothers were dashed in pieces with their children" (10:14), and "The pangs of childbirth come for [Ephraim], but…at the proper time he does not present himself at the mouth of the womb" (13:13), and of Samaria, "their little ones shall be dashed in pieces, and their pregnant women ripped open" (14:1). Through Hosea's brutal diction, the mother becomes a monstrous figure of horror. Pregnancy—new life—becomes a proleptic sign of death. The power of the (male) audience is rendered impotent,[23] and the potential fruitfulness of children is deformed into a specter of wrenching loss and calamity.

23. Nuanced cases have been argued by Ken Stone and Susan E. Haddox that Hosea's feminizing metaphors, mockery of "Baal's" failure to provide grain, wine, and oil, and indictments of male leaders' weakness would have had an emasculating effect on the male Israelite audience. See Susan E. Haddox, "(E)Masculinity in Hosea's Political Rhetoric," in *Israel's Prophets and Israel's Past: Essays on the Relationship of Prophetic Texts and Israelite History in Honor of John H. Hayes* (ed. Brad. E. Kelle and Megan Bishop Moore; LHBOTS 446; New York: T&T Clark International, 2006), 174–200.

The faithless audience cannot respond. The children are commanded to speak, yet their voices are silenced each time we hear them in the book of Hosea. Does the implied audience dare "contend," really? Consider the stern injunction in 4:4, "let no one contend!" The text ostensibly permits response but undercuts it at every turn, for every rhetorical move toward dialogue we see in Hosea is abortive. The confused Israelites, lacking in knowledge of the LORD, are characterized as being about to say, "Come, let us return to the LORD, for it is he who has torn, and he will heal us..." (6:1–3). A response is on the tips of their metaphorical tongues, but their answer is derided pre-emptively. Their putative repentance—the possibility of their ever repenting, ever saying the right words—is immediately ironized by Hosea's uncompromising rebuke: "your love is like a morning cloud, like the dew that goes away early" (6:4). Their voice is turned against them as inherently unreliable. They try to speak again, double-voiced by a scornful Hosea: "My God, we know you!" (8:2). But their stammering attempts to claim God go unheeded. The prophet speaks over them implacably, leveling indictment upon indictment.

Israel's claim of intimate relational connection with God is refused by the prophet. Infidelity, not love, is the real truth of the relationship. Jeremiah Wright makes an analogous homiletical move at the climax of his indictment of American racism:

> The government gives them the drugs, builds bigger prisons, passes a three-strike law, and then wants us to sing *God bless America*. No, no, no! Not "God bless America," "God damn America"—that's in the Bible—for killing innocent people! God damn America for treating her citizens as less than human! God damn America as long as she tries to act like she is God and she is supreme.[24]

Loyalty would be ludicrous under these circumstances of unrelenting disempowerment. No singing of "God Bless America" can be possible for African-Americans and their allies, according to Wright, so long as betrayal goes unacknowledged at the heart of America's historical treatment of people of color. Gestures toward reconciliation will be false, unreliable, so long as the sin of racism goes unremedied.

Reconciliation in Hosea is problematized as well. The final example of "dialogue" in Hosea comes at the end of the book, when the people are commanded to speak words that will return them to the LORD. The people are compelled by the prophetic imperative to return to a God who rends and tears like a leopard, who to them is like maggots (5:12), like

---

24. Wright, "Confusing God and Government."

lion and leopard and bear (13:7–8), like Death and Sheol (13:14). "In you the orphan finds mercy," the people are commanded to say as part of the "words" they are to bring with them to God. But their agency has been destroyed; they cannot speak.

Hosea 4 insisted that the people of Israel lack knowledge of God, hence they will be forgotten and devoured. The diction of Hosea has proceeded, then, to do just that: Israel's tradition-history is swallowed whole by a rapacious and unforgiving God. The place names that map their identity are sites of dismemberment and devouring. Other aspects of Israelite history fare no better. Kingship? No salvation there, among this people whose bloody coups have made a mockery of royal authority (5:1–2; 7:3–7, 16; 8:4, 10; 10:7; 13:10–11). Deliverance from Egypt? No: the people will return to Egypt as slaves (8:13). Repentance? Not acceptable—that possibility has been derided as "mist," unreliable and evanescent. The people learn who their God is through the relentless semantic pressure of four identical verbs in Hos 13:7, 10 and 14 (×2): *ʾĕhî, ʾĕhî, ʾĕhî, ʾĕhî*. And what they learn is terrifying: "I will be to them like a lion," "I will be your king," "I will be your plagues, O Death; I will be your pestilence, O Sheol!" The destroying power of God's actions is connected with the destroying power of God's words through Hosea. The term *dĕbārêka* in 13:14 is graphically and aurally polyvalent, suggesting not only "plagues" but also "words." The God of Hosea thunders, "I have hewn them by the prophets" (6:5), and "through the prophets I will bring destruction" (12:10). The implied audience finds, to its horror, that this is true of the performative power of the book of Hosea itself as they encounter it.

Hosea's Homiletical Aesthetic

Through imitation, the sacred past reasserts itself.[25]

Turn to your neighbor and say, "God does not change!"[26]

Through stories, we tell ourselves who we have been and who we ought to be. Jeremiah Wright sets up a polarity for his American-identified audience in which the United States government is figured in opposition to God. Governments inevitably change ("sometimes for the good and sometimes for the bad") and hence they are unreliable. Political power can be "messed up," Wright says, whether in the case of welfare legislation under President Clinton or in the Bush administration's sustained

25. McClure, *Other-Wise Preaching*, 33.
26. Wright, "Confusing God and Government."

efforts against affirmative action, health care, benefits for the military, and an equitable tax structure. Wright's audience is invited to redirect its hope for redemption away from the story of (uncritical) American identity and toward a new identity formed in response to God's sovereignty. "We" are to be people of God, not people identified with the historical inequities and iniquities of our earthly government. Thus is official American history, the history that does not adequately acknowledge White racism, deconstructed. Wright's homiletic creates a space for those identified with the suffering of slavery to stand up and resist contemporary exploitation. It also invites those who identify themselves with the power structures of this country—those who enjoy White privilege—to realign themselves with the prophetic word of judgment against racism. We can speak a new word, for "God does not change," and God has always been a God of love and justice.

Hosea's audience, too, is lured into reconstructing its own historical identity in condemnatory terms. The audience has been forced to watch the death of its "mother" (tradition history) and "children," its own misunderstandings being the offspring that are rhetorically threatened, aborted, and miscarried throughout the book. History deconstructs itself in Hosea, and with it goes the inadequate identity of the audience that relied on those dominant historical narratives. Israel has always understood itself through the narration of its history; remembering its Pentateuchal and Deuteronomistic traditions is a divinely mandated exercise in identity formation (Deut 6:6–8; 8:2). The prophet narrates a formative history through his cartographic subtext too, but the stories he adumbrates are stories that lacerate and bruise Israel's self-confidence. The implied hearers and readers of this text are repelled each time they reach for a reliance on tradition history and thereby seek a false god, a god who has no choice but to destroy them.

John McClure writes that "homiletic countermemory is a prolonged moment of erasure, when preachers allow their own well-formed memory, and the memories of their hearers, to dissolve into *proximity* to others, present and past, whose bodies begin to signify things unremembered."[27] Much has lain dormant in Israel's culture, "unremembered" until Hosea brings it to light with his counter-history of transgression. The whore/mother/offspring metaphor complex deconstructs the audience in Hosea, leaving them with a God in whom the "orphan finds mercy" only if the orphaned audience rejects its own history of transgression. The prophet threatened to "destroy your mother" (4:5), and so he has. The "mother" of idolatrous Israel lies dead—dismembered among

27. McClure, *Other-Wise Preaching*, 43.

shards of razor-sharp prophetic discourse. The metaphorical orphan children must cling now to something else: to the true God who has always been their real mother. In Hos 14, a new set of images for God emerges: beautiful botanical images displace the god who had been savage batterer and ravening wild animal to Israel. God will be like dew to Israel, and like an evergreen cypress. "O Ephraim, what more do I have to do with idols? I have answered and I will look after him" (14:9). The violent god required by Israel's transgressive constructions of identity is not the God whom Hosea would have Israel know. Forced to reconfigure itself, Israel learns to renounce the god that had wreaked such havoc on its cultural body.

Philosopher Richard Kearney muses,

> Are there not signs of life to be found even in the...images of a dying culture? ...Disinherited of our certainties, deprived of any fixed point of view, are we not being challenged by such images to open ourselves to *other* ways of imagining? Is our bafflement at the dismantling of any predictable relationship between image and reality not itself an occasion to de-centre our self-possessed knowledge in response to an otherness which surpasses us...?[28]

Both Hosea and Jeremiah Wright invite their audiences into "*other* ways of imagining" as response to a godly "otherness" that surpasses the malformed and violated identity Israel had constructed for itself. Kearney suggests elsewhere that a "poetics of the 'living word'" may serve as "an antidote to the proliferation of mirror images and mirror texts that characterizes contemporary culture," for "the best answer to the parodic imagination is an auditory imagination critical of its own images and attuned to what exceeds them."[29] The violent discourse of Hosea constitutes a "living word" that disinherits Israel from its official historical perspective and points the way to an "otherness" that can exceed the misunderstandings of the people. Kearney's words are relevant also for the homiletical aesthetic of Wright, which subverts the official narrative of United States history by means of its incisive critique of racism. Wright invites his audience to imagine a new future, one that exceeds the roles historically prescribed for African-Americans by the distorted power relations of White privilege. Hosea, too, invites his audience to

28. Richard Kearney, *The Wake of Imagination: Toward a Postmodern Culture* (London: Routledge, 1988), 397.

29. Richard Kearney, "Levinas and the Ethics of Imagining," in *Between Ethics and Aesthetics: Crossing the Boundaries* (ed. Dorota Glowacka and Stephen Boos; Albany: State University of New York Press, 2002), 93.

envision a new theology, a new fruitfulness that is possible only with a God who is not an idol created by Israel's own faithlessness and corrupt politics.

Both Hosea and Wright have invited their audiences to reconstruct themselves apart from a prior distorted epistemology and the strangle-hold of grim cultural memories. And both prophets use violence as an aesthetic texture of their discourse to maximize the effectiveness of their invitations. Wright's audience hears "'God damn America'—that's in the Bible!," something that constitutes a frontal assault on American political identity and an evisceration of what passes for patriotism in the dominant discourse of contemporary American politics. Hosea's rhetoric is even more violent because he attacks his people directly, dismember-ing their identity. Hosea's prophesying presents a potent challenge to his implied audience. The challenge is for them to endure a "self-decon-structing imagination"[30] so that they can learn to rename themselves and discover who God is. A chief effect of Hosea's violent destabilization of the idols of the implied audience is a freeing of the imagination of his hearers. They are freed from the blood-soaked constraints of a past that had been imagined only in terms of illegitimate desire and the subse-quent rending of Israel's social body by a punitive God. Once they understand their own covenantal obligations aright, they see that God need not be that destroyer. God can be the source of fruitfulness and blossoming, the giver of shade and stability. True dialogue in the book of Hosea begins in earnest as the book closes: "Those who are wise under-stand these things...for the ways of the LORD are right, and the upright walk in them, but transgressors stumble in them" (14:10). The audience, ravaged and emancipated by the violent rhetoric of Hosea, can finally begin to respond.

Unofficial Transcript of an Excerpt from Jeremiah Wright's So-Called "God Damn America" Sermon[31]

"...Prior to Abraham Lincoln, the government in this country said it was legal to hold Africans in slavery in perpetuity. 'Perpetuity' is one of them University of Chicago words that means 'forever, from now on.' When Lincoln got in office, the government changed. Prior to the passing of the 13th, 14th, and 15th amendments to

30. Kearney, "Levinas," 90.
31. I have done my best to transcribe Wright's performance accurately. Because an official printed transcript of the sermon was not available to me, I have relied on aural cues to arrive at paragraph breaks and punctuation that I estimate to represent Wright's actual oral delivery.

the Constitution, the government defined Africans as slaves, as property. Property: people with no rights to be respected by any Whites anywhere. The Supreme Court of the government—same court, granddaddy court of the one that stole the 2000 election—Supreme Court said in its *Dred Scott* decision in the 1850s, no African anywhere in this country has any rights that any White person has to respect at any place, any time. That was the government's official position, backed up by the Supreme Court (that's the judiciary), backed up by the executive branch (that's the president), backed up by the legislative branch, and enforced by the military of the government.

But I stopped by to tell you tonight that governments change.

Prior to Harry Truman's government, the military in this country was segregated. But governments change.

Prior to the civil rights and equal accommodations laws of the government in this country, there was backed segregation by the country, legal discrimination by the government, prohibited Blacks from voting by the government, you had to eat in separate places by the government, you had to sit in different places from White folks because the government said so, and you had to be buried in a separate cemetery. It was apartheid American style, from the cradle to the grave, all because the government backed it up.

But guess what? Governments change.

Under Bill Clinton, we got a messed-up welfare-to-work bill, but under Clinton, Blacks had an intelligent friend in the Oval Office.

Oh, but governments change.

The election was stolen. We went from an intelligent friend to a dumb Dixiecrat, a rich Republican who has never held a job in his life, is against affirmative action, against education (I guess he is!), against health care, against benefits for his own military, and gives tax breaks to the wealthiest contributors to his campaign.

Governments change, sometimes for the good and sometimes for the bad. But 'I'm settin' to help you again'—turn back and say, 'He's settin' to help us again.'

Where governments change—write this down: Malachi 3:6. Malachi 3:6: 'Thus saith the LORD: For I am the LORD, and I change not.' That's the King James Version. The New Revised says, 'For I the LORD do not change.'

In other words, where governments change, God does not change. God is the same yesterday, today, and forever more. That's what His name 'I AM' means, you know: He does not change. There is no shadow of turning in God. One songwriter puts it this way: 'As Thou hast been, Thou forever will be. Thou changest not; Thy compassions, they fail not. Great is Thy faithfulness, Lord, unto me.'

God does not change! God was against slavery only yesterday, and God, who does not change, is still against slavery today. God was a God of love yesterday, and God, who does not change, is still a God of love today. God was a God of justice only yesterday, and God, who does not change, is still a God of justice today. Turn to your neighbor and say, 'God does not change!'

Where governments lie, God does not lie.

Where governments change, God does not change.

And I'm through now. But let me leave you with one more thing. Governments fail. The government in this text, comprised of Caesar, Quirinius, Pontius Pilate (*Pontius Pilate* [Latin pronunciation]): the Roman government failed. The British government used to rule from east to west. The British government had a Union Jack. She colonized Kenya, Ghana, Nigeria, Jamaica, Barbados, Trinidad, and Hong Kong. Her navies ruled the seven seas all the way down to the tip of Argentina in the Falklands. But the British government failed. The Russian government failed. The Japanese government failed. The German government failed.

And the United States of America government: when it came to treating her citizens of Indian descent fairly, she failed. She put them on reservations. When it came to treating her citizens of Japanese descent fairly, she failed. She put them in internment prison camps. When it came to treating the citizens of African descent fairly, America failed. She put them in chains. The government put them on slave quarters. Put them on auction blocks. Put them in cotton fields. Put them in inferior schools. Put them in substandard housing. Put them in scientific experiments. Put them in the lowest-paying jobs. Put them outside the equal protection of the law. Kept them out of their racist bastions of higher education, and locked them into positions of hopelessness and helplessness.

The government gives them the drugs, builds bigger prisons, passes a three-strike law, and then wants us to sing *God bless America*. No, no, no! Not "God bless America," "God damn America"—that's in the Bible—for killing innocent people! God damn America for treating her citizens as less than human! God damn America as long as she tries to act like she is God and she is supreme. The United States government has failed the vast majority of her citizens of African descent..."

ON THE PLEASURES OF PROPHETIC JUDGMENT: READING MICAH 1:6 AND 3:12 WITH STOKELY CARMICHAEL

Daniel L. Smith-Christopher

The Context of Two Threats in Micah 1–3

Two striking passages act like "book-ends" to Mic 1–3. These passages share a very similar use of images and are thus taken to indicate a "block" of material in the short prophetic book. In fact, there seems a widespread consensus on the blocks of material in the book of Micah.[1] It is not my concern here to explore the wider implications of making such literary divisions in a book like Micah, I only observe that chs. 1–3 are typically read as a unit such that our texts form a conceptual "*inclusio*."[2]

Andersen and Freedman refer to this first section as "The Book of Doom,"[3] and James Luther Mays identifies the first three chapters as

---

1. The following commentaries were consulted in the preparation of the present study: James Luther Mays, *Micah* (OTL; Philadelphia: Westminster, 1976); Hans Walter Wolff, *Micah the Prophet* (trans. Ralph D. Gehrke; Philadelphia: Fortress, 1981 [1978]), and *Micah: A Commentary* (trans. Gary Stansell; CCS; Minneapolis: Augsburg, 1990 [1982]); Delbert R. Hillers, *Micah* (Hermeneia; Philadelphia: Fortress, 1984); Ralph Smith, *Micah–Malachi* (WBC 32; Waco: Word, 1984); Daniel J. Simundson, "Micah," in *The New Interpreter's Bible Commentary*, vol. 7 (ed. Leander Keck et al.; Abingdon: Nashville, 1996), 531–90; William McKane, *The Book of Micah: Introduction and Commentary* (Edinburgh: T. & T. Clark, 1998); Francis I. Andersen and David Noel Freedman, *Micah* (AB 24E; New York: Doubleday, 2000); Ehud Ben Zvi, *Micah* (FOTL 21B; Grand Rapids: Eerdmans, 2000).

2. In my recent essay, "Are the Refashioned Weapons in Micah 4:1–4 a Sign of Peace or Conquest? Shifting the Contextual Borders of a 'Utopian' Prophetic Motif,'" I tried to discuss the implications of the various ways in which choices about literary "context" can be used to change the interpretation of a given passage. Similar arguments could apply to this passage as well. The essay appears in *Utopia and Dystopia in Prophetic Literature* (ed. Ehud Ben Zvi; Gottingen: Vandenhoeck & Ruprecht, 2006), 186–209.

3. Andersen and Freedman, *Micah*, 7.

"Judgment" within his proposed Section One.[4] We should note that Hillers expresses great caution about the variety of divisions proposed by various commentators, though he certainly notes the common phrases between the words of threat in Mic 1:6 and 3:12.[5]

The writer of the book of Micah famously opens chs. 1–3 with a call for a cosmic court to come to order and follows with an announcement that God is coming. Andersen and Freedman suggest, however, that this is more likely a picture of God going to war than his calling a court into order.[6] This theophany is accompanied with a very traditional series of catastrophic events (e.g. the leveling, or "melting" of mountains, Ps 97:5; Nah 1:5; Jdt 16:15; 2 Esd 8:23; 2 Pet 3:12). Next, there follows a series of accusations in v. 5 and then finally the proclamation of the punishments to be meted out to Samaria in v. 6: "Therefore I will make Samaria a heap [Andersen and Freedman suggest the implied meaning 'heap of stones'[7]] in the open country, a place for planting vineyards. I will pour down her stones into the valley, and uncover her foundations."

Why Jerusalem is not mentioned with Samaria at this point is curious when both the north and south seem to be implicated in v. 5, but perhaps this is precisely the idea of the enclosing thoughts of the entire section. It is only later in Micah that one finds the famous similar repetition of this judgment in 3:12, now applied to Jerusalem: "Therefore because of you Zion shall be plowed as a field; Jerusalem shall become a heap of ruins, and the mountain of the house a wooded height." The two texts are clearly similar, and the fact that one is cited in Jer 26 suggests a clear impact. But why are these two phrases so important? What, in short, is the "aesthetic" of these violent threats?

There are a number of ways one might exegete the phrase "aesthetics of violence," but my interest here is especially on a kind of socio-rhetorical reading of images in Micah. With regard to violent rhetoric, it is difficult to be absolutely certain that words represent events in an easy one-to-one relationship. Violent words, however, can certainly represent a kind of rhetoric. In sum, I am concerned with what Micah is reported to have said and how we may need to adjust our understanding of what he intended to imply with his violent rhetoric. I am less concerned here with the issue of whether Micah's words represent actual historic events.

4. That is, chs. 1–5; see Mays, *Micah*, 4–5.
5. Hillers, *Micah*, 8.
6. Andersen and Freedman, *Micah*, 137.
7. Ibid.

Two Brief Case Studies Concerning Violent Rhetoric:
Ancient and Modern

The Ban and Genocidal Threats in Ancient Texts

One example of the difficulty with regard to assessing the historical events behind the violent rhetoric in the Bible is provided in the work of K. Lawson Younger on the rhetoric of battle reports in the Bible and the ancient Near East.[8] In this work, Younger is particularly fascinating when he discusses the issue of the ban (*ḥērem*), as an aspect of ancient battle reports. When battle reports begin to become conventionalized as a rhetorical form, as it appears they do in ancient Near Eastern and biblical writings, how much can we confidently use such reports as historically reliable descriptions of the actual conduct of battle? This is especially interesting in the case of the ban, given that such genocidal violence becomes a common aspect of battle reports—not only Israelite battle reports but also notably that in the Moabite text known as the "Mesha Inscription."[9] However, very similar rhetoric of widespread and indiscriminate killing of even the families of warriors/male enemies turns up in decidedly different kinds of literature, such as narrative stories of the killing of the evil advisors ("they, their children, and their wives") in Dan 6:24 and the even more famous violence that concludes the story of Esther. We are justified, I think, in suspecting angry literary flourish rather than historical description in more than just the Daniel and Esther cases. It is precisely this suspicion that raises our questions about the "aesthetics of violence" in biblical literature and, in the case of this essay, the specific images used in Mic 1:6 and 3:12. Before turning to the texts I am particularly interested in, however, I would like to cite a further significant example in a bit more depth, because this modern case has proven particular suggestive in my own thoughts on the book of Micah's use of an aesthetics of violent imagery.

Stokely Carmichael and "Black Power"

We are quite familiar with violent rhetoric in the modern world, and it is not an unimportant factor in contemporary political discourse and decision making. The traditional Arab love for poetic exaggeration (e.g. "the

8.   See K. Lawson Younger, *Ancient Conquest Accounts: A Study in Ancient Near Eastern and Biblical History Writing* (JSOTSup 98; Sheffield: JSOT, 1990).

9.   See, on the Mesha Inscription, the interesting discussions by Simon Parker, *Stories in Scripture and Inscriptions: Comparative Studies on Narratives in Northwest Semitic Inscriptions and the Hebrew Bible* (New York: Oxford University Press, 1997).

mother of all battles") has not exactly given rise to subtle appreciations of rhetorical style in Western media, but rather to blunt assumptions that poetry equals policy. Although we can think of many examples of Western use of rhetorical exaggeration that are hardly ever assumed to be anything other than rhetorical flair (even elementary school teams refer to "killing" their opponents), I am interested in whether we sometimes make the same mistakes in modern violent rhetoric as in ancient rhetoric.

The rise of the phrase "Black Power" is associated with one of the most radical of the early 1960s' civil rights groups known as the Student Nonviolent Coordinating Committee (usually referred to simply as "Snick," pronouncing the acronym SNCC). The irony that the phrase arose within an organization bearing the words "nonviolent" is, of course, part of the fascinating history of SNCC.[10] The name usually associated with the move toward the use of the phrase "Black Power" is the fiery activist Stokely Carmichael, who died in Africa as the renamed Kwame Ture in November 1998.

Claybourne Carson explains that the rhetorical shift toward the use of the phrase "Black Power" was motivated by frustration:

> Disillusioned by their previous attempts to achieve change through non-violent tactics and interracial alliances, Carmichael and other outspoken militants in SNCC were no longer restrained by concern for the sensibilities of white people. By forthrightly expressing previously suppressed anger, Carmichael and others experienced a sense of "release" similar to that felt by black activists during the early days of the lunch counter sit-in movement. *SNCC workers' satisfaction with the black power slogan was based largely on the extent to which it aroused blacks and disturbed whites.*[11]

Christopher Strain further comments:

> When Carmichael and Ricks introduced...the phrase "Black Power," they alarmed white folks...[but]...for most black folks, the appeal of Black Power lay in its excitement and energy, not its threat... But as the notion of Black Power expanded and took on a life of its own, some black activists used its ominous overtones as a loosely veiled threat to whites.

---

10. I made use of two main sources for this brief case study, mainly because many of the works I consulted had little interest in the rhetorical impact of the phrase "Black Power." See Christopher B. Strain, *Pure Fire: Self-Defense as Activism in the Civil Rights Era* (Athens: University of Georgia Press, 2005), and Claybourne Carson, *In Struggle: SNCC and the Black Awakening of the 1960s* (rev. ed.; Cambridge, Mass.: Harvard University Press, 1995).

11. Carson, *In Struggle*, 216 (emphasis added).

> Conceptions of Black Power were hazy at best, and the phrase clearly
> meant different things to different people.[12]

Carson is careful to point out that Carmichael's statements of policy never advocated violence, much less unrestrained, frustrated rage, but at the same time he was keenly aware of the power of the rhetorical move toward the use of the phrase "Black Power."

Strain, along these lines, observes that "Black Power was an Afro-American expression of political and social empowerment, rather than an ideology of racial supremacy. It is worth nothing that, for most activists being pro-black did not mean being anti-white."[13] Carmichael, writes Strain, was quoted to say, "When you build your own house, it doesn't mean you tear down the house across the street."[14] Further, Strain uses the terms "self-determination," "self-sufficiency," and "self-protection" as terms that speak to the heart of the meaning of Black Power in the context of the early 1960s' civil rights movement.[15] Carson notes the observations of the black psychiatrist Alvin Poussaint, who observed that those who used the phrase "Black Power" "appeared to be seeking a sense of psychological emancipation from racism through self assertion and release of aggressive angry feelings."[16]

What is undeniable, however, is the power of the rhetoric itself. In his concluding observations about the legacy of SNCC in the civil rights movement, Poussaint writes that Carmichael's use of what other civil rights historians have referred to as "the rhetoric of rage" had a powerful impact:

> Stokely Carmichael had been one of SNCC's most effective organizers,
> but his fiery speeches rather than his activities in Mississippi and
> Alabama made him a nationally known leader.[17]

The amount of actual violence inspired by the language of "Black Power" is one of the ongoing debates about the civil rights movement. Strain even makes the fascinating observation that talk about guns was "more serviceable as rhetorical appendages than as tools of revolution, or even as devices of self-protection."[18]

---

12. Strain, *Pure Fire*, 149–50.
13. Ibid., 151.
14. Ibid.
15. Ibid.
16. Poussaint, in Carson, *In Struggle*, 237.
17. Ibid., 305.
18. Strain, *Pure Fire*, 178.

The reactions were obvious. Carson (and others) suggested that police and especially FBI involvement in civil rights issues took on a new level of earnestness following the rise of the angry rhetoric and not necessarily because of the rise of actual incidents of violence (and certainly not a result of the already decades-old levels of violence directed against African-Americans).

The point that I wish to draw attention to with this very briefly drawn "case study" is the actual power of the rhetoric of violence and its various functions within a social context. Words express anger and as such can be considered a release of emotion, but they also express a verbal form of force and thus rhetoric itself has a certain kind of power; as Strain pointedly observes, words *about* guns were arguably more powerful than the guns themselves.

By considering the case study of "Black Power" in the context of an otherwise explicitly nonviolent movement as defined not only by other civil rights organizations such as the Southern Christian Leadership Conference but also by the original founders of SNCC itself, we can clearly see how the shock of a new set of terms effectively changed the nature of the movement and certainly affected the reception of messages by the society at large.

Micah 1–3 and the Rhetoric of Violence

The significance of these case studies of politicized rhetoric[19] can be seen in the context of reading the first three chapters of Micah precisely because we have strong evidence of the impact of Micah's rhetoric. In preparing this study, I was struck by the imagery of some of the modern commentaries when trying to express the presumed impact of Micah's threats. Wolff writes: "It must have been like an exploding bomb when Micah hurled against these pietistic, self-satisfied opponents his final word of judgment, formulated in a direct address: 'Therefore, because of you!' "[20] And Ralph Smith writes: "What a bombshell this oracle must have been in Jerusalem."[21] Even rhetorical violence, apparently, begets rhetorical violence.

19. Certainly others could be studied. The powerful impact of General Booth's critique of English society entitled "In Darkest England," written at precisely the time with English society was deeply impressed with Stanley's "In Darkest Africa," would be another classic case. Paul's use of "Weapons of the Spirit" in Eph 6 is arguably another.
20. Wolff, *Micah*, 108.
21. Smith, *Micah–Malachi*, 35.

What about *ancient* reactions to the violent images of Micah? Rarely do any of the opponents of the prophets, for example, inform the modern reader what exactly angered them. Information is not entirely absent, of course, as in the case of Amaziah's reactions to Amos in Amos 7:10–14, but here we have the added difficulty that Amaziah does not appear to be quoting Amos explicitly, but only partially.

In contrast to this general circumstance, however, Jer 26:16–19 explicitly quotes Mic 3 (and indirectly, also Mic 1) in the context of a social reaction that gives us some measure of the social response to the rhetorical power of the prophet. Because of this quotation and the controversy that is reported in Jer 26, as well as the similarity of the language in Mic 1:6 and 3:12, I would argue that we are even further justified in using these texts to analyze the "aesthetics of violence" in Micah.

The Reinterpretation of Micah 3:12 in Jeremiah 26

While it is true that Micah is quoted in Jer 26, there are some problems. The second Micah passage we are concerned with here, naturally enough the one applied to Jerusalem, is cited in Jer 26:18 as a significant point of discussion when considering the ultimate fate of Jeremiah. Jeremiah's preaching against Judean elites a few generations later had upset a number of these leaders, particularly when his threats implied the destruction of the Temple. It is interesting to read the use of Micah in the context of the defense of Jeremiah:

> Then the officials and all the people said to the priests and the prophets, "This man does not deserve the sentence of death, for he has spoken to us in the name of the LORD our God." And some of the elders of the land arose and said to all the assembled people, "Micah of Moresheth, who prophesied during the days of King Hezekiah of Judah, said to all the people of Judah: 'Thus says the LORD of hosts, Zion shall be plowed as a field; Jerusalem shall become a heap of ruins, and the mountain of the house a wooded height.' Did King Hezekiah of Judah and all Judah actually put him to death? Did he not fear the LORD and entreat the favor of the LORD, and did not the LORD change his mind about the disaster that he had pronounced against them? But we are about to bring great disaster on ourselves!" (Jer 26:16–19)

In the Jeremiah passage, Jeremiah is being threatened with death for uttering his judgment, and the Micah passage is cited as a comparative case in Jeremiah's defense. It seems an odd argument, on reflection, to say that Jeremiah ought to be spared because, after all, we have heard such horrific threats before. Is it possible that the defense of Jeremiah works because those defending the sixth-century prophet are asking that people not become "too carried away with the rhetoric of violence" and miss the point that action ought to be taken? Or is this a good defense precisely because the threatened destruction of Jerusalem did *not* take place before and thus the "defense" is actually to dismiss the gravity of Jeremiah's words as merely that: words?

In any case, the problematic use of Micah is noted by recent commentators who point out that Jer 26 actually reinterprets the Micah passage to be a call to repentance, since the proposed repentance of Hezekiah is never indicated in the Micah passage.[22] It is thus not only quoted but reinterpreted, perhaps in the light of exilic events in which the devastation of Jerusalem is taken to be a lesson for the presumed future. Furthermore, the Jeremiah passage does not seem interested in the specifics of Micah's language, but only the threat. Like the wider reaction to "Black Power," "white interests" tended to focus on threat rather than asking who is angry and why.

In a sense, then, one could argue that the Jeremiah interpretation is similar to the way the Micah passages have been read by modern interpreters. Ben Zvi is quite correct to point out that historical markers are entirely missing from the Micah passage, which is why there has been so much guesswork with regard to the alleged historical circumstances of Micah's words.[23] But this has not stopped modern preoccupation with the apparent threat to the ancient powerful leaders and their city rather than with the outraged prophet and his interests. What might such attention to Micah's words look like?

In the case that I cited of "Black Power," violent rhetoric was used by a member of a group who arguably wanted to regain power in relation to a more powerful group. As such, it represented an uprising: the words themselves symbolized a change of status from people who previously would not dare speak in this manner. Micah has usually been understood as referring to God's 'interests"—not violence on behalf of a group but on behalf of God whose honor and divinity is impugned by the immoral behavior of the people listening to Micah. Micah is taken to be speaking for God.

Against this tendency, it is interesting to read Premnath's recent work on the eighth-century prophets,[24] wherein he raises the possibility that Micah's violent language may have more in common with Stokely Carmichael that we have previously appreciated.

22. Robert Carroll, *Jeremiah* (OTL; Philadelphia: Westminster, 1986), 518–19; Ben Zvi, *Micah*, 81–82.

23. Ben Zvi, *Micah*, 25, 32–32, 81.

24. D. N. Premnath, *Eighth Century Prophets: A Social Analysis* (St. Louis: Chalice, 2003).

The Language and Context of Micah 1:6 and 3:12:
A Socio-Rhetorical Reading

Premnath's argument involves, in part, an analysis of the causes of the social injustices and economic imbalances that prophets such as Isaiah and Micah were attacking. Premnath summarizes these injustices by analyzing latifundization in the eighth century—that is, the confiscation of small family agricultural lands and concentration of land and power in the hands of an increasingly powerful elite. Even more interesting, however, is Premnath's mention of militarization as one of the tools of this concentration of wealth and as a means of further disenfranchising the peasantry by forcing them into military service.[25]

For example, Premnath's reading of the famous "swords into plowshares" passage in Mic 4 (and Isa 2) suggests that the peasantry would be angry with the constant calls to serve in the military, and thus these passages envision a day when war will not be learned any more. Read in this way, Micah and Isaiah are speaking on behalf of a disenfranchised social class of eighth- and seventh-century Israel and Judah, the small family and clan-based farmers who would have been the social and economic majority of the population of early monarchical Israel and thus also the majority of the conscripted foot soldiers. One thinks here especially of the warnings against the monarchy in 1 Sam 8:11, including the threat that the kings will take "your sons" to be soldiers (in fact, they will "run before his chariots" and thus become the "cannon fodder" foot soldiers thrown out ahead to take the brunt of enemy punishment).

As we are here concerned with the "aesthetics" of violent language and with Premnath's analysis in mind, I would like briefly to draw further attention to a few suggestive aspects of these images: namely, the ruin of houses, the association of fields and vineyards, and the way in which we might understand the pre-eminence of agricultural imagery throughout this passage and even further in Micah.

The threat of destroying someone's home is not unknown in Scripture, of course, and along these lines we can cite not only personal homes but also the Temple:

> They will live in desolate cities, in houses that no one should inhabit, houses destined to become heaps of ruins. (Job 15:28)

> The king answered the Chaldeans, "This is a public decree: if you do not tell me both the dream and its interpretation, you shall be torn limb from limb, and your houses shall be laid in ruins." (Dan 2:5)

25. Ibid., 83–84, but especially 124–31.

> Therefore I make a decree: Any people, nation, or language that utters blasphemy against the God of Shadrach, Meshach, and Abednego shall be torn limb from limb, and their houses laid in ruins; for there is no other god who is able to deliver in this way. (Dan 3:29)

> This house [the Temple] will become a heap of ruins; everyone passing by it will be astonished, and will hiss; and they will say, "Why has the LORD done such a thing to this land and to this house?" (1 Kgs 9:8)

Some of the terminology in Mic 1:6 and 3:12 is of interest here. The form of the Hebrew term, ʿiy (from ʿnh; plural ʿiyn in 3:12), translated "ruin," is not used very often in the Hebrew Bible, although there is a series of interesting parallels to Micah's use, such as Ps 79:1:

> O God, the nations have come into your inheritance; they have defiled your holy temple; they have laid Jerusalem in ruins.

Psalm 79:1 uses the more expected plural form ʿiym instead of the widely noted *nun* ending in Micah. In a similar context of threat, the term is also used in a close parallel passage in Isa 17:1:

> An oracle concerning Damascus. See, Damascus will cease to be a city, and will become a heap of ruins.

And it is presumed to be intended in the threat of 1 Kgs 9:8:

> This house will become a heap of ruins; everyone passing by it will be astonished, and will hiss; and they will say, "Why has the LORD done such a thing to this land and to this house?"[26]

It is interesting to note that the threat to reduce cities or important buildings to "ruins" is widely noted in the Hebrew Bible, but usually using one of two terms: ḥorbâ (Pss 9:6; 109:10; Isa 44:26; 52:9; 61:4; Ezek 13:4; 26:20; 35:4; Ezra 9:9; Neh 2:17; Mal 1:4) or šāmmâ (Isa 24:12; Jer 4:7; 9:11). It is tempting to speculate that Micah chooses this rarer term because of its association with the destruction of the village of Ai: "So Joshua burned Ai, and made it forever a heap of ruins, as it is to this day" (Josh 8:28), although here the term šāmmâ renders the term for "ruin" perhaps to clarify the wordplay of the name of the village.

The term ʿiy is translated in the LXX as *opōrophulakion*. The term is used in some interesting places elsewhere, which suggests an interpretive

---

26. John Gray, *1 and 2 Kings* (OTL; Philadelphia: Westminster, 1970), 236 n. *h*; and 238. In this passage, Gray affirms his opposition to the LXX reading, "this house will become high," which accepted the Hebrew *elyon* ("height/high"), rather than the "more likely" reading of ʿiyyim ("shall become ruins"). The reading with "ruins" is supported, notes Gray, by Aquila's Greek, the Old Latin, and Old Syriac.

tradition in the Greek rendering with different associations than the Hebrew term which it translates. For example, in Isa 1:8 the term seems to suggest the modest structure of a temporary agricultural worker's dwelling, destined to fall and thus like a city destined to fall to attack:

> And daughter Zion is left like a booth in a vineyard, like a shelter in a cucumber field, like a besieged city.

True to Isaiah's use of agricultural metaphors throughout the book, the image is used again in the Greek translation of Isa 24:20:

> The earth staggers like a drunkard, it sways like a hut; its transgression lies heavy upon it, and it falls, and will not rise again.

There are other observations that are relevant here, especially with regard to the prominence of the agricultural motifs. Following McKane's analysis of the Greek terminology,[27] one may wonder if the idea might be that the *useless* elite structures are replaced by an agriculturally *useful* field-workers' hut.

The two activities of sowing fields (as in Mic 3:12) and planting vineyards (as in Mic 1:6) are often used together to signify simply cultivated lands—in law (Exod 22:5; Lev 25:3–4), narrative (Num 20:17; 21:22), and even in proverbial wisdom where the wife is praised when she appears to do all the work (cf. Prov 24:30):

> She considers a field and buys it; with the fruit of her hands she plants a vineyard. (Prov 31:16)

Finally, there is the matter of the final phrase of Mic 3:12. Hillers, McKane, and many others have noted the difficulty with the phrase "and the mountain of the house a wooded height," but Hillers' own work on this passage is particularly interesting. He notes previous suggestions that "wild animals" should be read here, as a close parallel to 5:7 (v. 8 in English) which partially reads "among the animals of the forest." Micah 3:12 would then read "animals in the forest" (*běhēmôt*) rather than "high place with trees" (*bāmôt*).[28]

If this correction is accepted, Hillers notes that this would be a further example of the theme of animals being present among the ruins of a former city as part of a classic threat. The Bible uses this threat of animals wandering among ruins as a part of a threats or curses. While the curse against Edom in Isa 34:11–17 may be the fullest form of this, other examples can be cited:

---

27. McKane, *The Book of Micah*, 114–15.
28. Hillers, *Micah*, 47 n. g.

Night and day it shall not be quenched; its smoke shall go up forever. From generation to generation it shall lie waste; no one shall pass through it forever and ever. But the hawk and the hedgehog shall possess it; the owl and the raven shall live in it. He shall stretch the line of confusion over it, and the plummet of chaos over its nobles. They shall name it No Kingdom There, and all its princes shall be nothing. Thorns shall grow over its strongholds, nettles and thistles in its fortresses. It shall be the haunt of jackals, an abode for ostriches. Wildcats shall meet with hyenas, goat-demons shall call to each other; there too Lilith shall repose, and find a place to rest. There shall the owl nest and lay and hatch and brood in its shadow; there too the buzzards shall gather, each one with its mate. (Isa 34:10–15)

Then the lambs shall graze as in their pasture, fatlings and kids shall feed among the ruins. (Isa 5:17)

I will make Jerusalem a heap of ruins, a lair of jackals; and I will make the towns of Judah a desolation, without inhabitant. (Jer 9:11)

and Babylon shall become a heap of ruins, a den of jackals, an object of horror and of hissing, without inhabitant. (Jer 51:37)

Related to these passages is Hillers's important 1964 study of such treaty curses and their relation to some of the details of prophetic oracles. Hillers noted that one can find examples of threats in the Sefire texts that include the threat that one's ruined house will become a dwelling place for animals.[29] He then relates this to passages such as Mic 3:12.

With regard to this list of three prophetic passages, however, one is tempted to wonder whether there is a significant difference between Isa 5:17 (where the ruins are productive land for domesticated animals) and Jer 9 and 51 (where the land is wild useless land, a home for dangerous animals). The difference between the two may hold the key to an argument that the treaty curses relate more to the Jeremiah passages than the Isaiah passage and, by extension, the Micah passages we are presently considering. In fact, running through the commentary literature is an interesting ambiguity about the images in Mic 1:6 and 3:12: Are the cities to be wasteland or agricultural land?

We could go further in summarizing previous work, but for my purposes here I simply want to observe that there are two common interpretive strategies with regard to these threats that I believe may be worth questioning. The first common approach has been the attempt to connect Micah's threats with known events of Assyrian imperialism in the west,

29. *Sefire* I A 32–33, cited in Delbert Hillers, *Treaty-Curses and the Old Testament Prophets* (Biblica et Orientalia 16; Rome: Pontifical Biblical Institute, 1964), 45–54.

as if Micah is speaking of threats to Jerusalem and Samaria from invading Assyrian armies. This would obviously "internationalize" the interpretation and lead into detailed discussions of the dating of Micah. Ben Zvi points out that readers of Micah

> tend to agree that the references or allusions made by the textually inscribed speaker to events such as the destruction of the city or town were directly and unequivocally related, at least in the original text, to actual, particular, historical events that happened either shortly before or soon after the composition of the text.[30]

McKane[31] and Andersen and Freedman each illustrate precisely this tendency. For example, Andersen and Freedman's summary discussion of the oracle against Jerusalem in Mic 3:12 is entirely focused on the various historical suggestions for dating the passage, and they conclude their entire analysis by despairing of the possibility of historical precision.[32] No other possibility for the meaning or significance of the oracles is considered at this stage, even though (as we shall see) they certainly toy with some potentially suggestive aspects of the similar passage in Mic 1:6 against Samaria. I agree with Ben Zvi and others who suggest that historical associations with Assyrian troop movements may not be the most productive direction to take for understanding the aesthetics of violence in these passages.[33] Furthermore, to emphasize the similarity with treaty curses is but another case of focusing on the threat rather than the speaker. The connection with Assyrian invasions or treaty-curses suggests to modern interpreters that the cities will be reduced to useless wasteland. But that is not exactly what Micah actually says.

The problem with either of these directions of interpretation is not that they fail to be suggestive but that they distract from the possibility that Micah is speaking on behalf of an internal, subordinated group within Judean society rather than about an Assyrian attack or on behalf of a judgmental God threatening all Judeans and Samarians by using capital cities as symbols of the entire population.[34] An example of this assumption is Andersen and Freedman's suggestion that

> Yahweh acts directly, and there are no foreign armies in the disasters he brings, although the anonymous agent of the invasion that causes the grief in vv 10–16 could be a foreign army.[35]

30. Ben Zvi, *Micah*, 25.
31. So McKane, *The Book of Micah*, 8, 19–20; Wolff, *Micah*, 21–22.
32. Andersen and Freedman, *Micah*, 386–87.
33. Ben Zvi, *Micah*, 80–81.
34. This seems implied in Smith's brief analysis, *Micah–Malachi*, 35.
35. Andersen and Freedman, *Micah*, 149.

To speak of ruins ought not necessarily to mean that these threats imply that the land is henceforth useless and abandoned, like Romans plowing salt into the fields surrounding Carthage so that it remains a useless ruin. Thus, I would dispute the view of Wolff,[36] who believes that 3:12 definitely implies a threat to turn the city into useless land rather than arable land. Wolff suggests that Micah's use of the term "field" is to be compared to Gen 27:3, which suggests a wilderness for hunting. Why, however, he restricts the term "field" in this way is not clear, since the same term has very common associations with agriculturally productive "fields" as well (Exod 22:4; Num 16:14; Prov 24:30).

Returning to the fascinating arguments of D. N. Premnath would help us develop the idea that the *specific images* used by Micah tend to suggest a social and political context that relates closely to the internal structures of eighth-century Israelite and Judean society. I suggest that if we disengage from attention on the threat then perhaps we can then listen to the angry imagery.

For example, in his analysis, Ben Zvi makes a number of important observations about the intended links between 3:12 and 4:1–4,[37] including repetition of terms such as "house," "mountain," and the phonic associations of "field of ruins" in 3:12 (*ᶜiyn*) and "days" (*ᶜamim*) in 4:1. Yet the subjects of the images are also related. The weaponry in Mic 4 is reformed into agricultural tools, and in the vision of Mic 4 and Isa 2 the weapons will once again return to useful agricultural implements. These are implements and tools, after all, that would be treasured possessions of peasant farmers—things that bring life rather than death, to paraphrase the Talmudic Rabbi Yohanon ben Zakkai speaking centuries later. But is this a further clue for reading Micah's threats in 1:6 and 3:12?

Noting the sheer number of agricultural metaphors and images used by the prophets of this period when they address issues of social injustice (e.g. Isa 5:8: "Woe to those who add house to house and field to field until there is room for no one but you"), Premnath's work raises interesting questions about the nature of the threat made by Micah. Is it possible that the threat was not so much reducing Jerusalem and Samaria to useless ruins in war but rather "taking back" the lands occupied by the elite, returning them to agriculturally productive land in the hands of the small farmer again? Rather than land in the hands of those who ruled from precisely these (now former) cities, is it possible that the real inspiration of these threats is not so much international treaties but rather jubilee-like

36. Wolff, *Micah*, 108.
37. Ben Zvi, *Micah*, 84–85.

redistribution of confiscated lands back into agriculturally productive land in the hands of the small farmers? Premnath writes:

> The cities, as the administrative centers of the state, functioned effec-
> tively in the process of penetrating and extracting the economic surplus
> from the rural areas. The ruling class used the economic surpluses to
> build palaces, fortifications, and temples; to build, equip, and maintain
> armies; and to underwrite their luxurious lifestyle.[38]

When Robert Carroll discusses the Micah quotation in Jer 26, he clearly points to the social dynamics of rival social groups involved in the later dispute. Carroll notes that representatives of the agricultural rural areas rise to cite Micah, and that this "indicates a history of attacks on the city from non-residents."[39]

Such a "social" reading of the imagery of "heap of stones" and "plant-ing a vineyard" in Mic 1:6 is, in fact, considered by Andersen and Freed-man but then dismissed. They write, "The associations of (grain)field and vineyard are positive and could represent the countryman's prejudice against urban development. Such a future for Samaria moderates the severity of the judgment, for then the land can be put to the use intended by God himself."[40]

They then, however, return to associating this destruction with war. While they recognize that there is "an implied comparison between the piles of stones such as one finds in the field, gathered out and heaped up by the farmer—a constructive act—and the ruined city,"[41] neverthe-less the writers conclusively observe that "Such a pleasing prospect, however, is hardly glimpsed; and it would not have been pleasing to the Samarians. The emphasis is on the destruction of buildings and on depopulation."[42] Premnath's class analysis strongly suggests that not everyone would be so upset about the fate of Samaria or about the fate of Jerusalem in 3:12. His analysis also works against Wolff's insistence on destruction and resulting wasteland. Potential farmland is only "wasted" to developers, just as iron used for ploughs and pruning hooks is only "wasted" to arms manufacturers.

If Micah's threats were seen less as threats of miraculous punishment of everyone by God than as threats of a God-inspired uprising against elite monopolies of land and power, then Micah's threats have more in

38. Premnath, *Eighth Century Prophets*, 117.
39. Carroll, *Jeremiah*, 518.
40. Andersen and Freedman, *Micah*, 177 (citing Jer 31:5).
41. Ibid.
42. Ibid.

common with "Black Power" than we have recognized: they are words intended to empower a disempowered Israelite/Judean social class rather than merely a Sunday School lesson in God's miraculous powers of judgment against sinners. The fact that Micah calls for a tribunal before this threat may lend further proof of the nature of the threat, since God is called upon to approve of the land transfer.

It is possible, then, that Stokely Carmichael's famous call for "Black Power" might be a worthy echo of a much older call for power to the farmer, both cases being examples of the rhetorical power of the aesthetics of violence. There is an aesthetic here not only because we may be able to "appreciate" the artistry of the terminology, but also because there was an entire class of the Judean population that was also deeply moved by Micah's rhetoric. Some "aesthetics" of violence are not equally threatening to all. Just as "Black Power" sounded hopeful to those who were not busy being terrified, so Micah's call to plow up Jerusalem may have been heard quite differently by those who dwelled in field-workers' huts near the cucumber patches (Isa 1:8). To them, it may have sounded like "Ploughman Power."

"TONGUE-LASHING"
OR A PROPHETIC AESTHETICS OF VIOLATION:
AN ANALYSIS OF PROPHETIC STRUCTURES
THAT REVERBERATE BEYOND THE BIBLICAL WORLD

Yvonne Sherwood

1. *Reflections on the Revival of Biblical Violence*

Invited to write a piece for a volume on biblical violence and, specifically, the aesthetics of violence in the Prophets, I realize that I've
barely written about anything else. My first book, *The Prostitute and the
Prophet*,[1] was, in more ways than I realized at the time, part of a burst of
feminist and womanist work that irrupted in the 1990s. My work on
metacommentary, feminist deconstruction, and the abuse of Gomer, wife
and conscripted symbol of the prophet Hosea, proved to be one element
in a collective body of work by critics including Athalya Brenner, Julia
O'Brien, Mary Shields, Renita Weems, Cheryl Exum and Fokkelein van
Dijk Hemmes. Such work exposed a repressed prophetic canon of female
exposure—women starved, imprisoned and paraded, "genitals" afflicted
with "violence (Jer 13:22), "virgin bosoms...handled" (Ezek 23:3),
Nineveh with skirts lifted up and excrement thrown at her like some kind
of exposed Nazi collaborator/sex slave (Nah 3:5–6). It concentrated all
its critical force on the heavy-handed metaphorical conjunction of
apostasy–idolatry–adultery and its violent effects. In subsequent work I
focused on what might be called, following Mikhail Bakhtin, the aggressive *monologism* of the prophetic corpus. By this I mean the inclusion of
oppositional or alternative voices only in the form of grotesques uttering
self-incriminating lines that too compliantly serve the main discourse.
These skewed scripts reduce the "other" to little more than the caricatured

---

1. Yvonne Sherwood, *The Prostitute and the Prophet: Hosea's Marriage in
Literary-Theoretical Perspective* (JSOTSup 212; Sheffield: Sheffield Academic,
1996); repr., as *The Prostitute and the Prophet: Reading Hosea in the Late Twentieth Century* (London: T&T Clark International, 2004).

villains of pantomime: those who even in token "opposition" are subservient to the main plot and who only function as long as they are needed, before being crushed, converted or ushered off the stage. So accustomed are they to this monologic prophetic model that when commentators encounter a major exception—the narrative anomaly of the book of Jonah—they instinctively translate it back into a properly monologic prophetic text. Thus, in an act of rhetorical and anti-Jewish aggression, the whimsical dialogic book of Jonah has been converted into a strident, bitter invective against the "Jews."[2] In 2004, I co-edited a collection on *Sanctified Aggression: Legacies of Biblical and Post-biblical Vocabularies of Violence*,[3] a collection that included studies of manifestations of biblical violence (for example, in the White Supremacist Bible[4] and Rwandan genocide[5]) and the investigation of broader paradigms of (for example) martyrdom, messianism and apocalyptic. Introducing this collection, I reflected how analysis of biblical violence entails much more than identifying "key minefields or troublespots in the biblical and postbiblical landscape" and "then attempt[ing] to diffuse them, put barbed wire around them, or hold peace summits around them" for the notion of a "violent" sub-canon can be a "strangely comforting" idea, reinforcing the dream of a neat dualistic separation between witness and perpetrator, good and evil, aggressor and victim.[6] The headquote to the collection, from Sylvia Plath's poem "Words," highlighted the imperceptible line or blade separating (mere) words from bodies:

Words
Axes
After whose stroke the wood rings,
And the echoes!

2. Yvonne Sherwood, *A Biblical Text and Its Afterlives: The Survival of Jonah in Western Culture* (Cambridge: Cambridge University Press, 2000).

3. Jonneke Bekkenkamp and Yvonne Sherwood, eds., *Sanctified Aggression: Legacies of Biblical and Post-Biblical Vocabularies of Violence* (JSOTSup 400; London: Continuum/T&T Clark International, 2004).

4. Timothy K. Beal, "The White Supremacist Bible and the Phineas Priesthood," in Bekkenkamp and Sherwood, eds., *Sanctified Aggression*, 120–31.

5. Malachie Munyaneza, "Genocide in the Name of 'Salvation': The Combined Contribution of Biblical Translation/Interpretation and the Indigenous Myth to the 1995 Rwandan Genocide," in Bekkenkamp and Sherwood, eds., *Sanctified Aggression*, 60–75.

6. Yvonne Sherwood and Jonneke Bekkenkamp, "Introduction: The Thin Blade of Difference between Real Swords and Words about 'Sharp-Edged Iron Things'— Reflections on How People Use the Word," in Bekkenkamp and Sherwood, eds., *Sanctified Aggression*, 1–9 (3).

I am currently on a "break" from the Prophets and obsessing about that iconic scene of (repressed?/censored?) biblical violence: the *Akedah* or "sacrifice of Isaac." And suddenly it strikes me as just a little odd that I've sought refuge from the Prophets on, of all places, Mt. Moriah.

I don't mean this as a self-serving *curriculum vitae* in article form. Rather, I'm interested in thinking about my own critical fascination with the dark, violent underbelly of the Bible as one symptom, of many, of a concerted return to the phenomenon of biblical and religious violence that has been gathering momentum since the 1990s. This seemingly sudden revival of an old question begs at least a moment's pause. The last time the spotlight was turned on the spectacle of biblical violence was during the so-called Enlightenment or Enlightenments of the late eighteenth century. Then, it served as the dark background against which the Enlightenment was made visible and also called forth, as necessity. Biblical myopia—and the chiaroscuro effects of the canon—required the transparency of Enlightenment light. In these Enlightenment contexts, the spectacle of biblical cruelty was used to loosen the hold of the biblical/Christian as universal and to slacken (without necessarily severing) the relationship between the biblical gods and the true God or Good.

The revival of the conjunction of Bible and violence two hundred years later is not simply a repetition. But it also relates to a sense of the Bible as cultural idol and putative universal in ways that are not entirely dissimilar to the late eighteenth-century debate. I have increasingly come to suspect that the recent concerted focus on the Bible and violence represents a mutiny from the stranglehold of what I've called, in a recent article, the "Liberal Bible"[7]—a bland consensus about the Bible that emerged in response to challenges to biblical authority, not least the so-called "Deist" debate. By the "Liberal Bible," I mean an all-pervasive reading of the Bible's benign exercise of power that is absolutely (if gently) dominant, among so-called liberals *and* conservatives. It is not a version or translation analogous to, say, the Geneva or King James Bibles, so much as an early modern innovation and a reinvention of the Bible's relation to morality and law. In the seventeenth century, it was commonplace to draw overt analogies between gods, kings and fathers. A work such as Sir Robert Filmer's *Patriarcha* (published ca. 1680) made a bare-faced "patriarchal" argument that later moderns might find hard to imagine, in all its non-liberal audacity. The founding premise is

---

7. "The God of Abraham and Exceptional States: The Early Modern Rise of the Whig/Liberal Bible," *JAAR* 76, no. 2 (2008): 312–43.

that the sovereign triumvirate of God, King and Father is/are[8] the origin of absolute power and that the absolute sovereignty of these figures is epitomised in their power to act beyond and above the law. In a legal case in England in the 1680s, Gen 22 was boldly interpreted as an example of the God of Abraham breaking his own law against murder, and thus as proof that the king (like God) had the divine power to break or suspend his own law.

What I'm calling the Liberal Bible is essentially a softer and more proto-democratic version of the Bible's politics, constructed in response to such audacious theological-political arguments. It represented a compromise settlement between the Bible and proto-democracy and signalled the transformation of Bible from a complex and variegated text to a cultural symbol or icon—a reduction of Bible to a few axiomatic politico-theological principles that could be liberally applied (excuse the pun) thereafter. The Bible became loosely and vaguely synonymous with justice, in the nascent, "Western" proto-democratic sense. This enabled the Bible to stay on, so to speak, as the putative foundation of modern culture. The Liberal Bible maintained that true scripture must be ethical and legal; it supported the universal and denounced the arbitrary and capricious; and it supported consensus and consultation and shunned acts of sovereign exceptionality and raw force.

The Liberal Bible effectively reduced questions of biblical violence to a mere ghost or irrelevance, now that the Bible was cast as a good citizen, subordinate to law and an icon of good force, within the law. What does the return, then, of this awkward spectre signal or portend?

Its return can be partly attributed, of course, to the perceived resurgence of religious terrorism. Much more could and should be said on the way in which religion (and, particularly, Islam) is currently perceived to have a special (if not unique) relationship to terror. As Slavoj Žižek has argued, we find it easier and more congenial to talk about "subjective violence"—with an easily identifiable agent—than structural violence. Moreover, the iconic *problem* and threat of religious violence can be used to fuel the myth of the redemptive secular and serve as a mask for violence perpetrated in the name of causes, nations, states.[9]

However, here I want to concentrate on a different point: the idea that the resurrection of that awkward pair "The Bible and Violence" constitutes a reaction against the bland consensus of the Liberal Bible. Looking back at my first book on Hosea, I note how keen I was to point out that

---

8. The three are as one, and the three are alternative names for the same origin. Analogies with the Christian trinity are tempting.
9. Slavoj Žižek, *Violence: Six Sideways Reflections* (London: Profile, 2008).

the text transgressed not just against the values of card-carrying feminists (always in danger of being viewed as a special concern), but against the foundational principles of liberal democratic society, based on the modern creed of equality, the protection of property and the sanctity of the body. "The text's relentless project of confinement not only offends against [contemporary] feminist ethics," I wrote, but "jars with the most fundamental claims of the Suffragette movement" and the principle now deemed incontestable that, as Sylvia Pankhurst put it, "a husband may not imprison his wife to enforce conjugal rights."[10] My point was not to extol liberalism in any simple way but to point to the overt tension. That I felt it necessary to state such an obvious point—and that the conjunction of "The Bible and Violence" seemed, then as now, at least a little shocking—testifies to the cultural victory of the Liberal Bible. But at the same time the Liberal Bible is a deeply ambiguous cultural force. On one level it may seem important to preserve and radicalize this more benign version: to make the Bible more and more ardent for human rights and social justice and so ever stronger in its stand against more sinister (and retro-theocratic) versions of the Bible's priorities and politics.[11] But, at the same time, such work feeds the idea of the Bible as ultimate foundation and authority. The well-meaning constructs of the Liberal Bible fold the specific sins and transgressions of the biblical (and the Christian) back into the Bible, the authority of which—and authority is a very interesting word in relation to violence—is yet sustained. Such work often draws on the now centuries-old mechanism whereby "violent" or "autocratic" readings are seen as a misreading of the Bible's true essence. Moreover, it tends to mask the fact that this politically benign Bible is a construct, and one of fairly recent origins. Consolidating the ideals of the Liberal Bible can thus make it more possible to displace religious violence onto that other, allegedly "pre-democratic" and "preliberal" religion, Islam.

Feminist criticism and critiques of biblical violence have hit a raw nerve precisely because they attack the compromise agreement of the Liberal Bible. They effectively argue that equating the Bible with general, universal, liberal ideas (like "justice") is not enough to diffuse the danger, and may actually backfire. They dissolve the benign icon back into a complex textuality and confront us with unpalatable images of

10.   Sylvia Pankhurst, *The Suffragette Movement* (London: Virago, 1978), 95, as discussed in Sherwood, *The Prostitute and the Prophet*, 301–2.

11.   Cf. Carole R. Fontaine, *With Eyes of Flesh: The Bible, Gender and Human Rights* (Sheffield: Sheffield Phoenix, 2008).

emphatically non-modern spectacles of force. The challenge of these exposés is far more disturbing these late modern days when, unlike earlier generations, we have come to equate the Bible with the Liberal Bible. The idea that violence is in the Bible or the Prophets is more shocking than it ever has been before.

2. *Escaping from the Confines of "the Literary Bible*

I want now to turn more explicitly to the question of aesthetics. Specifically, I want to think about how the prophetic corpus sins against another modern construct of the Bible that comes from a later date than the Liberal Bible. Let us call it the "Literary Bible." As the Liberal Bible represents the firm alliance between the Bible and a relatively benign form of power and politics, so the Literary Bible represents an alliance between the Bible and a restricted notion of literature and aesthetics.

Partly because Literary Criticism in Biblical Studies took the form of reactionary criticism against redaction criticism, the Literary Bible has been concerned with artfully crafted wholes and uniting authorial intentions. These overarching principles have meant that certain narrative examples became the showcase of the Literary Bible, while the awkward and fragmented Prophets were left out in the cold. The Literary Bible tended to promote high cultural conversation partners and analogies for the Bible, such as Shakespeare or modes of classical rhetoric. There are few literary studies of the Bible that seek out conversations with, say, the visceral and bloodied lines of Ted Hughes, the disjunctive rhythms of Gerard Hopkins, the mutating puns of James Joyce, the Gothic vision of Mary Shelley or the cryptic modernism of Ezra Pound.

Revealingly, the Literary Bible seems to share key dispositions with the Liberal Bible. The rise of reader-response theory as the most popular of "postmodern" approaches in literary biblical studies has, I believe, a great deal to do with the congeniality of the idea of a Bible that is hospitable and generous to the reader and that opens up space for his/her readerly *freedoms*. This is akin to the Liberal Bible's emphasis on making a space for freedom and democracy, as God and the Bible effectively devolve power. There is something very attractive, in modernity, about a Bible that makes space for reader-response.[12]

---

12. Cf. Yvonne Sherwood, "Abraham in London, Marburg-Istanbul and Israel: Between Theocracy and Democracy, Ancient Text and Modern State," *BibInt* 16 (2008): 105–53 (123).

The Prophets have proved relatively easy to squeeze into the ideals of the Liberal Bible. They have been restyled as defenders of the widow and the orphan and so early promoters of the equality of all citizens, extending even to the least among us. By highlighting scenes where God inveighs against war crimes such as ripping open the bodies of pregnant women, threshing bodies with threshing sledges and grinding bones to lime (Amos 1–2), and sidelining passages where (in the same book of "social justice") the Amorites are transformed into tree-things and "destroyed" as a sign of God's love for his people (2:9), or the national body is savaged as "two legs and a piece of an ear" salvaged from the divine-lion's mouth (3:12), God can be re-formed as the liberal protector and defender of the human body. In their commitment to social justice and their alleged hope for social amelioration, the Prophets can be easily grafted onto the modern, liberal project. Allegedly, "ethical monotheism"—the conflation or religion and morality or religion and legality that is the cornerstone of modern liberal religion—lies at their heart. In feminist critique, abused bodies have returned, so to speak, with a vengeance. But until very recently an exclusive concentration on the protection of certain vulnerable bodies rather effectively bracketed out the violation of national and individual bodies and very un-modern dimensions of the Prophets.

If the Prophets have proved able to conform to, or at least overlap with, the Liberal Bible, squeezing them into the ideals of the Literary Bible has proved far more difficult—which is why they were left out of the Bible and Literature revival of the 1970s and 1980s. Where literary readings of the Prophets have been attempted, the models drawn on have been those of Romanticism and Rhetoric.[13] But already at the end of my book of Hosea I was reflecting on how curious it was to try and cajole the Prophets into rhetorical models of seducing the reader, thinking of the needs and feelings of the reader, or penning a letter that begins "Dear Reader." I started searching out literary analogues that would help me to articulate a relationship between author and the reader/hearer that seemed antagonistic, violent, and that often involved a violation of all that the reader holds "dear." I turned to postmodern fiction and metafiction: dramatic breaks with what we might think of as the *covenant* between author and reader that lies at the foundation of the novel. I instinctively turned to John Barth, subjecting his reader to gratuitous abuse—"The reader! You dogged, uninsultable, print-oriented bastard, it's you I'm

---

13. Sherwood, "God of Abraham," 183–90.

addressing, who else, from inside this monstrous fiction";[14] William Gass taunting his reader, "Now that I've got you alone down here, you bastard, don't think I'm letting you get away easily, no sir, not you brother;"[15] Donald Barthelme, using "lexically and sexually exhibitionistic terms" in order to "get past the reader's hardworn armour";[16] and texts that deliberately confounded the reader by violating conceptual and chronological order so that "the story breaks in half, turns back, or jumps ahead."[17] These works, incidentally, were largely written in the 1960s and 1970s, when "the Bible and Literature" was just emerging as a viable movement and research agenda. This research area was, however, constructed around a more restricted canon of literary works.

Taking Yhwh's pairing of the prostitute and prophet as a cue, I went on to experiment with some of my own quasi-prophetic disjunctive pairings. In my attempt to analyze prophetic aesthetics without the confines of the Literary Bible, I drew on the inner-biblical distinction between the Prophets and Wisdom, and their own generic self-descriptions. Wisdom words are proffered as choice delicacies to be savoured, tried on the palate and combined in new thought-recipes (Job 12:11: "Does not the ear try words as the palate tastes food?"). They preserve decorum, respect boundaries and attempt to set *mots justes* in place, like "apples of gold in settings of silver" (Prov 25:11). Prophetic words, in contrast, frequently present themselves as slashing through the social fabric and the language that sustains it, presenting themselves as (s)words that slice the people in two, leaden weights that lie heavy on the land and fire that devours people like wood (Hos 6:5; Amos 7:10; Jer 5:14). Like Plath, such words explicitly cross the line between words and "axe." Given that prophetic words are graphic words—suspended between writing and vision—I also experimented with graphic analogies. I took passages from Amos out of their usual habitat "in a glass case in a museum of the Ancient Near East" and hung them in a gallery of modern art.[18] That curiously verbal vision of Amos 8:1–3, where a "basket of summer" proves, through

14. John Barth, *Lost in the Funhouse: Fiction for Print, Tape, Live Voice* (New York: Bantam, 1969), 123.

15. William H. Gass, *Willie Masters' Lonesome Wife* (Evanston, Ill.: Northwestern University Press, 1968), unnumbered.

16. T. Le Claire and L. MacCafferty, eds., *Anything Can Happen: Interviews with American Novelists* (Chicago: University of Chicago Press, 1983), 34.

17. Alain Robbe-Grillet, *Project for Revolution in New York* (trans. R. Howard; London: Caldar & Boyars, 1985), 132.

18. Yvonne Sherwood, "Of Fruit and Corpses and Wordplay Visions: Picturing Amos 8:3," *JSOT* 92 (2001): 5–27 (6).

punning remanipulation of key root letters, to mean death and decimation, mutated into a still life with fruit inscribed with the caption "Women
wailing; corpses lying everywhere" in the style of Belgian surrealist artist
René Magritte. In an attempt to "illustrate" how the Prophets transgress
against the aura of cultural sanctity that hovers around the Literary Bible,
I drew on forms of contemporary art that deliberately break the aura of
"ontological promotion akin to transubstantiation"[19] that accompanies the
High Cultural sanctity of the art museum.[20] Ezekiel 4 mutated into something like an exhibit in the controversial *Sensation*[21] exhibition: "*Siege I*:
wheat, barley, spelt, millet, cow dung, barber's razor, rope, human hair,
human flesh, cooking utensils, scales, measuring jug."[22]

In my imagination, the prophetic corpus was arranged around a
deflated, exposed and female body, not unlike Sarah Lucas's "Bunny."[23]
Like artists of the *readymade*, the prophets used brute matter (rope, a
soiled loincloth, lentils, a clay pot) in their performances and installa-
tions. In particular they incorporated bodies or parts of bodies: human
hair, a dead wife, a prostitute, three children, and the prophet's own
body, struck mute, stripped naked, paraded, rotated, tied down with
ropes, laid on its side. Eschewing milder descriptions of prophetic performances as "street-theatre"[24]—a word that seemed to suggest something light and touristy, like puppet shows or juggling at Covent
Garden—I turned to the work of contemporary performance artists such
as Ron Athey to explore the conscription, marking and humiliation of the
body. Other scholars have since joined this experiment to look for less
anodyne models of "prophetic theatre" in a dedicated journal edition on
Prophetic Performance Art.[25]

19. Pierre Bourdieu, *Distinction: A Social Critique of the Judgement of Taste*
(trans. R. Nice; Cambridge, Mass.: Harvard University Press, 1984), 5.

20. Yvonne Sherwood, "Prophetic Scatology: Prophecy and the Art of Sensation," in *In Search of the Present: The Bible through Cultural Studies* (ed. Stephen
D. Moore; Semeia 82; Atlanta: Society of Biblical Literature, 2000), 183–224.

21. The *Sensation* exhibition was an exhibition of the work of the so-called
"young British artists" from the Saatchi collection, exhibited at the Royal Academy
of Arts (London, 1997) the Hamburger Bahnhof Berlin (1998–1999) and the
Brooklyn Museum of Art, New York (1999).

22. Sherwood, "Prophetic Scatology."

23. See online: http://www.tate.org.uk/servelet/ViewWork?workid=26305.

24. Arthur L. Clements, ed., *John Donne's Poetry: Authoritative Texts, Criticism*
(New York: W. W. Norton, 1992), 6.

25. Yvonne Sherwood, ed., "Prophetic Performance Art," *The Bible and Critical
Theory* 2, no. 1 (2006).

3. Towards an Aesthetics of Violation:
Reading the Prophets with Donald Barthelme and John Donne

In this next section I want to discuss two potential literary companions for the Prophets that I have touched on in the past: one only in passing,[26] and the other in more detail.[27] Neither figure has featured prominently in contemporary liaisons between the Bible and Literature, but both have the potential to expose the intersection between violence, aesthetics and gender. And it is my contention that, though they are frequently treated in isolation, gender, aesthetics and force should not be forced apart.

I draw on these writers for their ability to highlight elements of pro- phetic literature that conventional study has—more than accidentally— occluded. So strong is the consensus of the Literary and Liberal Bibles that it takes a pre-Enlightenment writer like John Donne (writing well before these typically modern constructs of the Bible came into being) or a late modern writer like Donald Barthelme (not bound to these benign models of the Bible either confessionally or professionally) to bring the "masculine persuasive force"[28] of the Prophets back to the fore. Still in their relative infancy (or boyhood), studies of masculinity and the Bible have not yet extended into questions of style—specifically how one might write/speak as if writing/speaking for a god; how one might ven- triloquize the divine voice in the first person (as in the Prophets). Such "studies" have been conducted unofficially (and, in the case of the former, entirely unwittingly), by John Donne and Donald Barthelme as they explore how "language, [and audiences] are there to be fought and forced, not coaxed and wheedled, if one wishes to play the man."[29]

"A Tongue-Lashing" by Donald Barthelme (1931–1989) is a short, garrulous segment in his short story "A Manual for Sons." This "manual" is a compilation of quasi-encyclopaedic, eccentric, whimsical entries on the theme of "Fatherhood," performed in a complex variety of tones— comic, poignant, mock-didactic, sympathetic, bathetic—and in full and

---

26. Yvonne Sherwood, "Prophetic Literature," in *The Oxford Handbook of English Literature and Theology* (ed. David Jasper, Elizabeth Jay and Andrew Hass; Oxford University Press, 2005), 289–306 (303).

27. Yvonne Sherwood, "'Darke Texts Needs Notes': Prophetic Poetry, John Donne and the Baroque," *JSOT* 27 (2002): 47–74.

28. For "masculine persuasive force" as a famous attribute of Donne's poetry, see Helen Carr, "Donne's Masculine Persuasive Force," in *Jacobean Poetry and Prose Rhetoric: Representation and the Popular Imagination* (ed. Clive Bloom; Basingstoke: Macmillan, 1988), 96–118.

29. Stevie Davies, *John Donne* (London: Northcote House, 1994), 32.

ironic awareness that "fathers" also double as "sons." The parodic con-
tents page for the chapter includes headings such as "Mad Fathers,"
"Fathers as Teachers," "Names of," "Sample Voice, A, B, C," "Hiram or
Saul," "Fanged etc.," "Colour of Fathers," "The Leaping Father," "The
Falling Father," "Death of" and "Patricide a poor idea, and summation."
Regarding patricide, the author makes the following recommendation:
"Patricide is a bad idea, first because it is contrary to law and custom and
secondly because it proves, beyond a doubt, that the father's every fluted
accusation against you was correct..."[30] The Manual includes the advice
that "If your father's name is Hiram or Saul, flee into the woods" for there
is "no one more blackhearted and surly than an ex-king" or "a person who
harbours, in the dark channels of his body, the memory of kingship."[31] It
also alludes to that biblical curiosity—the *Akedah*/"sacrifice of Isaac"—
in an equally curious passage on the colour of fathers:

> The liver-chestnut-colored father has a reputation for decency and good
> sense; if God commands him to take out his knife and slice through your
> neck with it, he will probably say "No, thanks." The dusty-chestnut father
> will reach for his knife. The light-chestnut father will look the other way,
> to the east, where another vegetation ceremony, with more interesting
> dances, is being held.[32]

"A tongue-lashing" comes as the climax to this pastiche on the power
of Fatherhood–Sovereignty–Divinity, cut-and-paste from biblical fragments. To achieve the full effect it needs to be cited and read (preferably
out loud, very loud) without pause for punctuation or breath:

> Whoever hath within himself the deceivableness of unrighteousness and
> hath pleasure in unrighteousness and walketh disorderly and hath turned
> aside into vain jangling and hath become a manstealer and liar and
> perjured person and hath given over himself to wrath and doubting and
> hath been unthankful and hath been a lover of his own self and hath
> gendered strife with foolish and unlearned questions and hath crept into
> houses leading away silly women with divers lusts and hath been the
> inventor of evil things and hath embraced contentiousness and obeyed
> slanderousness and hath filled his mouth with cursing and bitterness and
> hath made of this throat an open sepulchre and hath the poison of asps
> under his lips and hath boasted and hath hoped against hope and hath
> been weak in faith and hath polluted the land with his whoredoms and
> hath profaned holy things and hath despised mine holy things and hath
> committed lewdness and hath mocked and hath daubed himself with
> untempered mortars, and whosoever, if a woman, hath journeyed to the

30. Donald Barthelme, *Sixty Stories* (New York: Penguin, 1982), 270.
31. Ibid., 261.
32. Ibid., 262.

Assyrians there to have her breasts pressed by lovers clothed in blue, captains and rulers, desirable young men, horsemen riding upon horses, horsemen riding upon horses who lay upon her and discovered her nakedness and bruised the breasts of her virginity and poured their whoredoms upon her, and hath doted upon them captains and rulers clothed most gorgeously, horsemen riding upon horses, girdled with girdles upon their loins, and hath multiplied her whoredoms with her paramours whose flesh is as the flesh of asses and whose issue is like the issue of horses, great lords and rulers clothed in blue and riding on horses: This man and this woman I say shall be filled with drunkenness and sorrow like a pot whose scum is therein and whose scum hath not gone out of it and under which the pile for the fire is and on which the wood is heaped and the fire kindled and the pot spiced and the bones burned and then the pot set empty on the coals that the brass of it may be hot and may burn and that the filthiness of it may be molten in it, that the scum may be consumed, for ye have wearied yourselves with lies and your great scum went not forth out of you, your scum shall be in the fire and I will take away the desire of thine eyes. Remember ye not that when I was yet with you I told you these things?[33]

Plagiarizing from the Hebrew Prophets, with special reference to Ezekiel (see Ezek 16 and 23, and 24), Bartheleme compiles an inventory of the most shocking and graphic prophetisms. Crucially, the violence laid bare in the exposed human bodies—at the level of symbol—extends into the violence of form. Force is embodied in the performance of an absolutely sovereign and absolutely irrevocable/irresistible discourse: iteration, reiteration; the voice without limits, speaking and acting as if there were no other voices/bodies or counterforces in the world. The concept of "tongue-lashing" broaches the borders between body and voice, in imitation of the Prophets. It hints at a rhetorical divine right of kings (or fathers), or a scene of pseudo-torture, or perhaps the punishment of captives, in which the body or ear of the other dissolves or buckles beneath the voice or whip's force. As Emmanuel Lévinas once famously wrote,

violence is not to be found only in the collision of one billiard ball with another, or the storm that destroys the harvest, or the master who mistreats the slave, or a totalitarian State that vilifies its citizens, or the conquest or subjection of men in war. Violence is to be found in any action in which one acts as if one were alone to act; as if the rest of the universe were there only to receive the action; violence is consequently also any action which we endure without at every point collaborating in it.[34]

33. Ibid., 265–65.
34. Emmanuel Lévinas, *Difficult Freedom* (trans. Seán Hand; Baltimore: The Johns Hopkins University Press, 1990), 6.

In this sequence metaphors powered by their own momentum run away with themselves and cross the fragile border between word and body. The insubstantiality and negligibility of other bodies, except as a site to mark, or an ear to assault is articulated in the insistent, endless/eternal voice.

For Bartheleme, this prophetic voice functions as a kind of metonymy for the Bible in its role as cultural and religious idol, eternal, transcendent, inviolable voice. The Bible becomes the most obvious cultural manifestation of the voice of the Father which is an "instrument of the most terrible pertinaciousness."[35] Unlike the Literary Bible, which constantly yields itself to the reader and creates space for the reader— rather like a liberal parent, ceding power to the post-sixties generation— this Bible/Father deals in autocracy and never dies:

> The death of fathers: When a father dies, his fatherhood is returned to the All-Father, who is the sum of all dead fathers taken together. (This is not a definition of the Dead Father, only an aspect of his being.) The fatherhood is returned to the All-Father, first because that is where it belongs and secondly in order that it may be denied to you. Transfers of power of this kind are marked with appropriate ceremonies; top hats are burned. Fatherless now, you must deal with the memory of a father. Often that memory is more potent than the living presence of a father, is an inner voice commanding, haranguing, yes-ing and no-ing—a binary code, yes no yes no yes no yes no yes no, governing your every, your slightest movement, mental or physical. At what point do you become yourself? Never, wholly, you are always partly him. That privileged position in your inner ear is his last "perk" and no father has ever passed it by.[36]

Freud and Christian theology blur in this mock paean to the massiveness of the Father. The voice of the Fathers/the Bible is the Super-Ego or Over-I who shrinks the I by inhabiting it, outliving it and magnifying inadequacy and sin to hyperbolic excess. The comic aside that the Dead Father cannot be defined, except in one of his aspects, seems to parody the inaccessibility of God the Father in mystical or negative theologies and the disproportion of power in which he is infinitely above us, and exceeds us. The godlikeness of the father can be seen in the fact that he never dies (in a sense) and also in concepts of fatherhood as an ideal (perfect) state. "Many fathers are blameless in all ways," muses Bartheleme, "and these fathers are either sacred relics people are touched with to heal incurable illnesses, or texts to be studied, generation after generation, to determine how this idiosyncrasy may be maximised."[37] The reference to

35. Bartheleme, *Sixty Stories*, 255.
36. Ibid., 270.
37. Ibid., 255.

"a text to be studied" and/or "a sacred relic" seems to invoke the Bible in its dual role as a text to be studied and an icon of salvation. Bartheleme's mock-statement of faith in the miraculous exception—the occasionally perfect/holy father—begs the question of our faith in the biblical and the gods and fathers it represents. Is it beyond the powers even of God— perhaps especially of God—to escape to a realm of absolute innocence and absolute exemption from the cruder discourses of masculinity and power and their violent effects?

Writing in the late twentieth century, Bartheleme concludes with a poignant exhortation to turn down the temptations of fatherhood or, para- doxically, be a less good father, according to the traditional definitions of the task:

> Your true task, as a son, is to reproduce every one of the enormities [committed by your father], but in attenuated form. You must become your father, but a paler, weaker version of him. The enormities go with the job, but close study will allow you to perform the job less well than it has previously been done, thus moving toward a golden age of decency, quiet, and calmed fevers. Your contribution will not be a small one, but "small" is one of the concepts you should shoot for... Begin by whisper- ing, in front of a mirror, for thirty minutes a day. Then tie your hands behind your back for thirty minutes a day, or get someone else to do this for you. Then, choose one of your most deeply held beliefs, such as the belief that your honors and awards have something to do with you, and abjure it. Friends will help you abjure it, and can be telephoned if you begin to backslide. You see the pattern, put it into practice. *Fatherhood can be, if not conquered, at least "turned down" in this generation*—by the combined efforts of all of us together. Rejoice.[38]

Writing four centuries earlier, John Donne is blissfully unaware of gender criticism and is entirely outside and prior to the general discourse of liberalism from which it originates. He is keen to perform what he perceives as the "masculine perswasive force" of the Bible in a helpfully unselfconscious fashion, and to amplify the power of the Gods of the Bible, writ large.[39] As John Carey puts it, "Donne's God is a heavenly powerhouse, with all circuits ablaze. He is an explosion of energy, His eye is hotter than the sun, and melts people... His voice is unimaginably loud..." Even his angels can "molder" a rock into its "atoms" with the ease of bodybuilders tearing up telephone directories.[40] Like the prophets and their God, Donne does not flinch from proclaiming his woman/his

---

38. Ibid., 230–71 (original emphasis).
39. "On his Mistress" (Elegy XVI) l. 4.
40. John Carey, *John Donne: Life, Mind and Art* (London: Faber & Faber, 1981), 122–23.

kingdom, his "America," his "mine of precious stones" and "empery." Donne, God and the prophets also concur that women (actual and metaphorical) are "safeliest when with one man manned."[41]

I first paired Donne with the Prophets because both seemed to share a predilection for "baroque," counterintuitive metaphorical conjunctions–disjunctions and for what could be thought of as a poetics of force. As poet, Donne was praised for committing "holy rapes upon our wills."[42] He sought to "teare/the tender labyrinth of the ear"[43] and bragged of his "masculine perswasive force." He frequently portrayed the poet as slicing through oppositional surrounding voices: thus "The Canonisation" opened, "For God's sake, hold your tongue, and let me love." His poetic persona bragged of not soliciting the pleasure of the reader, in fact quite the opposite: "I sing not siren-like to tempt for I/Am harsh."[44]

As Dean of St. Pauls, Donne was prone to highlight the stranger figures in the prophetic corpus: God as lion and bear, mangling the body of the people in Hos 13:8; God whistling for the fly-Assyria in Isa 7:18. (Donne may have particularly relished the latter for its similarities for his own extended metaphysical conceit on "The Flea.") He glossed these passages in ways that might make late moderns squeamish: "*I will meet them*, says God (when hee is pleased, he says, he will wait for them), as a *Bear* (no longer a Dove), *as a Bear robbed of her whelpes*, (sensible of his injuries) and *I will rent the caule of their hearts* (shiver them in peeces with a dispersion, with a discerption)." And, "If he doe but *sibilare muscam*, hisse and whisper for the flye, and the Bee, there is nothing so little in his hand, as cannot discomfort thee, discomfit thee, dissolve and pow'r out, attenuate and annihilate the very marrow of thy soul."[45]

Force is amplified and is made visible in the graphic impact on the body. In what feels like a ceaseless inventory of effects of dissolution and decomposition in Donne's sermons, the human body is "scattered, melted" and subject to entropy, or the frail body is "ground to powder," or seeps and melts away like wet mud."[46] In a highly apposite phrase,

41. "To His Mistress Going to Bed" (Elegy, XIX).
42. Thomas Carew, "Elegie Upon the Death of the Deane of Pauls," ll. 38–39 in Clements, ed., *John Donne's Poetry*, 139–41.
43. Satire II in John Donne, *The Satires, Epigrams and Verse Letters* (ed. W. Milgate; Oxford: Oxford University Press, 1967).
44. John Donne, *The Satires, Epigrams and Verse Letters* (ed. W. Milgate; Oxford: Oxford University Press, 1967), 66.
45. George R. Potter and Evelyn M. Simpson, eds., *The Sermons of John Donne 1572–1631* (10 vols.; Berkeley: University of California Press, 1953–62), 3:86.
46. Jonathan Dollimore, *Death, Desire and Loss in Western Culture* (New York: Routledge, 1998), 75; Potter, *The Sermons*, 188.

T. S. Eliot described Donne's writing as seizing the audience by the *"cerebral cortex, the nervous system and the digestive tracts."*[47] It turns the body inside out, even as it confounds the understanding and exposes the fragility of the mind.

These expositions of biblical effects and Donne's own poetry map helpfully onto prophetic literature, pointing towards a less anodyne conception of prophetic aesthetics. In prophecy, the presence of words that have been allegedly "stout/strong" or "harsh" against God and the prophet (cf. Mal 3:13) are often invoked to validate the use of extra-ordinary force. Divine force is presented as counter-force: always provoked, and always total. In a meta-comment on his own words, Yhwh declares "I have split/slain them by the prophets/I have murdered them with the words of my mouth" (Hos 6:5). Alongside the book of Deuter-onomy's rather banal and rather vulnerable definition of true prophecy (true prophecy is that which is fulfilled in the future; see Deut 13:1–5 and 18:15–22), the prophetic corpus points to a more interesting distinction between true and false prophecy on aesthetic grounds, or, as we might say, on the grounds of *"reception."* Whereas false prophecy white-washes, soothes and takes the form of "pretty songs" and smooth words (Jer 6:14; Ezek 13:8–13), true prophecy can be recognized through its unbearability and the recoil of its audience. Ezekiel is desperately concerned *not* to be praised for "skilfully executed love songs, or pretty [flute] songs" and mere (?) metaphor-making (Ezek 20:49; 33:30–32). The audience's counter-cries for an entirely different kind of discourse (see Isa 30:11) are part of the aesthetic identity of true prophecy. That prophecy is too ugly, too disturbing and too vulgar is more than an accidental side-protest; it is an integral part of the genre's self-definition. If one definition of true prophecy is that it comes true in the future, another more interesting definition is that—in terms of pleasing or winning its audience—it fails.

It may be tempting to see feminist and gender critique as a special interest occupation and to view the problem passages as lapses in the prophetic corpus—perhaps bruises or blemishes on an otherwise pristine body that can be operated on by cosmetic surgery. But it seems that here as elsewhere (not least in heated contemporary debates where "sexuality" acts as surrogate and stand-in for a whole nexus of issues, and positions taken on sexuality, abortion and the family act as the ultimate marker of religious identity) questions of gender take us to the very heart of what is at stake. A feminist critique of prophetic violence can and must be extended into a broader study of *violation*, which is at once a matter of

---

47. T. S. Elliot, *Collected Essays* (London: Faber & Faber, 1963), 290.

gender and of aesthetics. The opening chapters of Hosea centre on the abuse of a woman *and* a wild metaphor, an overtly improper pairing of a prostitute and a prophet. The abuse of the woman and the abuse of convention and propriety are connected through the theme of violation. Prophecy seeks out an aesthetics of violation. It seeks to violate the body of decorum and to inflict all kinds of shock and damage on the body, eye, ear, mind.

4. *The Body as the Place Where the Force of the Invisible Is Marked*

Without in any way wanting to relativize a distinctively feminist critique and absorb it back into generalizations—least of all wanting to be misunderstood as making the bland equality case that "men suffer too"— I do nevertheless want to claim that the well-known litany of porno-prophetic images can be helpfully reconceived as the most obvious and graphic symbols of a concerted assault on the corpus of decorum and the body, female, male and national. There is something a little queer about the abused woman who has been the figurehead for our campaigns against biblical violence. "She" is also a male body and a male audience feminized and denigrated as a prostitute or whore. Most importantly, "she"—the abused and raped female body—*is the most obvious figure produced by a general aesthetics of violation/damage and a rhetoric of overcoming exerted by the inexorable and irresistible voice/will.*

Beyond the "purely" female body, prophecy, like Donne's poetry and sermons, is full of decomposing and dissipating bodies, that seeth, writh and slop. Whether it is being slopped like liquid from one container to another (Jer 48:11); lying covered with bleeding sores, Job-like (Isa 1:6; cf. Jer 30:12); shaved and humiliated by Assyria the metaphorical genital-razor (Isa 7:20); subjected to the internal force of a God who inhabits the body like dry rot, maggots or oozing infection (Hos 5:12–13); or reduced to a sardonic pastiche of the "remnant" as "two legs and a piece of an ear" salvaged from a lion's mouth (Amos 3:12), the national body is profoundly volatile. The flesh and the cerebral cortex can only reel from the shock of these violent and violating images, rather than process, control and understand. In a previous article I tried to figure this *sensation* of prophetic literature—this immensely vulnerable national and prophetic and textual body—in Marc Quinn's *Self* (1991),[48] a sculpture

---

48. See Sherwood, "Prophetic Scatology." Quinn's "Self" can be found online at http://arts.guardian.co.uk/pictures/image/0,8543–1130464117,00.html.

of the artist's own head made from his own frozen blood. At a flick of the refrigeration switch, the highly unstable "Self" will decompose.

In prophecy, everything tells us that we are less than agents, a sensation figured in the dissipating body. The figures (in the sense of meta- phors) are brutally disfigured, as if language is exceeding us. Relatedly, the prophet's body and voice is frequently sacrificed, distorted, disabled, as if he were personifying the distortion, shame and damage at the heart or gut of the prophetic corpus. Subject to an imperative not his own, the prophet must: go naked and barefoot, have sex with a prostitute, betray what he "is" by transgressing priestly prohibitions, and offer up (sacri- fice?) parts of his own body as physical stage for prophetic tropes (Jer 13; Hos 1:1; Ezek 4 and 5; Jer 27 and 28). As if by way of demonstration of "holy rapes upon our will" Jeremiah protests that he's been "had" in both senses of the word (Jer 20:7).

Why does the prophetic corpus center, so relentlessly, on the body? The body is not just one trope among others. The body has a particular power to "beseech[ ] and pulverise[ ] the subject" and create a "vortex of summons and repulsion," and create a "violent, dark, revolt of being," that turns the subject "inside out."[49] As Julia Kristeva writes:

> A wound with blood and pus, or the sickly acrid smell of sweat, of decay, does not signify death. In the presence of signified death—a flat encepha- lograph, for instance—I would understand, react or accept. No, as in true theatre, without makeup or masks, refuse and corpses show me what I permanently thrust aside in order to live. These body fluids, this defile- ment, this shit are what life withstands, hardly and with difficulty, on the part of death... Such wastes drop so that I might live, until, from loss to loss, nothing remains in me and my entire body falls beyond the limit— *cadere*, cadaver.[50]

As Peter Brooks puts it, the body's end, in death, is "not simply a dis- cursive concept." Mortality "may be that against which all discourse defines itself, as a protest or as attempted recovery and preservation of the human spirit, but it puts a stark biological limit to human construc- tions."[51] Collapsed and dissipating corporal figures draw us in with the pleasures of *schadenfreud* and voyeurism, because we are yet composed enough to hear, watch, read. They also elicit recoil, the reflex cry for "pretty songs"—thus convicting us of that which the Prophets accuse us:

---

49. Julia Kristeva, *Powers of Horror: An Essay on Abjection* (New York: Columbia University Press, 1982), 1, 3, 5.

50. Ibid., 3.

51. Peter Brooks, *Body Work: Objects of Desire in Modern Narrative* (Cambridge, Mass.: Harvard University Press, 1993), 7.

the desire for escapism and beauty. (One is reminded of Bartheleme's *Catch 22* on "patricide,"[52] in which we find ourselves doing that of which we are accused.) They take us to beyond meaning and construction, and elicit corporeal empathy, a desire to bind wounds with bandages and sooth them with oil (cf. Isa 1:6). Bodies that are raped, that ooze, that slop and are covered in excrement may also release the desire to wipe, heal, pull down the skirts, protect.

There may be another reason for all these bodies. The Prophets reach for bodies in their attempt to make the invisible divine voice or acts manifest, through its *effects*. As Elaine Scarry has argued in her *The Body in Pain*, the invisible God of the Hebrew Bible is habitually made manifest through the alteration of, and the impact on, landscapes and, particularly and especially, bodies,[53] particularly through scenes of supernatural reproduction and un-natural death.

Intriguingly, this is also the way in which the force we describe as "violence" becomes visible: through exceptional and forceful *effects*. The book of Amos experiments with making an abstract noun of violence, *hms*, when it speaks, metaphorically, of those who stockpile "violence" and store up "robbery" (Amos 3:6). But as Michael Taussig points out, violence is not "a substance," "so many ergs of spermatic effluvial power that the father exerts in the fastness of his family," for example.[54] Violence is nothing without an object, a scene of impact. Violence is seen most clearly—indeed is defined by—its object, its victim, its effects. In its attempts to make "violence" appear, at least within a space cleared by definition, the *Shorter Oxford Dictionary* reaches out for objects and for bodies, just like the Prophets:

> *Violent* 1. Having a marked or powerful (esp. physical) effect; (of pain, a reaction, etc.) very strong, severe, extreme. b. Of colour: intense, vivid. 2. Of an action: involving or using great physical force or strength, esp. in order to cause injury; not gentle or moderate. 3. Of a storm or other natural force: operating with great force or strength, now esp. destructively. b. Of a noise: extremely loud. 4. Of a person: habitually using physical force or violence, esp. in order to injure or intimidate others. Formerly also, acting illegally. 5. Due or subject to constraint; involuntary, forced. b. Of death: caused by external force or poison; unnatural. 6 Characterised by or displaying passion or intense emotion; vehement, furious.

52. Ibid., 9.
53. I opt out of her argument that the "Old" and "New" Testaments function as scenes of wounding and healing, respectively.
54. Michael Taussig, *The Nervous System* (London: Routledge, 1992), 116.

These definitions are then followed by a revealing selection of examples, including violent storms, a violent coughing fit, violent offenders (the criminal), lipstick of a "violent mulberry colour," and "making violent love"— the kind of "love" that comes close to rape.

Notably, violence is defined as "powerful (*esp. physical*) effect." It appears through its action on an object and it seems to find its favoured object in the body. Though it *can* be seen in convulsions of the cosmos and the violent storm, it finds it most natural and graphic sign in the body that receives injury or the body that is forced to act (or that is acted on) beyond its own volition. A violent coughing fit sends the body into involuntary convulsions, and makes it do things beyond its will, as if an invisible force were acting upon it. (Hos 5:12–13 equates the lack of control in illness with the force and punishment of God.) Even when violence is applied, metaphorically, to, say, a voice or a colour, it is marked by recoil, the implied image of a viewer or hearer staggering backwards under the impact of what has been seen or heard.

Revealingly, the particular range of examples used by the Dictionary is essentially the same basic image set habitually used in the Prophets— so much so that this cumulative definition seems to read almost as a contents page or précis. Think of those theophanies or kratophanies where the Lord roars and sends the world into convulsion (e.g. Amos 1:2); stockpiles of images of unnatural death ("corpses lying everywhere," Amos 8:3); images of being bound, imprisoned, unable to escape (Hos 2:6–7; Jer 27:2; Ezek 4:8; Amos 9:2); and all those curious commands to act against the law, and *to portray God himself as exceeding or breaking the law*. Thus a prophet marries a prostitute, a priest breaks Levitical prohibitions and God appears to commit incest as in Ezek 16 as "the rescuing midwife God observes that his nursling now has breasts and becomes the sexual partner of the infant he has raised."[55]

My point here is not simply that God is violence (but nor is it that God is not). I want to thwart the easy and oft-rehearsed argument that religions and their scriptures have an exceptionally and particularly close relationship to violence and terror. It is a fundamentally unsafe illusion that, having scapegoated the religious-violent or the fundamentalist terrorist, we can escape to a safer, purer, place. At the same time, it seems that violence is not an accidental accretion in the prophetic and biblical corpus. Rather, "it" is built in to its structures. To return to Levinas's description that "violence is to be found in any action in which one acts as if one were alone to act; as if the rest of the universe were there only

---

55. Fontaine, *Eyes of Flesh*, 277.

to receive the action,"[56] is this not a description of the basic conditions of *monotheism?* (Lévinas, who tries to create a special place for what he terms "spiritual violence," would want to resist this conclusion.) In the world of radical monotheism, divine actions and words become, by definition, that which "we endure without at every point collaborating." (If the inhabitants of the world of the Prophets do "collaborate" in that which happens to them, it is generally in the form of providing the culpability and counter-power that legitimates the use of divine power by way of response.) The word and voice of God is performed as massive, irresistible, unanswerable, hypermasculine—a world away from the collaborative environment of the Liberal and Literary Bibles, with their models of reader-response. Images of God and his representatives breaking the law invoke what Kierkegaard and others have termed the *horror religiosus*: the sacred as that which is not reducible to moral obligation and ethics, and that, to prove that this is so, risks moments where God and the just and the proportionate clearly come apart.[57] The dare of the illegal as supra-legal is mirrored in the scandal of spilt and stockpiled bodies, or the raped and exposed female body. In prophetic logic it is often almost impossible to separate decreation/destruction and recreation/transformation, making and breaking. To make space for the new, old worlds are torn apart.

Though "he" might be a numinous spirit beyond the body and beyond representation, the fact that the God of the Hebrew Bible does have a body does not mean that he does not have the power to overwhelm our bodies. On the contrary: the very invisibility of God seems to beg for these repeated manifestations. *God makes himself felt in the world as an irresistible force meeting an infinitely moveable and impressionable object.* The is-ness of God is made manifest in the strong impression that he makes on the world and our body, through the exertion of the will/ voice/act that can bring us to our knees. As the body doubles up under the force of that which acts on it, God becomes most tangible, felt, visible. The difference between God and human beings—that causes considerable anxiety at certain points in the Hebrew Bible—is most clearly etched in the contrast between the eternal transcendent and inviolate and the vulnerable, contingent, human body, a distinction later perfected and fine-tuned in Christian theology, where omniscience, omnipotence and omnipresence define Godness over and against the

---

56. Lévinas, *Difficult Freedom*, 6.
57. Hent De Vries, *Religion and Violence: Philosophical Perspectives from Kant to Derrida* (Baltimore: The Johns Hopkins University Press, 2002).

limits and edges of the human body. Unlike human bodies, God is not susceptible to hunger or thirst; he cannot be mutilated by a wild animal, or speared, or burnt. His skin cannot rot. He cannot decoagulate, turn back into water, breath, dust. According to a certain theo-logic, God is most clearly God when he iterates the edges of the human body; the tightly bound limits of human agency. Thus scenes of wounding and unnatural death function as a mode of negative theology—the marking of the weakness of the body that God has not.

In this reading, fundamental structures such as the divinity of God, the nature of the prophetic word and the creation of new and better worlds partake, through their very structures, in what we call "violence." Nor is this a particularly unique observation, though it may be particularly striking (violent?) in the way I have phrased it. When it comes to the Bible, we would rather speak German rather than French or English and use a word like *Gewalt*—a word that can mean violence *and* power, and therefore can always be understood in the more neutral sense. The kinds of points I am making in this essay have been kept at bay not by ignoring them but by repeatedly making them in a more anodyne and euphemistic form, to the point where they have become a well-worn, harmless commonplace. The Bible and the Prophets are habitually cast as striking or irresistible. In almost dead metaphors that have lost their connection to the boxing glove, the biblical text regularly "pulls no punches" or "hits home." Rare are the voices in modernity that, with Erich Auerbach, write of the Bible's autocracy, sovereignty (*Allenherrschaft*) and the power to sweep aside the rights of its addresses and its characters.[58] The argument has been made (and nullified), in a "decaffeinated" version, to borrow a metaphor from Žižek.[59] In a culture of "Alpha Courses"—where God graciously seeks to elicit our believing, take our questions into account, and convince us—we prefer "the still small voice" to the Barthelmian boom.

The only thing that can keep God's power on the good side of "power, apart from violence, is our trust, our believing: our belief that these new worlds are worth the levelling and destruction of the old ones; our belief that divine force has indeed been called forth and provoked by vast counter-forces that pre-existed it, and that needed to be flattened, punished or eliminated; our belief that the manifestation that seems illegal

---

58. Erich Auerbach, *Mimesis: The Representation of Reality in Western Literature* (Princeton: Princeton University Press, 1953), 15.

59. Žižek, "Passion: Regular or Decaf?," online: http://www.lacan.com/zizek-passion.htm (2004), accessed 1 March 2008.

only breaks or momentarily suspends the law in the greater name of justice. Clearly, these structures of believing do not simply apply to the Bible or religion. They are replicated in the structures of law, state and liberalism itself. For example, torture can be seen not as violence but as a legitimate practice of power "provided that its sole purpose is preventing future harms," creating better, safer, more liberal worlds in the future.[60] The law can be suspended in the name of "justice" (and it can be said that justice, like God, is never really outside the law, but rather redefines it). Similarly acts of seemingly disproportionate aggression can be believed to be inevitable and proportionate, called forth by a preceding act of violence; an example of the global/cosmic order righting itself, by way of retaliation or legitimate defence.

Rather than thinking the biblical and the religious as worlds apart—the very opposite of politics, according to modern definitions—it would be interesting to follow thinkers such as Walter Benjamin, Jacques Derrida, Michael Taussig and Slavoj Žižek as they attempt to put the state, the sacred, the legal, the divine and the violent together in different experimental formulations (without simply using the religious as the scapegoat of the violent and so the saviour of the state). They point, for example, to the "intrinsically mysterious, mystifying, convoluting, plain scary, mythical and arcane" dimension of the "power of violence," particularly "violence" construed as "an end in itself"—whereupon it becomes a "sign" of the existence of the gods."[61] (The word "gods" here is not intended to equate, in any straightforward way, with the Gods of the Christian, Jewish or biblical traditions, or the purely religious, as construed as distinct from the state.) Confusing the traditional separation of Gods and states, Žižek argues that power would not be power if it were to elicit rational submission from its subjects, if we were only to submit after carefully reasoning "[t]his is justice." Taussig writes of the coming together of "reason-and-violence" that creates, in a secular and modern world, the "auratic and quasisacred quality" of the big State, capital S. The conjunction of reason and violence in the State is at once frightening and reassuring: frightening because we "cling to reason" as the safeguard against violence; reassuring because we need to know that reason "has violence at its disposal, because we feel that that very anomie and chaos will respond to naught else."[62] In attempting to grope for thoughts of a paradoxical, pure non-violent violence, that is to say a

---

60. David Luban, "Liberalism, Torture and the Ticking Bomb," *Virginia Law Review* 91 (2005): 1436.

61. Taussig, *Nervous System*, 116, drawing on Benjamin.

62. Žižek, *Sublime Object*, 37; Taussig, *Nervous System*, 115–16, 119.

non-coercive, bloodless or revolutionary violence, Žižek and Benjamin use the term, coined by Benjamin, "divine violence."[63] This "divine violence," conceived as the cataclysmic, purifying violence of the sovereign ethical deed, may be found, Žižek claims, in the slum favelas in Rio de Janeiro disturbing the peace of bourgeois neighbourhoods. For Benjamin, it is seen in the vision of a general proletariat strike as a mode of violence that has no clear *telos*, no calculation, and that is free from the economics and projections of ends. I am reminded again of a book like Amos, inveighing against all those war crimes, all those acts of calculation and intra-human violence and exploitation, and trying to dream a purer, better counter-violence, a destruction/purification that is nameless, that has no clear content. (Yhwh repeatedly only tells his hearers that "it"—unspecified—is coming, and shows the coming of "it" through the paralysis and decimation of those who reel before "it"; see Amos 2:13–16). In Benjamin and Žižek, as in Amos, I find it impossible to construe or dream of this pure non-violent violence. Even if there is no objective, no calculation, there must still be the possibility of, at the very least, "collateral damage." Amos projects massive collateral damage in its vision of transformation; indeed, the absence of the future content means that "it" becomes most visible and manifest in the destruction of the present order and present bodies. There is something terrifying about this violence without clear form or name.

My argument is not that we should believe, or dissent from, the structures and logics in the Bible and the Prophets (what kind of rhetorical power/[violence?] would be required to enforce that kind of argument, or that decision on anyone else's behalf?), but that we should become more conscious of the relationship between acts of violence (or power) and acts of faith. Structures and logics within the biblical and theological are regularly applied in the world outside the Bible's covers. States and nations may elicit modes of faith that the biblical and theological Gods have lost, not least as a result of certain Enlightenment moves that turned the Bible/religion into the locus of violence and unreason. Conversely, structures and logics that we assent to within the Bible may, when replicated in the "political," provoke our ardent dissent.

63. Walter Benjamin, "Critique of Violence," in *Selected Writings*. Vol. 1, *1913–1926* (ed. Marcus Bullock and Michael W. Jennings; Cambridge, Mass.: Harvard University Press, 1996), 236–53.

VIOLENT PICTURES, VIOLENT CULTURES?
THE "AESTHETICS OF VIOLENCE" IN CONTEMPORARY FILM AND IN ANCIENT PROPHETIC TEXTS

Julia M. O'Brien

Nahum's Violence and Its "Historical" Solution

The book of Nahum has long been noted for its fascination with war and for the glee with which it calls for revenge. Graphic depictions of the siege of Nineveh describe war in bloody detail, and, throughout, the piece refuses any empathy or care for those about to be destroyed. Nahum does not merely describe war and its toil; it revels in imagining the panic and death of the Assyrian foe. In addition, feminist interpreters have highlighted the highly sexualized nature of Nahum's violence. In ch. 3, Nineveh, personified as a woman, is called a whore (Hebrew *zona*) and is threatened with exposure and assault by none other than Israel's deity, while others are goaded to watch and taunt. Many commentators have remained content simply to remark upon and subsequently to distance themselves from book's violence. Such a response was especially common among Christian commentators prior to the 1950s, who saw Nahum's nationalism and desire for vengeance as the antithesis to the loving, forgiving spirit of a universal Christianity. In the 1903 *Expositor's Bible*, for example, G. A. Smith deemed Nahum's sentiments as "Oriental" and "Jewish," far from the refined sensibilities of the West,[1] and in 1911, J. M. P. Smith rated Nahum as inferior to "ethical" prophets such as Jeremiah.[2] For these commentators, the only thing to say about Nahum's violence is that it is wrong.

But particularly since the late twentieth century, Nahum's violent rhetoric has been explained, even justified, by an appeal to its historical

---

1. G. A. Smith, "Nahum," in *The Expositor's Bible* (New York: A. C. Armstrong & Son, 1903), 91–92.

2. J. M. P. Smith, "Nahum," in *A Critical and Exegetical Commentary on Micah, Zephaniah, Nahum, Habakkuk, Obadiah, and Joel* (ed. J. M. P. Smith, W. H. Ward, and J. A. Brewer; New York: Charles Scribner's Sons, 1911), 281.

context. When Nahum is read in the context of Assyrian oppression, its opposition to Nineveh becomes understandable—indeed holy—resistance. According to Peter Craigie,

> If, from the comfort of study or pew, we complain that the sentiments of this book are neither noble nor uplifting, we need to remind ourselves that we have not suffered at Assyrian hands.[3]

More recently, Willie Wessels has identified Nahum as "resistance literature," which, like the protest poetry of the anti-apartheid movements in South Africa, challenges the dominant hegemonic system by construing an alternative ideological world.[4] Clearly, for these latter commentators, historical contextualization in general and an Assyrian-period dating in particular are crucial for an appreciation of Nahum's message. Assyria must be a real and present threat for the rhetoric of Nahum to function as resistance literature, for it to challenge the dominant and hegemonic discourse of an occupying or colonizing power. For these interpreters, the dating of Nahum takes on a moral dimension.

One of the primary arguments advanced by commentators arguing for the Assyrian-period dating of Nahum rests upon an aesthetic feature of the book: its "realism." J. R. Macarthur vividly describes just how "realistic" the book sounds:

> The superb strong word-pictures and the astoundingly impetuous movement place the author among the world's great literary artists. We still can see the flaming chariots with their scarlet-clad warriors; we still can hear the noise of the whip and the noise of the rattling of the wheels, and of the prancing horses, and of the jumping chariots. Brilliant pictures, replete with vivid realism, follow in quick succession—the preparation, the repulses, the flight, the spoils, the heaps of corpses.[5]

For the commentators I have been discussing, the realism that Macarthur describes is not simply an artistic feature: the aesthetics of Nahum is the key to its dating, evidence of its chronological proximity to the Assyrian period. Because the scenes are so vivid, so realistic, so the argument goes, they *must* derive from actual situations.

---

3. Peter Craigie, *Twelve Prophets*, vol. 2 (The Daily Study Bible Series; Philadelphia: Westminster, 1985), 59.

4. Wilhelm Wessels, "Nahum, an Uneasy Expression of Yahweh's Power," *OTE* 11 (1998): 615–28 (625).

5. J. R. Macarthur, *Biblical Literature and Its Backgrounds* (New York: Appleton, 1936), cited in *The Hebrew Bible in Literary Criticism* (ed. Arthur Preminger and E. L. Greenstein; New York: Ungar, 1986), 505.

My goal in this essay is not to engage directly with arguments for Nahum's dating. Rather, my aim is to address the chain of assumptions that I have attempted to set forth: that the realistic nature of Nahum's poetry necessarily indicates an Assyrian-period setting, which in turn explains and/or justifies its use of the violent image.

I seek to address those assumptions by exploring the multiple ways that the violent image can function in art, other purposes to which "realism" can be directed. And, to do so, I turn to an unlikely conversation partner: contemporary film theory.

Why Film Theory?

To invoke contemporary film theory in an effort to think through the violence of Nahum is not an obvious move to make. Clearly, the media are not the same. Ancient texts are not movies; they employ a medium that is not primarily visual; and they emerged within the context of ancient Near Eastern social movements and politics rather than in those of the twentieth or twenty-first centuries. Moreover, many of the analytical categories of film theory are not unique to that discipline. Film criticism's discussion of Freudian and Lacanian psychology, its debates over the essentializing vs. queering of gender, as well as its Marxist questions of the function of race and class, are quite familiar to other branches of the humanities—and are in fact borrowed from them. Many angles of vision offered by film studies offer little that is new to studies of prophetic texts.

I would like to suggest, however, that at least two dimensions of current film studies raise interesting possibilities for those of us who study prophetic texts. First is their focus on the stylistic dimensions of portrayals of violence. Film studies, as I aim to demonstrate, provide useful categories beyond literary-critical ones for talking about the artistic dimensions of violence rather than about their discursive content. Film critics pay attention not only to what films include, what scenes they show, but also with how those scenes are crafted, how they are cut.

Second, and perhaps of greater concern to those who are interested in how prophetic texts resonated in their ancient contexts, study of a contemporary art form such as film offers a testing ground for considering the socio-political dimensions of the violent image. Film has the obvious advantage of being recent. We know when films were produced and what was going on in the world at the time of their production. We often have access to the thoughts of their writers, producers, and directors through live or published interviews. The contemporaneity of film makes it a New Historicist's dream, a playground for testing different understandings of the relationships between images and the socio-political climate in which they were produced.

When it comes to the particular question of violence in film, we also have a wealth of literature theorizing about how film violence correlates to societal violence. No film violence is gratuitous: violence in film performs a function, even if that function is to generate an audience. But exactly *what* work film violence does, as we shall see, is disputed. As I will outline, a survey of film theory suggests that the violent image can "work" in multiple ways.

In what follows, I survey some of the theoretical approaches to film violence and ask what each may contribute to our reflection on how depictions of violence function in Nahum. The hope is that thinking about how the images on the screen do and do not simply reproduce the conflicts, the mores, and the problems of the world outside the theater may allow us a new way of viewing ancient texts.

Feminist Film Theory

Feminist film theory has obvious potential for study of Nahum, given that both objects of study depict violence in highly gendered ways. In film, women are victims of violence—from the slasher movie, to the-hero-saves-the-day movie, to bondage film. In Nahum, Woman Nineveh also is a sexualized victim, and enemy males are demeaned by being compared to women.

Feminist Psychoanalytic Approaches

Laura Mulvey's 1975 article "Visual Pleasure and Narrative Cinema" is widely recognized at the first major step in feminist film criticism.[6] In it, Mulvey explores how film taps into two primary psychoanalytic processes. The first is scopophilia, looking as a source of pleasure. The darkness of a theater encourages our scopophilia: though side by side with others, we feel as if we are alone in a darkened theater and are able to look without being seen. The second psychological dimension of film is narcissism, as we identify with the image we see. As in the mirror stage of a child's development, through our identification with the ideal main character on the screen we perceive ourselves as more complete than we really are.

---

6. Laura Mulvey, "Visual Pleasure and Narrative Cinema," *Screen* 16 (1975): 6–18.

Mulvey's claim is that these psychoanalytic processes are encoded with patriarchy. In terms of scopophilia, the gaze that the camera constructs is male: we see from the male point of view, and the object of our gaze is female. In terms of narcissism, the camera leads us to identify with the ideal male, the violent conquering hero. We find the violence against the film woman pleasurable because in this fetishizing and punishing of a woman, male castration anxiety is "resolved."

That Mulvey's categories well describe the male orientation of most mainstream film is clear. One need think only of Hitchcock's *Rear Window*, in which the audience becomes a voyeur by identifying with Jimmy Stewart, a voyeur himself who like us is stuck sitting in a chair observing others' lives. In the film, Stewart's girlfriend, the beautiful and glamorous Grace Kelly, only becomes interesting to him when she is seen from his binoculars, when "he sees her as a guilty intruder exposed by a dangerous man threatening her with punishment and finally saves her."[7]

Mulvey's focus on scopophilia and narcissism carry over into an understanding of Nah 3 in fairly obvious ways. As Pamela Gordon and Harold Washington argue, in Nahum erotic pleasure and sexual violence are linked most clearly in 3:4–7, where Woman Nineveh, who is raped before the gaze of onlookers, is described as desirable, "full of grace" (3:4).[8] Cynthia Chapman's work as well as my own have stressed the sexualization of Nineveh's punishment and the scope of the male gaze in Nah 3: readers, like Nineveh's enemies, are invited to gaze at her when Yahweh lifts up her skirts over her face.[9] She is indeed a spectacle (3:6). Scopophilic, the reader takes pleasure in looking; narcissistic, the reader identifies with the male agent and takes pleasure in the eroticized violence carried out against the female character.

For psychoanalytic approaches such as that of Mulvey, an image of violence against a woman does not simply signify violence against a woman: while anti-female violence is embedded in patriarchy, it is refracted through psychoanalytic processes. The punishment of Nineveh is pleasurable to the male viewer and to the male-identified female viewer

---

7. Ibid., 9.
8. Pamela Gordon and Harold Washington, "Rape as a Military Metaphor in the Hebrew Bible," in *A Feminist Companion to the Latter Prophets* (ed. Athalya Brenner; Sheffield: Sheffield Academic, 1995), 308–25.
9. Cynthia Chapman, *The Gendered Language of Warfare in the Israelite–Assyrian Encounter* (HSM 62; Winona Lake, Ind.: Eisenbrauns, 2004); Julia Myers O'Brien, *Nahum* (Readings; Sheffield: Sheffield Academic, 2002).

not simply because we like to see women hurt, but because psychologically her punishment resolves a crisis within our own psyche. Patriarchy, for Mulvey, is an underlying ideology, but not necessarily the manifest content of the image of violence against women.

Feminist Critique of Mulvey
Mulvey has been roundly pummeled for her assumption of gender- and psychological-essentialism, for assuming that gender is a fixed, biological given and that psychological processes are universal, unfiltered through the experiences of sexual orientation, race, or class.

Race. Jane Gaines and bell hooks have argued that Mulvey's theory assumes that what is true for white women (and men) is true for all women (and men). hooks complains that the psychoanalytic categories Mulvey applies are ahistorical, blind to how life and looking relations have differed depending on positions of power.[10] Historically, for example, black males could look at a white woman on screen in ways they could not do publicly, and black female spectators have not automatically identified with the white female on the screen; they have not seen themselves in the role of the Scarlett O'Hara who depends on Mammy or scolds Prissy in *Gone with the Wind*, or the Mae West who in her moment of triumph orders her black maid, "Beulah, peel me a grape" in *I'm No Angel.* hooks argues that

> Identifying with neither the phallocentric gaze not the construction of white womanhood as lack, critical black female spectators construct a theory of looking relations where cinematic visual delight is the pleasure of interrogation.[11]

That is, the refusal to identify with the white woman on the screen allows the African American woman a sense of agency, the ability to step outside of the script and critique it—to make of it what she will.

Like hooks, Gaines argues that there is little "universal" about gender or, indeed, about male control.[12] While Mulvey claims that the woman on the screen is the object of the male gaze, Gaines explains how the formula is "queered" when we posit a lesbian viewer, who finds the woman on screen attractive as well. And, while Mulvey treats patriarchy as a

10. bell hooks, "The Oppositional Gaze: Black Female Spectators," in *Feminist Film Theory: A Reader* (ed. Sue Thornham; New York: New York University Press, 1999), 307–20.

11. Ibid., 316.

12. Jane Gaines, "White Privilege and Looking Relations: Race and Gender in Feminist Film Theory," in Thornham, ed., *Feminist Film Theory*, 293–306.

monolithic, universal phenomenon, Gaines emphasizes how the adoption of the bourgeois, male-headed household has functioned differently for black and white men: the adoption of male control of the African American family after Reconstruction was an attempt to claim an agency for black men that slavery had denied them.[13]

The critiques of Mulvey by hooks and Gaines underscore that film violence functions differently according to the materialist conditions of the viewer. There is nothing automatic or "natural" about the message that a viewer takes from a film. When such approaches are applied to Nahum, the power dimensions of the gaze are highlighted. Who in Nahum is permitted to look? Within the narrative world of the book, Nah 3:5–6 threatens Nineveh with the gaze of the nations:

> I will let nations look (*rʾ*) on your nakedness//kingdoms on your shame…
> I will make you a spectacle (*rʾ*)… Behold (*hnh*) your troops: they are women in your midst.

And, yet, the readers are the ones who truly see Nineveh's shame. Ancient readers were allowed to gaze on assaulted Nineveh; they saw the feminization of Assyrian troops. Like a darkened theater, the reading event allowed readers to experience something to which they would not have had access in the light of day. No longer the oppressed with their eyes downcast or diverted, the readers looked directly at Nineveh; they became not the downtrodden but equals with nations and kingdoms who got to see the spectacle of Assyria's defeat.

At the same time, the cautions of Gaines and hooks suggest that neither ancient nor modern readers "naturally" identify with any single figure in the book. Although Judah is the female addressed by Nahum, the one told to celebrate her festivals, the one encouraged to cheer Nineveh's fall, the reader, depending on his or her location, might identify with Nineveh or perhaps with that other devastated woman—Thebes, whose children were dashed at the head of every street (Nah 3:10).

When read through the lens of hooks and Gaines, the effect of Nahum's violence becomes unstable. The reader does not automatically identify with Judah, with the "us" whom the deity rescues. Assyria is not necessarily the other, the foreign one, if we understand ourselves to be outsiders as well.

Mulvey's "man problems." Following the more contemporary move away from gender as a biological given to gender as a socially constructed—and always unstable—category, film critics also have gone beyond

13. Ibid., 300.

Mulvey in considering the complications of masculinity in film. As Steve Neale observes, the male reader's narcissistic identification with the ideal male character on screen is always threatening: "The image of the male body as object of a look is fraught with ambivalences, repressions and denials," and "the erotic element in looking at the male body has to be repressed and disavowed so as to avoid any implications of male homosexuality."[14] The potential homoerotic crisis is resolved, often, by "highly ritualized scenes of male struggle which deflect the look away from the male body to the scene of the spectacular fight."[15] The male on the screen must be remasculinized so that the male viewer may be as well. In this understanding, images of male-on-male violence serve the purpose of protecting masculinity, of showing that the man remains a real man.

For Nahum, this understanding would underscore the role of violence in the masculine construction of the deity. The concern with protecting Yahweh's masculinity runs throughout Nahum. In other work, I have argued that the book of Nahum is a contest of masculinity between Israel's deity and the king of Assyria, the male figure addressed implicitly as "you" at the end of ch. 1 and explicitly at the end of chs. 2 and 3.[16] I and others also have argued that the violence against Woman Nineveh reflects a contest between males: like a lion who cannot protect his den (Nah 2:12 MT), the king of Assyria is shown unable to protect his own.

Yet Neale's argument that violent fight scenes serve as resolution for homoerotic tension suggests something else about Nahum: that the image of Yahweh the Divine Warrior moves to include violence just when the image itself becomes too attractive. Although the extended look at Yahweh the Divine Warrior in Nah 1 does not focus particularly on Yahweh's body, it is noteworthy that attention to Yahweh's appearance turns quickly to scenes of combat and heterosexual assault. In Nah 1:12, the deity says to the feminine Judah, "I have afflicted you; I will afflict you no more." The verb here is ʿnh, also the one used elsewhere in the Hebrew Bible for rape. Moreover, Nah 1 ends with the deity's explicit challenge to the rival male: "I will make your grave, for you are worthless" (1:14).

---

14. Steve Neale, "Masculinity as Spectacle," *Screen* 24 (1983): 2–16, quoted in Anneke Smelik, "Feminist Film Theory." Online: http://www.let.uu.nl/womens_ studies/anneke/filmtheory.html (accessed September 14, 2006).

15. Ibid.

16. O'Brien, *Nahum*.

The fluidity of gender. The fluidity of gender has been explored further by other film critics. Carol Clover, for example, takes on the genre of the slasher movie and finds significance in the classic slasher plot. In films such as *Halloween* and *Friday the 13th*, she observes, "no male character of any stature lives to tell the tale."[17] All males are killed, as are all promiscuous girls. The Final Girl alone survives.

Clover explains the cinematic techniques that encourage us to identify with that Final Girl. Through the use of the "I-camera" (the one from whose vantage point the scene is viewed), we most often see from her point of view. When the I-camera films from the position of the killer viewing the Final Girl, we identify with her terror, just as in *Jaws* the I-camera films from the viewpoint of the shark in order that we might see the victim's terror and identify with it.[18]

Important to Clover's argument is that in slasher films the Final Girl is ambiguously gendered. Unlike the girls who die early in the action, she is not sexual; and, in order to triumph, she takes on stereotypically masculine traits, often using weapons shaped like a phallus to kill the monster. Clover maintains that the bisexual nature of the Final Girl indicates that, psychologically, she is the stand-in for the adolescent male: the movie works out adolescent male concerns through the embodiment of the Final Girl. According to Clover,

> It may be through the female body that the body of the audience is sensationalised, but the sensation is entirely a male affair… What is represented as male-on-female violence, in short, is figuratively speaking male-on-male sex.[19]

For Clover, the Final Girl's survival and ability to save herself is not a feminist triumph but rather the triumph of the male fending off the threat of penetration through the "agreed-upon fiction" of the girl on the screen.[20] Although she could be described as exhibiting her own version of psychological essentialism, Clover differs from Mulvey in arguing that the gender of a film character can function as a trope, a convention, rather than necessarily mirroring biological gender.

Linda Williams extends Clover's discussion to consider how three film genres utilize female characters not only to represent emotion but also to evoke bodily states. These "body genres," as Williams calls them, depict states of bodily excess:

17. Carol Clover, "Her Body, Himself: Gender in the Slasher Film," in Thornham, ed., *Feminist Film Theory*, 234–50 (236).
18. Ibid.
19. Ibid., 241.
20. Ibid., 242.

- Pornography depicts the body in an excess state of orgasm.
- Horror film depicts the body in an excess state of terror.
- Melodrama depicts the body in an excess state of weeping.[21]

In each case, the success of the film depends upon its success in manipulating the viewer's body to replicate the sensation being depicted. The successful horror film is, literally, a fear jerker; the successful melodrama, a tear jerker; successful pornography, well, encourages other kinds of jerking. The aim of these films is to collapse the emotional distance between screen and viewer and make the viewer experience the appropriate sensation.

Following Foucault, Williams also traces the "sexual saturation of the female body,"[22] how each of these states (fear, weeping, and sexual ecstasy) are modeled by the female character on the screen. Women weep when we are supposed to weep. They scream for us—in pain and in ecstasy—when we are asked to scream.

When read through the lens of Clover and Williams, Nahum's female characters represent not simply women but also the emotional states that the writer seeks to create in the reader. In 2:1, Judah, addressed in feminine imperatives and represented by feminine pronouns, models the state of relief and celebration that the reader of the book is supposed to feel upon hearing of Nineveh's fall. She is the Final Girl: "no longer will Belial pass through you; all of him is cut off" (2:1). With the promiscuous Nineveh raped and destroyed (3:6), the woman-as-example Thebes long ago having suffered her fate (3:8–10), Judah alone is left standing when the terror is over. Williams's approach, however, suggests that Judah does not just represent herself. Nahum 2:3 makes this clear: "Because the Lord has restored the glory of Jacob, along with the glory of Israel, even though devastators have devastated them and ruined their branches." Jacob's glory is being restored, but female Judah must embody it.

Moreover, I would suggest that the "I-camera" of the book of Nahum sees from the perspective of Judah. It is Judah who is invited to see the Divine Warrior, to see the images of Nineveh's destruction, to overhear the taunts against the king of Assyria. Nahum-as-movie is told from the perspective of what Judah is seeing, hearing, experiencing. And we are asked to let hers be the character with which we see, hear and experience as well.

---

21. Linda Williams, "Film Bodies: Gender, Genre, and Excess," in Thornham, ed., *Feminist Film Theory*, 267–80.
22. Ibid., 270.

Noteworthy, however, is the way in which Nahum differs from the classic slasher genre. While in *Halloween* and *Friday the 13th* the Final Girl takes on masculine characteristics in order to save herself, in Nahum, the only savior is Yahweh the Warrior. Yahweh remains the only real man in the book, as the masculinity of the king of Assyria is taunted and Jacob never rises to defend himself. According to Clover's line of thought, that also means that Jacob never fends off the implied threat of penetration, and we never get the satisfaction of feeling that we have conquered, that we are secure. We remain dependent on Yahweh—for good and for ill: "I afflicted you," says Yahweh in 1:12, but "I will not afflict you further."

Judah might be encouraged to cheer Nineveh's demise, but she remains vulnerable to the same Yahweh, open also to being called a *zona* and sexually assaulted. The images of violence against Nineveh perpetually remain a threat against Judah. In the slasher movie, the Final Girl is threatened with the same fate as the slut, but in the end takes up the phallic object and triumphs. In Nahum, where Judah is never allowed to become masculine, the threat remains, so that Woman Nineveh embodies our terror as well.

In the approach of Clover and Williams, Nineveh is a woman because the emotions we are asked to feel are modeled through women. And the violence is there to evoke both the reader's celebration and terror.

Other Approaches to Film Violence

Thus far I have focused on how various strands of feminist and gender-focused film theory have interpreted violence in film. We have seen the violent image function to resolve male psychological processes, to protect the male character from the potential for homoerotic focus on his appearance, and to evoke particular emotional states by embodying them as women. We have also been warned that the social location of viewers challenges our assumptions of how a reader "naturally" chooses a character with whom to identify.

I turn now to several other approaches to screen violence and to a consideration of how they may shed light on Nahum.

Margaret Bruder

In "Aestheticizing Violence, or How to Do Things with Style," Margaret Bruder stresses that the viewer experiences violence not only according to the content of a film, but also according to its style. Echoing Rick Trader Witcombe's phrase "the brutality of the camera eye," she highlights how the point of view from which a scene is shot affects our experience of the film.[23] In movies such as Jean Claude Vann Damm's *Hard Target*, in which the viewer is bombarded with forty-nine shots in one minute of film, the constant repositioning of the camera is itself an assault. The viewer suffers not only by observing violent content, but also by, in a return to the language of Clover and Williams, being literally "jerked" around. According to Bruder,

> Like the attackers, we are thrust down by extreme low angles, hurdled forward by fast tracking, slapped up against bodies through low angled closeups emphasized by slow motion and further exaggerated by over-lapping editing. Few of the awkward framings and re-framings remain on screen for more than a second or two. It is little wonder, then, that by the time we leave the theater, we are both exhilarated and exhausted.[24]

In her exploration of the cultural functions of violent images, Bruder challenges the distinction made by Devin McKinney between "weak" and "strong" violence in films—the latter referring to violence as it is used to provide social commentary in serious films and the former to violence that is made into a spectacle, calling attention to itself rather than to a message. Bruder maintains that the focus in New Hollywood movies on the spectacle of violence, via the cinematic techniques of slow motion or the "shock cut," not only reflects a change in filmmaking away from the plot-driven classic film formula, but also a change in American society toward a more postmodern sensibility toward signs and their multiform and often indirect significations.

In her discussion of how film violence can function non-mimetically, Bruder offers a political comparison. She notes that Clinton's tough anti-crime bill was passed in 1993—*after* two years of declining crime rates. The bill drew from the vocabulary, images, and motifs of earlier presidents to portray Clinton as tough on crime; and yet, significantly, Bruder argues, the bill bore no direct correlation to what was going on in society. Rather than addressing social problems directly, Clinton's bill was stylized, putting into play "disconnected signifiers taken up to suit the needs of the moment or the individual."[25] Both Clinton's crime bill and violent movie blockbusters such as *Hard Target*, Bruder argues, deal with social issues only indirectly; in both "we can notice both a

23. Margaret Ervin Bruder, "Aestheticizing Violence, or How to Do Things with Style," 1998, online: http://www.gradnet.de/papers/pomo2.archives/pomo98.papers/mtbruder98.htm (accessed September 2006).
24. Ibid.
25. Ibid.

fetishization of past discourses and a willingness to disconnect and reconnect current connotations."[26]

Bruder maintains that the spectacles of violence in much modern film also function to activate genre recognition: one kind of violence marks the Western; another the road movie; yet another the muscular action film. Yet modern film, unlike classical film, rarely stays true to the genre which it invokes. Rather, genre itself becomes a sign, a vocabulary, an intertext:

> this film [*Tombstone*], like *Hard Target* and *True Romance*, seems more concerned with how such cultural ideas have come to form a stockpile of images which, when assembled, form our cultural identity.[27]

According to Bruder, "The recent increase in the stylization of violence in the mainstream cinema must have something to say about the culture consuming and producing it."[28] That violence, however, does not necessarily reveal that our culture has become more violent or numb to violence. Rather, it indicates that violence has become part of our vocabulary, our cultural language.

A direct application of Bruder's theory to the book of Nahum is challenging. Bruder herself argues that this non-narrative, intertextual play of violent images is a new phenomenon, at least in film. Postmodern bricolage is certainly not a cultural constant. And, yet, chronology might not provide an impenetrable barrier to our project. Bersani and Dutoit, for example, have argued that the violent images of neo-Assyrian palace reliefs are themselves non-mimetic, that the motif of war and images of phalanxes of marching soldiers provided Assyrian artists with space for visual play:

> The artists' use of repeated forms, the play of curve and line, the incongruous details (for example, a lion whose haunches—through varying depths of relief—are both inside and outside of a cage) not only engage the eye but also take attention away from the story being narrated... The force of this violent subject is, then, contravened by visual abstractions which disrupt the spectator's reading of the subject.[29]

What Bersani and Dutoit do *not* do, however, is argue as Bruder does that the non-narrative violent image resonates socio-culturally.

---

26. Ibid.
27. Ibid.
28. Ibid.
29. Leo Bersani and Ulysse Dutoit, *The Forms of Violence: Narrative in Assyrian Art and Modern Culture* (New York: Schocken, 1985), 9.

Bruder's claim is that "in not addressing issues directly we might be engaging them circuitously."[30] If that is true in the case of Nahum, several implications follow. First and foremost, it underscores that Nahum need not be understood as an Assyrian-period book. The list of stock images in Nahum is long: it opens like a prophetic book; it includes a Divine Warrior hymn; it feminizes the enemy; and it uses *zona* as epithet against Nineveh, even though the language is more traditionally leveled against Judah/Israel than a foreign nation. These are features that could be borrowed from other ancient literature as much as from any immediate experience of the neo-Assyrian armies. Clearly, that the book "sounds" urgent and immediate testifies far more to the spectacularization of violence than to any concrete dating scheme.

In light of Bruder's analysis, Nahum need not have been produced for the same purpose as other Oracles Against the Nations. It might not even primarily be concerned with Assyria. Violent images and anti-Assyrian language may mirror the repertoire of stock cultural images rather than mark authorial intent. Similarly, the genres within the book may have been chosen because they allowed the author to portray a certain kind of scene. The Oracle Against the Nations motif, the Divine Warrior hymn, the rape scene against a feminized city called a *zona*—all would have provided an author with the opportunity to be graphic with violence, since all are genres in which the reader expects violence to occur.

What would that say about the society in which Nahum was written? That violence had become part of the vocabulary? That literate scribes were bored with classical texts and wanted the equivalent of watching an action movie? That violence was itself seen as the answer to social problems, and not a necessary evil? Bruder's scheme does not allow us to answer those questions, but it does disrupt an easy correlation between Nahum and particular social settings.

In such an approach, biblical historians are left with little on which to base the dating of a book. While Bruder can refer to movies and political scenarios within our own time and thus show the disjuncture between cultural performances and social realities, historians are left with texts that the approach itself makes more difficult to locate chronologically.

Combat Film

For my final foray into film theory, I turn to analysis of a particular film genre: the combat film. Because Nahum's theme (or, if Bruder is right, one of its stock images) is warfare, the discussion of how combat film relates to larger social issues appears fruitful.

---

30. Bruder, "Aestheticizing Violence."

Anthony McCosker's "Suffering with Honour: The Visual Brutality of Realism in the Combat Film" approaches film much in the same manner as Bruder.[31] Like her, he stresses how violence is inscribed on a viewer not only through the content of film but also through cinematic technique. His case study is *Saving Private Ryan* and its extended opening scene of the invasion of Normandy. According to McCosker, the viewer is assaulted not just by blood and guts of this 25-minute-long barrage, but also by the jerkiness of the camera, which seeks to recreate in the viewer the sense of the disorientation of battle. For *Private Ryan* and other war movies since World War II, he argues, "the quality of suffering and brutality is both the subject matter of these films and their realistic affect"; the violent image on the screen is a "way of reinscribing the wound of war upon contemporary audiences."[32]

One way in which the director inflicts this wound on the audience is through evoking the perception of realism. In *Private Ryan*, for example, director Stephen Spielberg consciously modeled the opening sequence on documentaries of World War II, and even the famous still shots taken by photographer Robert Capa during the assault on Omaha Beach:

> The cinematography of the initial landing scene and the combat-adventure that follows is saturated with pallid olive, khaki, greys and browns in a fashion that brings it closer to Capa's photography and other World War II documentary films than recent Vietnam War combat films.[33]

"Drawing on the aesthetic characteristics and 'authenticity' of documentary photography and footage," McCosker claims, Spielberg used a stylistic device that signifies "realism" in the eyes of the viewer.[34]

McCosker argues, however, that this impression of "realism" is itself a construal of reality. To claim that the brutality of the opening scene appears simply because "that's the way it was" obscures the ideological dimensions of the film: the "mythologizing tendencies in the classical dramatization of the plight and value of the individual, and its historical inaccuracies in erasing soldiers of any other nationality from the D-Day invasion and elsewhere in the film."[35] Realism is a special effect.

---

31. Anthony McCosker, "Suffering with Honour: The Visual Brutality of Realism in the Combat Film," *Scope: online journal of film studies*, Issue 2 (2006): online, http://www.scope.nottingham.ac.uk/article.php?issue=2&id=70 (accessed September 2006).
32. Ibid.
33. Ibid.
34. Ibid.
35. Ibid.

The brutally violent opening scene of *Private Ryan*, McCosker claims, "works" both in the film and in the society in which it appeared. In the film, the opening violence serves as the backdrop for the primary narrative—that of the attempt to save one young soldier lest his mother suffer too much. Only with the hellishness of war so deeply inscribed onto viewers' psyches can they truly appreciate the heroism of the American soldiers, the ability of races to come together to accomplish a noble task, and the value of the individual. The violence shows that war is hell; the narrative shows that soldiers can also be honorable and do the right thing.

In society, combat films can do different kinds of work. Some combat films, especially those produced by and for those currently at war, serve as blatant propaganda; examples include Leni Riefenstahl's *Triumph of the Will*, which aimed to deify Adolph Hitler; and Frank Capra's documentary series *Why We Fight*, which attempted to convince American soldiers, and later civilians, of the need for the U.S. to fight in World War II. Other combat films, according to McCosker, serve as an act of protest by showing civilians what military officials attempt to keep from them—Vietnam War films such as *Platoon*, *Full Metal Jacket*, and *Hamburger Hill*, for example, "were a vehicle for an even more intimate, and often more critical view of the physical repercussions of war."[36]

The violence in *Private Ryan*, McCosker claims, serves to persuade the viewer that World War II was a necessary evil. He refers to published interviews with Spielberg to suggest that "[the film's] body horror and violence is justified as an act of demoralization, as a way of shocking 'complacent' U.S. and Western audiences into a new process of remembering the past and confirming the moral right of 'the good war.'"[37]

Why would a 1998 film seek to convince viewers of the rightness of a war that had ended fifty years earlier? McCosker does not raise or address this question directly. His analysis, however, suggests a line of thought: if I believe that World War II was a necessary war, and if I believe that this right war was fought for the values of individualism and compassion, then I will be more likely to believe that future wars fought for the same values are right as well.

I would extend McCosker's argument by observing that, despite their very different styles and different social functions, Spielberg's *Private Ryan* and Capra's *Why We Fight* both sought to make the case that World War II was fought for the right values. For *Why We Fight*, convincing an

36. Ibid.
37. Ibid.

audience served an immediate purpose: after being assigned to the Morale Branch of the U.S. Army in 1942, Capra was ordered to

> make a series of documented, factual-information films—the first in our history—that will explain to our boys in the Army why we are fighting, and the principles for which we are fighting.[38]

In the film, what the "boys" needed to believe was explicitly stated and illustrated with stark graphics produced by the Walt Disney company: *our* world (shown in white) is fighting *their* world (shown in black) for the sake of the freedom of religion, for the value of the individual, for democracy, for freedom. *Why We Fight* shows violence, but only that of the enemy: through seeing *their* violence, the viewer could be frightened by the enemy threat and be convinced of the need for armed response.

Fifty years later, *Private Ryan* made a similar case through a different use of violence. Unlike *Why We Fight*, *Private Ryan* graphically depicts American soldiers in the agony of combat and death, but, in the context of the film, the purpose is to show that American values are worth those tragic losses. In *Private Ryan*, violent scenes serve to embody the message that *Why We Fight* verbalizes. Disney graphics have been replaced by elaborate, graphic images: jerking scenes of bullet-ridden bodies recreate the horror of war, while the images of one grieving mother and the quest for her one remaining son seek to evoke in us the belief that the individual is worth all the carnage. Here, as in the body genres discussed by Williams and Clover above, the female does our grieving, our pathos for us.

How might these reflections on the social resonance of violent scenes in *Saving Private Ryan* invite us to reflect on violent scenes in the book of Nahum?

First, the comparison between the two underscores what is missing in Nahum—the image of successful human armies. The only human soldiers depicted are those of the routed enemy. In 2:6–11 (MT), the enemy scatters in chaos; in 3:14, the enemy's attempts at defense prove futile. The only victorious solider throughout is Yahweh the Warrior.

In scene after scene in Nahum, Yahweh is the only one who fights successfully. In the opening theophany, his power is shown as invincible—he overpowers mountains, rivers, hills. Nahum 1:7–8 makes the point clear: nothing can harm those who take refuge in this soldier. Those who oppose him have no chance. And each successive chapter serves to

---

38. Steven Schoenherr, "Why We Fight," Film notes of the Department of History of San Diego, 2000. Online: http://history.sandiego.edu/GEN/filmnotes/whywefight.html (accessed September 8, 2008).

make the same point more and more powerfully. In Nah 2, through the use of "body language," we experience with the enemy armies the futility of resisting the divine army: along with them, our hearts faint and knees tremble (2:11). Nahum 3 intensifies the depiction of the terror Yahweh inflicts; phrases heap up like the dead bodies they describe, and in the rape of Whore Nineveh we experience the violation that Yahweh can inflict, just as we feel the parting taunt of the king of Assyria. The violence of Nahum is not compartmentalized in the opening scene, as in *Private Ryan*, but escalates as the book progresses. In contrast to *Private Ryan*, in which the violent opening shows the cost of the values that the rest of the film will portray, in Nahum the invincibility of Yahweh the Warrior is the book's unceasing theme.

McCosker's exploration of *Private Ryan* also provides a powerful contemporary example of how important it can be to one generation to understand in a particular way a conflict from its past. It raises the possibility that Nahum may reflect a writer of a post-Assyrian generation attempting to convince his audience—and for them to feel in their guts— that the fall of Nineveh, a well-known event from the past, was the act of Yahweh on Judah's behalf. Yahweh was the sole cause for Nineveh's demise.

Why would such a thing be important to believe, especially after the fact?

If I believe that Yahweh alone felled Nineveh, then I might believe these things as well:

- That the end of Assyrian hegemony is not an indicator of Babylonian strength, but of that of Yahweh, and that when Yahweh says in 1:12, "I will afflict you no more," that means that Judah need not fear Babylonian strength.
- That a national policy that purports to rely on Yahweh will provide sufficient military strength.
- That if powerful Assyria can fall to Yahweh, so can other apparently invincible empires—Babylonian or Persian.
- That a country does not require an army for its oppressor to fall.

Each of those beliefs bears profound political ramifications.

McCosker claims that the violence of *Private Ryan* served to bolster "American" values, such as the worth of the individual. What values does Nahum bolster? Clearly, Nahum does not care about *individuals*— we hear instead about heaps of bodies, and the only real characters besides Yahweh is personified Nineveh. Obviously, Nahum is not inter- ested in *democracy*—Yahweh alone has power, and there is no mention of any human who speaks for or fights with this all-powerful Warrior.

Unlike *Private Ryan*, Nahum gives little from which to reconstruct the values Yahweh is fighting for. The charges against Nineveh are generic; Nineveh is a *zona*; the king is evil; and "you" plotted evil against Yahweh (Nah 1:11). Only a brief comment suggests that Yahweh's actions will restore Jacob's honor (2:3).

But while the ancient context of Nahum is not revealed by its comparison to combat film, such a comparison does encourage us to consider how a particular "take" on the fall of Nineveh may have been produced in later scenarios—Neo-Babylonian or Persian. Just as a late-twentieth-century film can enlist the interpretation of a past war for the sake of contemporary politics, so too Nahum may reflect a perspective on the Assyrian period from a politically charged later vantage point.

Conclusion

That possibility deserves much more concentrated attention, as do many of the analyses that I have presented here. In bringing Nahum studies into conversation with contemporary film studies, my goal has been to evoke different avenues of thinking rather than to claim that methods of film analysis provide grand answers to our questions about Nahum and how it resonated in its ancient context(s).

I do, however, find these studies particularly helpful in challenging an easy solution (historical or otherwise) to Nahum's violence. If the comparison between Nahum and film has any merit, then it becomes clear that violence in art—be that film, literature, or biblical texts—functions in very different ways. Violence can be psychological integration; it can be trope; and/or it can be a frame for understanding cultural values. As Bruder maintains, there is no "gratuitous" violence in art, even while we cannot always determine with confidence what indirect "work" it does.

For Nahum, this means that we need to keep asking what "work" the violence does and how that "work" would have resonated in ancient cultures. Our exploration of that question may need to proceed heuristically, as we ask what social/political climates might resonate most compellingly with Nahum's insistence that Assyria fell to Yahweh and that Yahweh fights alone.

At the very least, film studies underscores that violence can function non-mimetically, representing something else. And, as we continue to explore and imagine the ancient contexts of prophetic texts, our goal is to multiply the angles of vision, the takes, the lenses from which we view the past.

THE BEAUTY OF THE BLOODY GOD:
THE DIVINE WARRIOR IN PROPHETIC LITERATURE*

Corrine Carvalho

Confessions of a Violence Junky

Research is an act of self-understanding. Sometimes the ego-centric element is hidden beneath the rhetoric of objectivity or scholarly debate, but ultimately the scholar pursues her own questions, fleshes out his own agenda. This essay is unapologetically personal, because it arises from my inability to find myself in discussions about the Bible and violence. I confess that I am a consumer of violence. I love action pictures, war movies, football. I thrill at the mythic violence of *The Lord of the Rings* and am moved by the realistic violence of *The Killing Fields*. I am fascinated by the biblical texts that involve violence, while my favorite ancient Near Eastern deity is Anat. And, although many biblical scholars abhor these same texts (ancient and modern), I am not alone; I know many people who share these interests.

When I read explanations for violence, though, I rarely see myself.[1] René Girard tells me that my fascination keeps my violence in check.[2] Daniel Smith-Christopher suggests that I am coping with trauma.[3] And

* A version of this study was presented at the 2006 Annual Meeting of the Society of Biblical Literature (Prophetic Texts in their Ancient Context session). I also presented a version to the Old Testament Colloquium in February, 2008. I would like to thank everyone for their helpful suggestions, especially Kathleen O'Connor. All deficiencies, however, remain my own.

1. See, for example, Barbara Whitmer, *The Violence Mythos* (Albany: SUNY Press, 1997), and James G. Williams, *The Bible, Violence and the Sacred: Liberation from the Myth of Sanctioned Violence* (San Francisco: HarperSanFrancisco, 1991); Mark H. Ellis, *Unholy Alliance: Religion and Atrocity in Our Time* (Minneapolis: Fortress, 1997); and Jack Nelson-Pallmeyer, *Is Religion Killing Us? Violence in the Bible and the Quran* (Harrisburg, Pa.: Trinity Press International, 2003).

2. René Girard, *The Scapegoat* (Baltimore: The Johns Hopkins University Press, 1986).

3. Daniel Smith-Christopher, *A Biblical Theology of Exile* (Overtures to Biblical Theology; Minneapolis: Fortress, 2002).

David Halperin probably thinks I was abused as a child.[4] A few people reading this may be convinced that I am becoming so used to violence that I am destined for an uncontrolled shooting spree soon. Or maybe I'm just a mouthpiece for an uncritical consumption of patriarchal values.[5]

Yet I can assure you that none of this is true. I am a liberal feminist who thinks war is an evil, corporal punishment models aggression, and the death penalty is morally wrong. I own no guns, and among my violence-consuming friends I am not unusual. I would aver that there is a significant portion of consumers of violence who are like me: those who abhor actual violence, have never committed a violent act, but sometimes employ violent language in a rhetoric of resistance rather than as an affirmation of coercive control. My experience tells me that the typical way biblical scholars address divine violence in the Bible, then, is only partially adequate.

This study seeks to decentralize academic discourse about divine violence in the prophetic corpus. In this essay I will explore three prophetic texts that describe a violent God: Zeph 1:7–18; Nah 3:1–7; and Isa 63:1–6. Although I acknowledge that the term "violence" is ambiguous,[6] I will not address the question whether any act of coercion is a violent act, nor will I treat mythic violence such as lies behind some theophanic texts and eschatological apocalypses. Instead, I am choosing to focus on the most obvious depictions of divine violence: those involving human victims. These texts focus on the reality of physical, military violence, stressing the messiness of hand-to-hand combat. I will argue that, although at least parts of these texts might have addressed an original traumatized audience, they contain a "beauty" that accounts for their continued appeal to a wide variety of audiences.[7]

4. David Halperin, *Seeking Ezekiel: Text and Psychology* (University Park, Pa.: Pennsylvania State University Press, 1993).

5. See, for example, Susan Thistlethwaite, "'May You Enjoy the Spoil of Your Enemies': Rape as a Biblical Metaphor for War," *Semeia* 61 (1993): 59–75; Renita J. Weems, *Battered Love: Marriage, Sex, and Violence in the Hebrew Prophets* (Minneapolis: Fortress, 1995); J. Cheryl Exum, "The Ethics of Biblical Violence against Women," in *The Bible in Ethics: The Second Sheffield Colloquium* (ed. John W. Rogerson et al.; JSOTSup 207; Sheffield: Sheffield Academic, 1995), 248–71; Julia M. O'Brien, *Nahum* (Readings: A New Biblical Commentary; Sheffield: Sheffield Academic, 2002), 87–103; and Jonneke Bekkenkamp and Yvonne Sherwood, eds., *Sanctified Aggression: Legacies of Biblical and Post-biblical Vocabularies of Violence* (JSOTSup 400; London: T&T Clark International, 2003).

6. See the discussion in Hans Boersma, *Violence, Hospitality, and the Cross: Reappropriating the Atonement Tradition* (Grand Rapids: Baker, 2004).

7. I am not arguing here that those who repudiate these texts are misinterpreting them. Their reasons to repudiate them are well-founded. Nor would I argue that

Violence and Victory (or "God at the Movies")

There is general agreement among theologians, film critics, and anthropologists that positive depictions of violence are a problem.[8] Many presume that these depictions contribute to a more violent society and cause, either directly or indirectly, violent societies, or that they mediate psychological states, such as trauma[9] or violent tendencies. In the wake of 9/11, the discussion has focused on the connection between religion and violence.[10] As Boersma succinctly puts it, "The underlying assumption in many discussions of divine violence appears to be that violence is inherently evil and immoral: a violent God necessarily leads to a violent society, since 'what happens above happens below.'"[11] While some studies stress that the two are inherently linked, even within Judaism and Christianity,[12] others note that religion and violence are tangled in a much more complex web of social and political assumptions.[13]

everyone "should" see the beauty of these texts. Rather, I am attempting to explore the theological connections for those, like myself, who do not wish to repudiate them.

8. On violence in film, see, for example, Stephen Hunter, *Violent Screen: A Critic's 13 Years on the Front Lines of Movie Mayhem* (New York: Delta, 1995); Sissela Bok, *Mayhem: Violence as Public Entertainment* (Reading, Mass.: Addison-Wesley, 1998); Christopher Sharrett, ed., *Mythologies of Violence in Postmodern Media* (Detroit: Wayne State University Press, 1999); Martin Barker and J. Petley, eds., *Ill Effects: The Media/Violence Debate* (Communication and Society; London: Routledge, 2001); and Karen Boyle, *Media and Violence: Gendering the Debates* (London: Sage, 2005).

9. On trauma and film, see, for example, Elizabeth S. Goldberg, "Splitting Difference: Global Identity Politics and the Representation of Torture in the Counter-historical Dramatic Film," in *Violence and American Cinema* (ed. D. J. Slocum; New York: Routledge, 2001), 245–70.

10. For a cross-section of essays dealing with religion and violence, see the four-volume work *The Destructive Power of Religion: Violence in Judaism, Christianity, and Islam* (ed. J. Harold Ellens; Contemporary Psychology; Westport, Conn.: Praeger, 2004).

11. Boersma, *Violence, Hospitality, and the Cross*, 43.

12. See, for example, Ellis, *Unholy Alliance*.

13. See R. Scott Appleby, *Ambivalence of the Sacred: Religion, Violence, and Reconciliation* (Carnegie Commission on Preventing Deadly Conflict; Lanham: Rowman & Littlefield, 2000); Mark Juergensmeyer, *Terror in the Mind of God: The Global Rise of Religious Violence* (3d ed.; Berkeley: University of California Press, 2003); Steve Bruce, "Religion and Violence: What Can Sociology Offer?," and Francisco Diez del Velasco, "Theoretical Reflections on Violence and Religion: Identity, Power, Privilege and Difference (with Reference to the Hispanic World)," in *Numen* 52 (2005): 5–28 and 87–115, respectively.

Christian biblical scholars have a particular set of issues to address. On the one hand, they are trained to read the texts within their historical contexts. Such reading reveals the rather obvious point that divine violence wasn't the same problem for the ancient audience. Texts that describe warrior gods are rather *de rigueur* in the ancient record. Kang traces the references to the Divine Warrior across the Fertile Crescent from the pre-Dynastic period to the Exile.[14] These military metaphors utilize all of the elements of human war: preparations for battle, use of specific weapons, even the gathering of the spoils of war. The depictions of Yahweh as a warrior unselfconsciously share this common language.[15] The Old Testament scholar is forced to accept the fact that these images of divine violence are a treasured part of the biblical record. The "problem" of divine violence is a hermeneutical problem, not an historical one.[16]

On the other hand, contemporary Christianity likes to think of itself as a voice for peaceful resolution of conflicts, whether this is in the form of a just war theory or a full-blown pacifism.[17] While many Christians

14. Sa-Moon Kang, *Divine War in the Old Testament and in the Ancient Near East* (BZAW 177; Berlin: de Gruyter, 1989).

15. There are many studies of holy war and the divine warrior in ancient Israel. See, among them, Patrick D. Miller, *The Divine Warrior in Early Israel* (HSM 5: Cambridge, Mass.: Harvard University Press, 1973); Millard Lind, *Yahweh Is a Warrior: The Theology of Warfare in Ancient Israel* (A Christian Peace Shelf Selection; Scottsdale, Pa.: Herald, 1980); Susan Niditch, *War in the Hebrew Bible: A Study in the Ethics of Violence* (Oxford: Oxford University Press, 1993); Lori L. Rowlett, *Joshua and the Rhetoric of Violence: A New Historicist Approach* (JSOTSup 226; Sheffield: Sheffield Academic, 1996); Eckhart Otto, *Krieg und Frieden in der Hebräischer Bibel und im Alten Orient: Aspekte für eine Friedensordnung in der Moderne* (Theologie und Frieden 18; Stuttgart: Kohlhammer, 1999); and Ronald E. Clements, "Achan's Sin: Warfare and Holiness," in *Shall Not the Judge of All the Earth Do What Is Right? Studies on the Nature of God in Tribute to James L. Crenshaw* (ed. David Penchansky and Paul L. Redditt; Winona Lake: Eisenbrauns, 2000), 113–26.

16. For a recent essay dealing with the hermeneutics of violence, see John J. Collins, "The Zeal of Phinehas: The Bible and the Legitimation of Violence," *JBL* 122 (2003): 3–21.

17. This is an issue for Judaism as well, but it cannot be denied that Christianity has tended to view its hermeneutical position as unique because of the resurrection. I contend that this position, while accurately presenting a particular tradition, actually sets up a false dichotomy. As we will see below, the tension between divine love and divine violence is not unique to Christianity. On the anti-Jewish element in many Christian attempts to deal with divine violence, see Erich Zenger, *A God of Vengeance? Understanding the Psalms of Divine Wrath* (trans. Linda Maloney; Louisville: Westminster John Knox, 1996), 13–22.

have traced this legacy to material in the New Testament,[18] recent critiques of atonement theology uncover the question of whether Jesus' violent death reveals unconscious assumptions about an inherently violent god, one who demands the violent sacrifice of a son in order for the sins of humanity to be repaid.[19] The hidden and overt violence of much of the biblical tradition is made manifest in a variety of ways; Christian historians note their own religion's complicity in violence throughout its history, from the Crusades to the Holocaust.

Christian theologians seem to want a pacifist messiah, a non-bloody kingdom, an effortless victory. And yet the success of contemporary films reveals the deficiency of this view of non-violent salvation for many believers. American audiences, at least, like our messiahs to have rippling muscles, sweat-dripped arms, and a well-stocked arsenal. The most obvious example of this is Neo from *The Matrix*, a messianic figure, packing heat.[20] His violence is portrayed as beautiful: physically impossible feats depicted in slow motion, allowing the audience to savor every justified moment of the kill. But his heroism follows in a long line of American heroic figures from Old West cowboys to futuristic "sci-fi" warriors.

The desire for not just a super-hero, but a violent messiah, is even more evident in the audience response to Yoda's battles in the *Star Wars* trilogy. These cosmic Jedi-battles satisfied the audience's desire for a violent encounter with evil. This enthusiastic reaction, which I shared, fascinates me, because I wonder why I was so happy to see a rather Zen-like character suddenly take up the proverbial battle-axe. There was something poetically fitting about the scene, and there was a beauty to the encounters. Such satisfaction resonates with Chris Hedges' observations

18. Although, see the discussion in Rich Bowman and R. W. Swanson, "Samson and the Son of God or Dead Heroes and Dead Goats: Ethical Readings of Narrative Violence in Judges and Matthew," *Semeia* 77 (1997): 59–73.

19. For critiques of atonement theology, see, for example, Rita Nakashima Brock and Rebecca A. Parker, *Proverbs of Ashes: Violence, Redemptive Suffering and the Search for What Saves Us* (Boston: Beacon, 2001).

20. A lot has been written on the Christian resonances in "The Matrix." See, for example, Jeremy Punt, "Messianic Victims or Victimized Messiah? Biblical Allusion and Violence in *The Matrix*," in Bekkenkamp and Sherwood, eds., *Sanctified Aggression*, 139–55. On biblical parallels with Spaghetti Westerns, see Eric S. Christianson, "A Fistful of Shekels: Scrutinizing Ehud's Entertaining Violence (Judges 3:12–30)," *BibInt* 11 (2003): 53–78. There have also been a few books written on biblical apocalyptic and film. See, for example, John W. Martens, *The End of the World: The Apocalyptic Imagination in Film and Television* (Winnipeg: J. Gordon Shillingford, 2003). For the Bible in film, see Adele Reinhartz, *Scripture on the Silver Screen* (Louisville: Westminster John Knox, 2003).

that war has the qualities of "excitement, exoticism, power, chances to rise above our small stations in life, and a bizarre and fantastic universe that has a grotesque and dark beauty."[21]

I do not view my reaction to God's bloody return from the killing fields of Edom in Isa 63 as qualitatively different from my satisfaction with on-screen violence as a movie-goer. The popularity of films such as *The Matrix* and *Star Wars* belies the incomplete explanations about divine violence that I so often encounter in the works of biblical scholars. Those buying the tickets are a lot more like me than they are like the reconstructed ancient Israelite audience of biblical scholarship. We don't enjoy *Star Wars* because we are trying to work out the cognitive dissonance of the fall of our city or because we are expressing hope in a just God in light of our miserable conditions. We go because we enjoy it, both visually and ideologically. What follows is not meant to deny that texts describing divine violence can be used to justify human violence. Rather, I pose the simple theological question: Can these texts be revelatory in the contemporary world?

Painting the Picture of the Bloody God

Julia O'Brien in her commentary on Nahum points out that the prophetic oracle describing God's defeat of Nineveh creates a visual picture.[22] Texts such as Nah 3 also engage our other senses: the sounds of the battle, the taste of the feast. I would venture that it is precisely these sensory elements that evoke such a strong reaction: as viewers we can picture the blood-soaked garments, the stripped whore, the disemboweled soldiers. We can smell the roasted meat of the sacrifice and taste the heady wine. We can hear the yells of the warrior and the cries of the victims. We just can't always picture the God of our holy cards as the agent of this violence.

Zephaniah 1:7–18 depicts God's battle against Judah and Jerusalem.[23] Whether this is viewed as a vision of a threatened punishment or the recollection of a traumatic defeat, the images are painted in realistic colors, complete with an accompanying soundtrack. The verbal forms in

21. Chris Hedges, *War Is a Force that Gives Us Meaning* (New York: Public Affairs, 2002), 3.

22. O'Brien, *Nahum*, esp. 58–63.

23. For a study of a variety of texts describing God's attack on Israel, see R. Norman Whybray, "'Shall Not the Judge of All the Earth Do What Is Just?' God's Oppression of the Innocent in the Old Testament," in Penchansky and Redditt, eds., *Shall Not the Judge of All the Earth Do What Is Right?*, 1–19.

the passage contribute to a sense of time warp. Most of the verbs are perfects with a prefixed *waw*. These should most probably be translated in the future tense, but they could also be statives or immanent presents, bringing to the fore the "tenseless" aspect of Hebrew verbs. These verbs are coupled with tenseless participles, adding to the timeless or even repetitive possibility of God's punishment.[24]

The poem is structured by a series of repetitions and *inclusios*.[25] The text emphasizes the "day of Yahweh," repeating the word "day" fourteen times. This repetition provides a rhythmic beat that starts out gradually and then speeds up to an almost frenzied pace in vv. 15–16, mirroring the message of the text that the day is ever more hurriedly approaching. Whether this "day of Yahweh" alludes to the earlier prophecies of Amos or simply the annual ritual festival, the text does presume an ironic use of the term.[26] The prophet speaks of the "day" as if everyone knows what it is, but the awaited day is ominous, not joyful. The phrasing surrounding the "day" contributes to the temporal slippage. It "draws near" (v. 7 and 14) quickly (v. 14), although it seems to be associated with the specific ritual activity of a scheduled festival (vv. 7, 8, 9). This specificity slips away following v. 15's announcement that, "A day of fury; that is the day."[27] The hastened pace of the poem culminates in an over-the-top ending. By the end of the poem, it is not just the elite who will be sacrificed; rather, God's fury will extend to the "whole earth" and to "all the inhabitants of the earth" (v. 18).[28]

In conjunction with this emphasis on a cultic day, the passage uses an ironic *inclusio* in its references to sacrifice. The pericope begins with a

---

24. This is distinct from Marvin Sweeney's view that the verb forms are futures. On this basis, he concludes that the bulk of the text stems from the reign of Josiah and is part of a program in support of the king's religious reforms (*Zephaniah: A Commentary* [Hermeneia; Minneapolis: Fortress, 2003]).

25. On the question of the poetic nature of the book, see Adele Berlin, *Zephaniah: A New Translation with Introduction and Commentary* (AB 25A; New York: Doubleday, 1994), 11–13. On reading the text as a "prophetic drama," see Paul R. House, *Zephaniah: A Prophetic Drama* (JSOTSup 69; Bible and Literature, 16; Sheffield: Almond, 1988). A rhetorical analysis can be found in Ivan J. Ball, *A Rhetorical Study of Zephaniah* (Berkeley: BIBAL, 1988).

26. J. J. M. Roberts, *Nahum, Habakkuk, and Zephaniah* (OTL; Louisville: Westminster John Knox, 1991), 176–81. This assumption differs from that of Meir Weiss, "The Origin of the 'Day of the Lord' Reconsidered," *HUCA* 38 (1966): 29–63. Rex Mason (*Zephaniah, Habakkuk, Joel* [Old Testament Guides; Sheffield: JSOT, 1994], 16–58) notes the use of cultic language throughout the whole book.

27. All biblical translations are my own.

28. Berlin (*Zephaniah*, 81–84) connects this with a theme of creation and cult.

prophetic invitation to a sacrifice that Yahweh has appointed and the purification of the participants (v. 7). Yet immediately the text launches into an indictment of these invitees: they wear "foreign" clothing (v. 8),[29] practice improper rituals (v. 9), and hold Yahweh in disdain (v. 11). Because of these sins, the real purpose of the sacrifice is gradually and repetitively revealed.[30] From v. 9 on, it becomes clear that this is no celebration. The verses lead to the text's punch line. The invitees, unable to be ransomed, are slaughtered (vv. 17–18). Their blood soaks into the earth and their ritually impure body parts (guts/intestines/bowels) become unholy piles of carnal garbage.

The passage also conjures up auditory images. The passage begins with an onomatopoeic call for silence as the sacrifice begins.[31] Yet, the sounds of cries, wails, and crashes from the outskirts of the city can be heard in v. 10. From the silence of the temple mount, the attendees can hear the anguish of God's first victims, as the bi-located God gathers victims throughout Jerusalem. They hear the terrifying yell of the victorious warrior, like a big-time wrestler entering the arena in v. 14. That sound is described as "bitter." The final sound in the passage is the trumpet blast and battle cry of v. 16. The warrior has entered the ring; death ensues.

The question of whether this is a threat pronounced in the days of Josiah or a recollection from an exilic or post-exilic perspective does not mitigate the effect of the violent imagery.[32] An abused wife still experiences terror when her husband describes in graphic detail what he will do to her if she "steps out of line." The fact that God is willing to do this to Judah adds to the horror of the violence.[33] The imagery creates a

29. The reference to "foreign" clothes might be a reference to alliances with other nations. Ben Zvi (*A Historical-Critical Study of the Book of Zephaniah* [BZAW 198; Berlin: de Gruyter, 1991] 278–82) connects the reference to competing social groups. In light of the use of the term "foreign" in Ezek 44, I would suggest that it refers to anything not allowed within the temple precinct. "Foreign" could include things socially Israelite (such as a resident alien) but not ritually Yahwistic (at least from the perspective of the authors).

30. Berlin, *Zephaniah*, 78–79.

31. J. Vlaardingerbroek, *Zephaniah* (HCOT; Leuven: Peeters, 1999), 83.

32. On the various options given for the date of the book, see the discussion of Berlin, *Zephaniah*, 33–43. Since my discussion of the prophetic texts is asking about how they appeal to multiple audiences, my interpretation of these texts is not dependent on a specific date.

33. There have been a few studies of the application of "horror" theory to the Bible. See, for example, Gary Aichele and Tina Pippin, eds., *The Monstrous and the Unspeakable: The Bible as Fantastic Literature* (Playing the Texts 1; Sheffield: Sheffield Academic, 1997); Timothy K. Beal, *Religion and Its Monsters* (New York:

collage, not a single panel. The places of killing include the Fish Gate, the Mishneh, the hills, "Mortar," the marketplace, places of hiding, places where people drink, the homes of the wealthy, the vineyards, the fortified cities—in sum, "the whole earth" (v. 18). The net effect is that the reader recognizes that the text is a well-crafted poem. Its use of sensory elements, repetition, and an ironic *inclusio* creates an incredibly moving portrait of a God bent on destruction.

Because the audience identifies with the victim, one might be tempted to view this as some kind of redemptive suffering. Certainly in discussions of the violence of the cross, the assumption is that the violence makes us more sympathetic to victims of violence because the audience is expected to identify with that victim. Similarly, the depictions of the Suffering Servant in Isaiah and, perhaps, the personification of the city in Lamentations move the audience to pity and moral outrage at its unjust suffering. However, this violence does not have the same rhetorical effect. We are asked to identify with God and, like David confronted by Nathan, pronounce a verdict against ourselves. The cumulative effect assumes that the audience admires or at least acquiesces to the violent retribution.

The texts from both Nahum and Isaiah, on the other hand, describe God's vengeance against Israel's enemies: Nineveh and Edom respectively. The depiction of God's violence against Nineveh has been well-studied by O'Brien, to whose work mine is indebted. O'Brien also rejects the too-easy explanation of trauma as the effect of the language.[34] Noting that the final form of the book addresses a non-traumatized audience, she rightly points to how limiting such an explanation can be.[35]

Routledge, 2002); and Amy B. Kalmanofsky, *Terror All Around: Horror, Monsters, and Theology in the Book of Jeremiah* (LHBOTS 390; New York: T&T Clark International, 2008). The problem with horror theory for me is that it renders God as evil and deficient, which is not the intention of either the author, nor the conclusion of those who read these texts as uplifting. God, while terrifying, is no Freddie Kruger, meant to instill revulsion. Even Kalmanofsky must change the category of "disgust" to that of "shame" to make the theory fit the literature. However, for an attempt to see the monstrous characterization as essentially subversive, see David Penchansky, "God the Monster: Fantasy in the Garden of Eden," in Aichele and Pippin, eds., *The Monstrous and the Unspeakable*, 43–69.

34. O'Brien, *Nahum*, 116–17.

35. This is not to deny that many texts describing violence do stem from trauma and fit the kind of creative re-imagining described by Smith-Christopher, Elaine Scarry (*The Body in Pain: The Making and Unmaking of the World* [New York: Oxford University Press, 1985]), and others. I also recognize that trauma can be intergenerational; see, for a modern example, Joy D. Leary, *Post-Traumatic Slave*

O'Brien nowhere shies away from the detailed violence of Nah 3:1–7 and uncomfortably reveals how the language derives from certain assumptions about gender. Even so, she notes the poem's beauty.[36] The staccato phrasing most prominent in vv. 1–3 creates impressionistic glimpses into an on-going battle, not a chronological battle account.[37] The poem also includes parallel halves. The beginning focus on the city of blood (vv. 1–3) is matched by the metaphor of the whore (vv. 4–7), while the depictions of Nineveh's military machine is undone in the description of its shameful fall. The two halves present an ironic twist of fate at the hand of a God who is not only great but also crafty: "he" knows best how to design the most fitting punishment. The parallelisms of the poem weave together a sensory experience of the fall of a city, one that echoes the iconographic remnants we have of siege warfare. This picture satisfies an Israelite audience who has experienced first-hand the Assyrian violence preserved in the reliefs.

Instead of a soundtrack, the audience is treated to a slide show. In an ironic opening, a doomed Nineveh sits covered in the blood of its own victories, surrounded by the spoils of its wars, unaware that its death penalty has already been pronounced. The slide show picks up images from the battlefield: "Here's a picture of the chariots (click), here's the cavalry (click). Oh, and look, bodies!" But not just bodies: "*tons* of wounded, *a heap* of corpses; there is *no end* to the dead bodies—they *stumble* over the bodies!" (v. 3). We almost expect a pile of severed heads with soldiers playing catch, such as we find in the Assyrian reliefs.

But in place of the masculanized male ruler,[38] we are treated to the image of a whore. Here the text lingers, exploiting the emotions of the male gaze: she is both desired and destructive, tempting and evil, every-thing you don't want your daughter to be, no matter how much you would

---

Syndrome: America's Legacy of Enduring Injury and Healing (Milwaukie, Ore.: Uptone, 2005). I presume all of this is true, but these theories fail to address other sources for the image of divine violence, and nor do they address the hermeneutical question that I am raising, which is whether there can be an appreciation of texts depicting divine violence that do not stem from personal or empathetic trauma that renders God the source of evil.

36. O'Brien, *Nahum*, 127–28. See also Klaas Spronk, *Nahum* (HCOT; Kampen: Kok Pharos, 1997), 111–26, who observes "the remark by Jerome on vv. 1–4, that no translation can do justice to the beauty of its language" (p. 115).

37. See the comment on v. 3 in Roberts, *Nahum, Habakkuk, and Zephaniah*, 72–73.

38. See Cynthia R. Chapman, *The Gendered Language of Warfare in the Israel-ite–Assyrian Encounter* (HSM 62; Winona Lake: Eisenbrauns, 2004), esp. 20–59, as well as O'Brien, *Nahum*, 97.

have paid to spend some time with her (or make a political alliance with her, whatever side of the metaphor you would like to be on). So what do we do with this visceral image? We turn her into a pornographic image and cover her in feces. After all, as v. 7 tells us, that's the only way to repulse her former allies (read Judah).

Is there anything redeeming in such a vision? Because this text and the one from Isa 63 are tied to Israel's salvation, a typical way of dealing with the texts is to say that they are necessary parts of God's salvation. Therefore these texts are about divine justice, not divine violence. They encapsulate Israel's nationalistic exaltation of God's defeat of their enemy. After all, we do know that Nineveh's cruelty was similar to that of Nazi Germany. Why not give a cheer for this divinely orchestrated destruction?

This interpretation is ready at hand for Isa 63 as well. Its relationship to chs. 34, 59, and 60–62 links this verbal icon to the promise of salvation in the earlier chapters.[39] This poem is again consciously crafted, and the satisfaction that the audience feels depends just as much on its literary placement as it does on its historical background. Isaiah 34:1–10 introduces a theme that ch. 63 completes, predicting the fall of Edom/ Bozrah in more gory detail than ch. 63. The enemy will be slaughtered, its dead bodies left rotting on the field. The mountains will be soaked in blood and the dirt will soak up their fat. The text makes clear that the agent of this destruction is Yahweh, with his sword dripping in blood, and, in language echoing Zeph 1:7–18, the destruction is called a sacrifice in vv. 6–7.

The fulfillment of this oracle begins in 59:15b–20. Here the reader is treated to the image of the warrior suiting up for battle. God puts on breastplate and helmet, but these are divine fatigues: a "breastplate of righteousness" and a "helmet of salvation" (v. 17). The immanent appearance of the Divine Warrior will inspire fear (v. 19). Chapters 60–62 delay

39. There have been many studies on the redactional interconnections within Isaiah. See, for example, Seiko Sekine, *Die Tritojesajanische Sammlung (Jes 56–66) redaktionsgeschichtlich Untersucht* (BZAW 175; Berlin: de Gruyter, 1989); Odil H. Steck, *Studien zu Tritojesaja* (BZAW 203; Berlin: de Gruyter, 1991); Wolfgang Lau, *Schriftgelehrte Prophetie in Jes 56–66: Eine Untersuchung zu den literarischen Bezügen in den letzten elf Kapiteln des Jesajabuches* (BZAW 225; Berlin: de Gruyter, 1994); Paul A. Smith, *Rhetoric and Redaction in Trito-Isaiah: The Structure, Growth and Authorship of Isaiah 56–66* (VTSup 62; Leiden: Brill, 1995); and J. C. de Moor, "Structure and Redaction: Isaiah 60,1–63,6," in *Studies in the Book of Isaiah: Festschrift Willem A. M. Beuken* (ed. J. van Ruiten and M. Vervenne; BETL 132; Leuven: University Press, 1997), 325–46.

the text's denouement but fill out what ch. 34 introduced: divine vengeance is an essential element for Israel's salvation. Like a pre-battle
speech, God declares, "For the sake of Zion, I will not be silent; for the
sake of Jerusalem I will not be quiet" (62:1). By using phrases found in
chs. 34, 59, and 60–62, the poem reads as the final scene of a sub-plot
about Edom.[40]

In ch. 63 the reader is treated to the return of the bloody and bruised
warrior. The actual fighting has taken place off-camera, although the
reader has the description ready-at-hand in ch. 34's preview. What is so
brilliant about ch. 63 is that it does not just repeat the battle, as is so
common to ancient near eastern literature, nor does it present a glorious
warrior untouched by an effortless victory. Instead, we have a sullied
soldier whose appearance raises the question, "Who is this?" (v. 1).

The text paints a picture but does so through dialogue. The questions
of vv. 1 and 2 pull the reader along. They focus attention on the clothing
of the warrior,[41] setting up the parallel between grape-juice and blood,
wine offering and ritual slaughter. The questions elicit a divine response.
This warrior talks, and it is not just a battle cry. We hear Yahweh's com-
plaint that no one showed up to help with the battle, introduced in v. 3
and filled out in v. 5.[42] I agree with Sawyer that this emphasis on God's
solitary activity makes the reading of God's gait in v. 1 more clear: this
is a soldier who has barely won the battle.[43] The scope of the battle and
threat of this cosmic enemy is communicated by the warrior's appearance: bloodstained and stooped.[44] In addition, the dialogue creates an
unusual sympathy for a character whose usual mode is the untouched
hero.[45]

40. On the complex intertextuality of these passages, see Brevard S. Childs,
Isaiah (OTL; Louisville: Westminster John Knox, 2001), 514–19.

41. Claire R. Mathews, *Defending Zion* (BZAW 236; Berlin: de Gruyter, 1995),
80.

42. Terrence E. Fretheim contends that depictions of divine violence in the
prophets highlight God's relationship with humanity; see his "'I Was Only a Little
Angry': Divine Violence in the Prophets," *Int* 58 (2004): 365–75.

43. John F. A. Sawyer, "Radical Imagery of Yahweh in Isaiah 63," in *Among the
Prophets: Language, Image and Structure in the Prophetic Writings* (ed. Philip R.
Davies and David J. A. Clines; JSOTSup 144; Sheffield: Sheffield Academic, 1993),
72–82.

44. For Edom as an arch-enemy, see Mathews, *Defending Zion*, 80–86; and Jan
L. Koole, *Isaiah.* Vol. 3, *Isaiah Chapters 56–66* (HCOT; Leuven: Peeters, 2001),
327–43.

45. For a discussion of God as a character within texts of divine abandonment,
see Walter Brueggemann, "Texts that Linger, Not Yet Overcome," in Penchansky
and Redditt, eds., *Shall Not the Judge of All the Earth Do What Is Right?*, 21–41.

Once again, the blood of the victim gains special attention. It stains the warrior's garments (v. 1) and soaks into the ground (v. 6). The repeated references to the winepress also paint a picture. If God treads the Edomites like a farmer treads grapes, then we imagine God stepping on their heads, blood squirting out, like juice from the over-ripe fruit. The text also resonates with the language of wine: not only is God treading the grape-heads, but he first gets them drunk (v. 6). These interplaying images once again reveal a skillful author weaving interconnections both within this poem and across the book as a whole. It may be a disturbing picture, but it is beautifully crafted. It glorifies God by its very depiction of a spent warrior.

God dripping in blood, feasting on victims, and stripping the enemy provides ready fodder to reinforce abhorrent social values. Even this consumer of violence cannot imagine exalting God as the one shaming the prisoners, like we saw at Abu Graibh. These texts do participate in a particular hierarchical worldview that shares assumptions about gender, race, and class. One simplistic mechanism might be to note that the foreign identification of the victims in Nahum and Isaiah triggers right-eous outrage. Both texts speak to human fantasies of violent retribution, and, even though my fantasies may focus on the patriarchal elite, I can still use these texts as expressions of this same moral outrage. However, even that hermeneutical move would be too simplistic to capture the complex way that multiple readers have responded to these texts for centuries. Put simply: we see God in these texts, even if it is a god that simultaneously attracts and appalls us.

So, is the only alternative for someone who rejects those worldviews a pacifism that repudiates these texts? That's the question for me. It's not just about whether they're sacred; I can admit some texts are "sacred" without them being meaningful. Do I have to conclude that the fact that I am moved by these texts means I am not sufficiently conscious of their hidden toxic assumptions? Can't I enjoy them? Can't I say they have a terrible beauty about them, a terrible beauty that is characteristic of my experience of the divine?

Wading in Blood: A Grotesque God(dess)

What is beauty, and can it ever be "terrible"? This is a question many theologians have asked.[46] García-Rivera relates beauty to Augustine's

---

46. See, for example, Alejandro Garcia-Rivera, *The Community of the Beautiful: A Theological Aesthetics* (Collegeville: Michael Glazier/Liturgical, 1999), and *A*

thought, concluding that the beautiful is what "moves the human heart,"[47] while Viladesau states that it is what reveals God, the source and definition of the beautiful.[48] The beautiful is a divine attribute distinct from Goodness, which evokes a moral response, and from Truth, which evokes an intellectual response.[49] Beauty evokes appreciation, recognition, resonance. In discussions of theological aesthetics, beauty challenges dualistic worldviews, certitude, and boundaries. "The beautiful encompasses the ugly and the pretty, the grotesque and the ordinary, the artist and the artist's community, the work of art and the work of craft, the natural and that made by human hands. Indeed, a living aesthetics is less a disinterested beholding of some alienated object than that which moves the heart."[50] Beauty plays both with the "edges," that is, that which cannot be reduced to words, and with connections, that is, the odd juxtaposition that reveals unexpected insights. As such, beauty is often associated with the mystical experience. It is the source of spiritual rapture.

Theologians who have explored aesthetics have similar problems with violence as biblical scholars do. They also tend to view the positive effect of a violent image to be the evocation of sympathy for the victim, and, thus, the development of an ethics of non-violence. And, yet, although I have not found a theory of violent images that traces their theological value *per se*, I find both the theological aesthetics of Hans Urs von Balthasar and of the grotesque offer a possible model for thinking about divine violence. The verbal icon of God's violent nature is glorious, grotesque, and ugly. In a word, it participates in a terrible beauty that finds resonance in our humanity.

Von Balthasar states that one of the results of viewing the beautiful is the recognition of God's glory. "All great art is religious, an act of

Wounded Innocence: Sketches for a Theology of Art (Collegeville: Michael Glazier/ Liturgical, 2003); and David B. Hart, *The Beauty of the Infinite: The Aesthetics of Christian Truth* (Grand Rapids: Eerdmans, 2003).

47. Garcia-Rivera, *Community of the Beautiful*, 9.

48. Richard Viladesau, *Beauty of the Cross: The Passion of Christ in Theology and the Arts, from the Catacombs to the Eve of the Renaissance* (New York: Oxford University Press, 2006), 10–12.

49. While the three categories are interrelated, I want to keep them distinct for the moment. See also my earlier work with theological aesthetics: Corrine L. Patton, "The Beauty of the Beast: Leviathan and Behemoth in Light of Catholic Theology," in *The Whirlwind: Essays on Job, Hermeneutics and Theology in Memory of Jane Morse* (ed. Stephen L. Cook, Corrine L. Patton and J. W. Watts; JSOTSup 336; London: Sheffield Academic, 2001), 142–67.

50. Garcia-Rivera, *A Wounded Innocence*, ix.

homage before the glory of what exists."[51] The verbal icon of God's violent nature in its ancient context was certainly glorious. From the wall reliefs of the neo-Assyrian kings we know that a leader's military prowess was an icon of exaltation. The Assyrian pictures communicate this by the level of detail that they devote to the gore of war. Like the slow-motioned martial arts of Neo in *The Matrix*, the reliefs invite the viewer to linger over the shameful death of the enemy: the naked corpses, the piles of severed heads, the vultures carrying off their entrails for their own sacrificial meal.[52] In the same way, the slowed pace of the poetry describing the shamed victim in Nahum reverses the fortunes of this Assyrian enemy.[53] Now we get to watch their shameful demise, as we see God defecate on them.

The verbal icon is also ugly in an ironically pleasing sort of way. The image implied in Zech 1 of God eating the elite of Jerusalem,[54] slow-roasted over a sacrificial fire, conjures up images of Goya's "Saturn Devouring One of His Children," a painting that "points to our capacity as human beings to destroy that which challenges our power, denies our immortality, questions our will to control."[55] It is not a God I find particularly attractive. And yet there is something satisfying in seeing the punishment of the elite who were so confident in their religious status. At God's banquet, just deserts are always the tastiest kind.

While classical discussions of beauty stress form, proportion, and that which is pleasing, contemporary discussions push at those categories, noting that those things which move us are often "ugly" but no less beautiful. For John Cook, art can deal with ugly content in a way that leads to an "aesthetic experience," that is, an experience that is meaningful and memorable.[56] Theologically, the "ugly" can reveal something

---

51. Hans Urs von Balthasar, *The Glory of the Lord* (San Francisco: Ignatius, 1989), 4:22.

52. See the similar image of birds of prey in Ezek 39:17–20.

53. See the discussion of "just desserts" in Ka Leung Wong, *The Idea of Retribution in the Book of Ezekiel* (VTSup 87; Leiden: Brill, 2001).

54. Michael Weigl's *Zefanja und das "Israel der Armen"* (Österreichische Biblische Studien 13; Klosterneuburg: Österreichisches Katholisches Bibelwerk, 1994) focuses on the economic theme that is at the center of Zephaniah.

55. Wilson Yates, "An Introduction to the Grotesque: Theoretical and Theological Considerations," in *The Grotesque in Art and Literature: Theological Reflections* (ed. James L. Adams and Wilson Yates; Grand Rapids: Eerdmans, 1997), 1–68 (45). I thank my colleague, Dr. Kim Vrudny, for leading me to the theories of the grotesque.

56. On the distinction, see John W. Cook, "Ugly Beauty in Christian Art," in Adams and Yates, eds., *The Grotesque in Art and Literature*, 125–41.

about the divine nature, such that our experience of God's "ugliness" is still an experience that is True and Good. As Viladesau states, "God's foolishness is wiser than humans, and God's weakness is stronger than humans," to which he adds, "And, by extension, presumably God's ugliness is more beautiful than human beauty."[57]

When I analyze my experience of divine violence through the lens of Beauty, I admit that the category feels inappropriate. And yet, this inappropriateness gives me one of two choices. On the one hand, these texts, which are part of a root metaphor that functions throughout the Bible, are not Beautiful, a conclusion which would mean they are also not revelatory. On the other hand, I can conclude that these texts may reveal the ways in which our categories are themselves inadequate, even inappropriate. I am far more willing to accept the conclusion that our theories fail than I am that the text has. Realizing that a human concept of beauty is inadequate when applied to God reminds me that the same can be said of the categories of goodness and truth. The purpose of these categories is not to tame God, but ultimately to reveal when we reach the end of our ability to capture that God.

The category of the "grotesque" highlights the way human artists can use incongruity to communicate the incomprehensibility of the divine realm.[58] "Grotesque" was originally a term used to describe art that entailed unexpected combinations creating surprising, even shocking visual images. In the early period, it referred to the visual images associated with the carnival, but more recently it has been applied to a wide variety of artifacts from the artwork of Bosch to the writing of Flannery O'Connor.

The impact of the grotesque comes specifically from the unease of the audience. Although some of the grotesque is simply humorous, often it is deeply disturbing: a crucified Jesus surrounded by fingers with mouths on their ends,[59] a frog judging the dead and defecating on those being sent to hell,[60] a ghost-child haunting former slaves.[61] Yates emphasizes its mythic and symbolic function,[62] while Scott examines the subversive

57. Viladesau, *The Beauty of the Cross*, 9.

58. For a similar view using the category of the monstrous, see Beal, *Religion and Its Monsters*, 6 and 53.

59. Francis Bacon, "Three Studies for Figure at the Base of a Crucifixion," 1944.

60. Hieronymus Bosch, "The Garden of Earthly Delights," ca. 1510.

61. See Susan Corey, "The Religious Dimensions of the Grotesque in Literature: Toni Morrison's *Beloved*," in Adams and Yates, eds., *The Grotesque in Art and Literature*, 227–42.

62. Yates, "An Introduction to the Grotesque," esp. 45.

intent of many "world-turned-upside-down" prints.[63] As symbol it points to something deeper, engaging the viewer in a primal experience beyond that which is taboo.

The grotesque expresses both continuity and discontinuity. It often includes elements that are quite familiar: human and animal body parts, landscapes, historical contexts. But, like a nightmare, that which is normal is distorted, either by metamorphasizing into something else— being joined to that which is incongruous—or by distortion of particular elements. Margaret Miles states that the grotesque utilizes three devices: caricature or distortion of individual elements, inversion of what is "natural," and hybridization, which refers to the random combination of natural elements.[64]

In one sense, these prophetic poems are grotesque. For example, logical disorder permeates the prophetic poems. In Zeph 1:7–18, God destroys those sacrificing inside the temple, while Yahweh also approaches the temple from the city gates. Nahum 1, like the Assyrian reliefs, simultaneously portrays the attack and its aftermath. Isaiah 63 communicates divine vulnerability, a need for human cooperation. There is another layer that contributes to the grotesque nature of ancient Near Eastern texts describing the Divine Warrior, though, and that is how they raise issues of divine gender.

Miles points out the ways in which, according to the medieval understanding of the human person, the female body in its natural state was "grotesque." Using the three characteristics of the grotesque (caricature, inversion, and hybridization), she notes that depictions of female bodies often include caricatures of female genitalia, view women's bodies as direct inversions of the male body, and randomly re-arrange female body parts to create hybrid bodies. The use of female genitalia (e.g. gaping vaginas sometimes lined with weapons), as well as social inversion (e.g. descriptions of Amazon women) express an anxiety about the female body from an andro-centric perspective. If the male body is "normal," then the protuberances and holes of the female body are a distortion of the normal. The use of gendered language, then, can be part of a depiction of the grotesque, and, as such, communicate through the use of incongruity divine incomprehensibility.

The pictures of the Divine Warrior in prophetic texts resonate with images of warrior goddesses. Ugaritic Anat and Mesopotamian Ishtar/

63. James C. Scott, *Domination and the Arts of Resistance: Hidden Transcripts* (New Haven: Yale University Press, 1990), 166–72.
64. Margaret Miles, "Carnal Abominations: The Female Body as Grotesque," in Adams and Yates, eds., *The Grotesque in Art and Literature*, 83–112.

Innana are warriors in much the same way as male warrior gods, but their fighting was set off from their male counterparts by its ferocity.[65] Innana is described as "mistress of the tumult" and "the terrible one" in neo-Assyrian inscriptions.[66] As their association with lions suggests, uncontrolled violence represented the carnage evident in leonine kills. Similarly, Anat's association with raptors, who feast on the corpses of the battlefield, is echoed in her enjoyment of the blood of her victims. Like a vulture, she hops around "knee-deep" in the blood of her post-battle banquet, a kind of "Old Country-kill Buffet."

Both goddesses are described as "Virgin," adding to the incongruity of their divine nature. They both embody a strange and dangerous beauty. Ishtar has many lovers, both human and semi-divine, including the king. Anat and Baal are lovers, even as she remains a "virgin."[67] Both goddesses also gender-bend: Ishtar is sometimes depicted with a beard, and Anat sets her fatal plan against Aqhat when he insinuates she is more "girly" than divine. This combination of hyper-femininization (virginal lovers) and male-like behavior (bloody warriors) fits the category of the grotesque, at least in the experience of the ancient world.

This language of a warrior goddess may have been one way these cultures communicated that the divine realm is not like the human realm. Surely, these texts were not intended to be models of ethical behavior for human women in the ancient Near East. This was no ethic of imitation.[68]

---

65. On the unique character of Anat's fighting, see Arvid S. Kapelrud, *The Violent Goddess: Anat in the Ras Shamra Texts* (Oslo: Scandinavian University Books, 1969), esp. 64–82, and Mark S. Smith, "Anat's Warfare Cannibalism and the West Semitic Ban," in *The Pitcher Is Broken: Memorial Essays for Gösta W. Ahlström* (ed. Steven W. Holloway and L. K. Handy; JSOTSup 190; Sheffield: Sheffield Academic, 1995), 368–86.

66. Kang, *Divine War*, 31–36. See also Tivka Frymer-Kensky, *In the Wake of the Goddesses: Women, Culture, and the Biblical Transformation of Pagan Myth* (New York: Macmillan, 1992), esp. 66–67.

67. Neal H. Walls (*The Goddess Anat in Ugaritic Myth* [SBLDS 135; Atlanta: Scholars Press, 1992) attributes these incongruities to her liminal status as an adolescent female. Beal (*Religions and Its Monsters*, 19–21) associates her with the monstrous.

68. For a discussion of different ethical models contained in the Old Testament, see John Barton, *Understanding Old Testament Ethics: Approaches and Explorations* (Louisville: Westminster John Knox, 2003). One of the models that he explores is that of "imitation of God" (see esp. 50–54): the dual assumptions that God's actions are, by definition, just, and, therefore that humans are supposed to act like God. It seems to me that these assumptions are inherently part of the hermeneutical problem of divine violence. I am arguing that the way God subverts human categories undercuts an ethic of divine imitation.

As Chapman's book points out, the glorification of the human king was accomplished by stressing his masculinity.[69] The motif of a warrior woman out-fighting a king would have involved shame for the monarch. And yet, it was appropriate for there to be a bloody goddess because it could remind the (primarily male) audience that they were *not* divine, and that what was appropriate for a god was not appropriate for a human.

The poetic texts echo this dichotomy. God returns from Edom like an Anat or an Ishtar covered in blood.[70] Is the question of Isa 63:1 ("Who is this...?") a question about God's gender? Does this divine being first look like the Virgin Anat or Maid Ishtar returning from their kills? Does the heightened gender identity of God's victims in Nah 3 and Zeph 3 reflect an anxiety over the grotesque notion that the bloody god could be a goddess? Was Yahweh as a warrior goddess a hybrid image that was too far beyond their aesthetic capacity to reconcile? In contrast to the human kings in the Assyrian reliefs, Yahweh seems to re-assert his maleness by sexually assaulting them.

And yet, God often fights like a goddess. He-she annihilates, loses control in the kill, has raptor agents, and flies like an eagle. Zephaniah 1:17 implies that Yahweh feasts on them in this unholy ritual.[71] God is a roaring lion and a slayer of Death. On top of that, Yahweh seems to be a more effective virgin than either Anat or Ishtar: after all, this deity never runs off to a field to fornicate like a bovine. He may beat his wives, but at least he doesn't sleep with them. Even his "rapes" end, not with penetration, but with the public exposures of the victim.

Such brutality raises the possibility of shame: Aqhat's refusal of the bow to Anat works on the assumption that female warriors are shameful. Either they are willfully transgressing social boundaries or they are forced to fight because their male patrons have been shamed. God's impotence (whether male or female) is also potentially shameful; his inability to rape his victim suggests, not mercy, but insufficient masculinity.[72] The warrior is either an insufficient male or a female improperly violent. And yet, they were not applied to God in a strategy to shame the

69. Chapman, *The Gendered Language of Warfare.*

70. Note, however, that John Day rejects parallels with Anat in *Yahweh and the Gods and Goddesses of Canaan* (JSOTSup 265; Sheffield: Sheffield Academic, 2000), 141–42.

71. See Paul D. Stern, "The 'Bloodbath of Anat' and Psalm XXIII," *VT* 44 (1994): 120–25.

72. Kent L. Brintnall argues that the violence in Quentin Tarantino films similarly negotiates anxiety about gender identification; see his "Tarantino's Incarnational Theology: *Reservoir Dogs*, Crucifixions and Spectacular Violence," *Cross Currents* 54 (2004): 66–75.

deity; instead, they highlight the ways that the divine warrior is not like a human one: acting as both a god and a goddess, yet not fulfilling either gender expectations fully. The depictions of God as a warrior, then, are part of the gender-bending language that we see applied to deities in the ancient Near East. This gender-bending is certainly "grotesque" not just in its content, but also in how it subverts the very binary opposites on which most analyses of violence flounder.

God's violence blurs the distinction between justice and sin, exalted and afflicted, honored and shamed, male and female. The readers entering these texts fall down the rabbit's hole of uncertainty. At the base of our anxiety is the question of what is an appropriate response: joy or terror, admiration or horror. At the end, all we can do is watch word-lessly, the quintessential mystical experience. The Warrior Goddess of Israel's uncontrolled kill, which undercuts the very dichotomous patriarchy on which gendered violence rests,[73] is potentially beautiful, revealing how the divine nature is beyond human categories of appropriate behavior.

Divine violence, like divine sexuality, is a metaphor borrowed from human experience of something that ultimately is indescribable. It is used in order to communicate the ultimately indescribable nature of the divine, but it does so not in language of tranquility and loss of emotion but rather in a way that re-confirms human experience as the best arena to explore the nature of God. I would argue that it leads to a notion of divinity that is not divorced from human experience but instead reveals that human experience is both revelatory of the divine nature and ultimately limited, imperfect, and flawed.[74]

When I analyze my own experience of this material in light of the transcendental categories of Truth, Goodness, and Beauty, I conclude that I read these texts as revealing something true about God's power

---

73. In this I differ from and disagree with Chapman. She does not entertain the ways in which the warrior goddesses and the use of the imagery in Israel have the potential to undermine the gender dichotomy that feeds patriarchy.

74. In the final chapter of Hedges' book, *War Is a Force that Give Us Meaning*, he asserts that love and war both offer a possible meaning to life through self-sacrifice and the nobility of a greater cause (pp. 157–85). He concludes, however, that war ultimately cannot give life meaning, only love can. In many ways I agree with him, although I would do so using theological language. I place emphasis here, however, on issues of divine transcendence and power, rather than love or mercy. I would also argue that Christian notions of the Incarnation flow from a similar belief in the appropriateness, although limitedness, of human categories for divine revelation.

and sovereignty. I experience this God as good, not evil, in the violence against enemies whether foreign or domestic. I find these portrayals appropriate, fitting, and satisfying. In addition, I am attracted to this kind of god, not because I want to be the victim of divine violence, and not because I am secure in my own righteousness, but because at the end of the day I want a God who cares enough to be angry, involved enough to do something, and divine enough to accomplish what humans shouldn't even try.

Sex, Violence, and Rock and Roll: The Devil's Playground, or Are We the Devil?

Are descriptions of violence always evil? Always beautiful? Certainly not. Violent images can simply be inflammatory, disgusting, and gratuitous. I would argue that language about violence, just like depictions of sexual activity, are not inherently good or bad; erotic or pornographic; glorious or gory. Rather, violent images can be used to resist, recover, entertain, inflame, or inspire. Therefore, while some violent texts provide an outlet for human violence or function as a therapeutic outlet for victims of violence, sometimes they provide an aesthetic experience. Are they beautiful? That would depend on one's definition of "beautiful." However, I do know that for many readers these texts are moving, memorable, complex, fascinating, emotive, satisfying, and an appropriate revelatory experience of God.

Although the question still remains of what social or psychic function these images serve, we cannot grapple with that question unless we first recognize that humans crave creative violence and often utilize it, not just to recover from trauma but also to express exaltation of that which is greater than us. And while we are a violent society, it is not enough to reduce depictions of divine violence to a direct cause of that real violence. The fact is that we use violent texts to justify acts we would commit anyway; the reality of human violence, just like the reality of sexual objectification, will always be with us, whether or not we have a Bible. We cannot expect a text to solve what we can't solve ourselves, no matter how "holy" it is.

Do Zephaniah, Nahum, and Isaiah make us violent? Would we have a better world if we stopped reading or imagining them? If eradicating violence in our society were that easy, we'd have been living in a bookless, aniconic Eden long ago. These books provide ready ammunition for violence, but they are not the finger on the trigger. For me, an Eden devoid of the passion that these images stir is as unsatisfying as a Barney-esque fantasy world. I can no more imagine a reign of God not won by victory than I can a heaven without sex. We can't get rid of sex or violence and remain human, and we can't remain human without misusing them. We remain on this side of reality where the grotesque is beautiful.[75]

75. Boersma (*Violence, Hospitality, and the Cross*, 257) talks of being on "this side of the eschaton."

DIVINE VIOLENCE IN THE BOOK OF AMOS

Mary Mills

This study intends to explore the theme of divine violence in the book of
Amos. In order to do so, a case will be made for viewing Amos as a text
in which violent behaviour is a central feature; this being so, the profile
of violence will be examined with regard, initially, to the field of cultural
geography, especially the topic of psycho-geography. In particular, the
work of Steve Pile[1] will be used as a reading tool for commentary on the
violence of Amos, with emphasis on his delineation of a vampiric urban
imaginary. The topic of the vampire will be expanded with reference to a
cultural study of the vampire figure carried out by Molly Williamson,[2] as
well as through consideration of the Monstrous and the Sublime. The
final goal of this study will be to comment on urban imagery in terms of
both positive and negative readings of the city.

The foundational layer of this reading of prophetic violence is the
concept of psycho-geography as employed by the urban geographer
Steve Pile, who, in his book *Real Cities*, intends to explore the manner in
which the use of Freudian thought can give fresh meaning to the content
of the city-as-concept.[3] He works with the topic of "urban imaginary,"
that is, the city as it is constructed by and through the imagination of its
inhabitants. In this approach, cities are viewed as social bodies whose
embodiment is constructed by the agency of their populations. The urban
imagination can be aligned with the Freudian theory of dreams, according to Pile, thus producing urban imaginaries which offer particular
urban identities.[4] In this perspective, cities are envisioned as being more

1. Steve Pile, *The Body and the City: Psychoanalysis, Subjectivity, Space* (New
York: Routledge, 1996).
2. Molly Williamson, *The Lure of the Vampire: Gender, Fiction and Fandom
from Bram Stoker to Buffy* (New York: Wallflower, 2005).
3. Pile's approach to geography is to focus on the theme of embodiment, viewing
the city as one example of this theme, namely, social embodiment. For an account of
this perspective, see Pile, *The Body*.
4. Pile's approach is to move from a focus on the manner in which cities are
connected with people's urban behaviour to the idea that cities themselves could be

than constructs from material artefacts; the city as "persona" becomes a matter for serious investigation since it produces a key aspect of urban identity.

In his book, Pile addresses the "city" both as a generic reality and as the particular city—New York, New Orleans, among other modern urban settings. It is possible to extend Pile's urban range to include the ancient city-state, and in particular the city of Samaria, as depicted in the book of Amos. This literary depiction will be understood as an example of an urban imaginary. It is possible to make this link between Pile and biblical text because Amos, like other books of written prophecy in the Hebrew Bible, has an assumed foundation in city-life. The first verses of Amos, for instance, refer to Jerusalem as the site of the prophetic voice; the major import of the book's message is a critique of the urban elite of Samaria. Within this context there is an alignment of city and temple/ sanctuary. Jerusalem is paired with Mt. Zion in Amos 1:2, a metaphor attached to the city to indicate its role as divine residence.[5] Amaziah's attack on Amos in ch. 7 provides an example of how the Samarian sanctuary functions to link its ruling classes with a divine patron. Deity and ruler, as indicated in this narratival pairing, are intimately connected.

As Pile pursues his topic of urban imaginaries constructed by dreams, he moves into the nature of violence as it operates within urban imagination. He draws on Freud's concept of the Uncanny to introduce the subject of the urban vampire. Vampires dwell within cities in the wider life of city spirituality and in the activities of leisure make-believe on the

said to have a state of mind, an emotional make up which determines their meaning. This leads on to the view that cities are like dreams, mysterious realities, and that the role of dreams is the exploration of inner existence. This activity is all the same a real event in city life. Pile's thought links with that of Robert Park in *The City: Suggestions for Investigation of Human Behaviour in the Urban Environment* (ed. R. Park; Chicago: University of Chicago Press, 1925) regarding the importance of state of mind as an interpretive tool for urban identity—giving rise to the concept of urban imaginary. For a recent treatment on the nature of urban imagination, see Amin Ash and Nigel Thrift, *Cities—Reimagining the Urban* (Malden, Mass.: Polity, 2002).

5. For the concept of Mt. Zion as embracing the aspects both of a divine residence and an historical city, Jerusalem, see, for example, Ps 132, where the idea of Davidic kingship is aligned with both city and temple. For an account of Zion in comparative religious thought in the ancient Near East, see John Walton, *Ancient Near Eastern Thought and the Old Testament: Introducing the Conceptual World of the Hebrew Bible* (Grand Rapids: Baker, 2006), 127–29. See also Richard Hess and Gordon Wenham, eds., *Zion, City of Our God* (Grand Rapids: Eerdmans, 1999), which explores Zion themes within a range of Old Testament material.

part of inhabitants. In turn, the city itself can be vampiric, enacting violence on its populace. The theme of dream vision leads Pile into the topic of the vampire both as an urban dweller and as an icon of city-space.[6] This image of the urban vampire can be applied to an exploration of the urban critique of the book of Amos, for this text deals with the violent aggression and blood-letting in which urban regimes can engage. In the case of Amos, the tone of the vampiric profile is one of destruction and defeat. Almost the entire contents of the book of Amos deal with the ruin of a society and the desperate fate of its elite. The prophet seeks to undermine a sense of confidence in divine support for the Establishment, turning the Day of the Lord from a sign of victory over enemies into a sign of the invalidity of the home society.[7] The fate of Samaria is aligned with the general urban crimes of violence and with the corresponding violent action on the part of the deity. Both city and deity, it can be argued, are agents of vampiric violence in the text of Amos.

6. Pile discusses this topic in the third chapter of his *The Body*. For Pile, the vampire is a social figure, through which the magical nature of a city can be expounded. Pile points to the reality of vampire cultures in certain cities, as well as moving to the view that a city can itself be characterized as a vampire in relation to its inhabitants. As such, the figure of the vampire explores those aspects of city-as-magic, which deal with human fears and anxieties. In this way Pile utilizes the legendary character of the vampire. For an account of folklore and history with regard to Dracula as vampire, see Matei Cazacu, *Dracula* (Paris: Tallandier Editions, 2004). Cazacu (pp. 341–48) notes two sources of vampire legend. The first deals with the topic of the "undead," that is, persons who have been excommunicated and whose soul cannot then separate from the body; the second is a version of the folklore of "evil eye," labelling someone as vampiric because of disease attacking village animals, for instance.

7. The Day of the Lord has been the subject of much scholarly debate, from the work of Gerhard von Rad on "Holy War" in *Holy War in Ancient Israel* (Grand Rapids, Mich.: Eerdmans, 1958) up to the present. For a link with the inherent nature of warfare in the ancient Near Eastern culture, see Ziony Zevit, "The Search for Violence in Israelite Culture and the Bible," in *Religion and Violence: The Biblical Heritage* (ed. J. Klawans and D. Bernat: Sheffield: Sheffield Phoenix, 2007), 1–15 (21), for a discussion of the concept of *ḥerem*. With regard to usage of the term in Amos, see Shalom Paul, *Amos* (Minneapolis: Augsburg Fortress, 1991), 182–84, where a survey is given of the main explanations of the term in scholarship. See also Hans Wolff, *Joel and Amos* (Philadelphia: Fortress, 1997), 254–55. Harry Mowvley, *The Books of Amos and Hosea* (London: Epworth, 1991), 60–61, links the topic with the feast of Tabernacles. Alberto Soggin, *The Prophet Amos* (London: SCM, 1987), 95, suggests that the Amos material represents the earliest written use of the theme and is a form of "popular eschatology" based on the profile of a theophanic Warrior God.

The initial profile of the book shows God to be the predator, with the use of the metaphor of God roaring like a lion, but it becomes clear that the city is the true foundation to the theme of violence, since chs. 1–2 focus on the actual harm done by city-states which call forth equivalent violence on the part of the deity. The book of Amos produces a violent urban imaginary in which an aggressive city calls into being a corresponding divine violence. The random violence of nature is harnessed to this so that God the creator/controller becomes a figure for a divine destroyer, as in the doxologies with their imagery of cosmic upheaval. It is the dual profile of human and divine violence which will be examined further in this study, through selected intertextual referencing to Pile's approach to the social activity of city populations.

Religious Violence and Biblical Texts

In a recent volume of essays on the topic of religion and violence, Jonathan Klawans notes a number of ways in which the biblical texts can be linked with the theme of religious violence.[8] Violent acts, including those of ethnic cleansing, are recorded in biblical books. Yet, as Klawans points out, the exact nature of the connection between images of violence and real acts of aggression is complex.[9] Religious texts may well not describe or prescribe actual aggressive behaviour, since "violent fantasies can in some situations serve to vent the rage that could otherwise be carried out."[10] Even the definition of the term "violence" is not simple. Ziony Zevit suggests that it should be used for "the use of extreme, sudden force to injure somebody, usually by surprise."[11] This definition certainly resonates with the presentation of the deity in Amos as a Being who lurks in the shadows ready to strike out suddenly. But is that enough to prove that the writer of Amos wants to endorse aggressive behaviour in its own right? Zevit argues that the Hebrew Bible text is full of violence: wars are described and justified, while the prophetic texts "call for and describe acts of violence"; yet that alone does not prove that the

---

8. Klawans, "Introduction," in Klawans and Bernat, eds., *Religion and Violence*, 16–37 (6–7).
9. Ibid., 9.
10. Ibid., 7–10.
11. The present study explores not only aggressive acts, but also a more continual state of economic oppression as a form of violence. These comments are made with regard to the text of Amos and do not assume a wider historical culture of oppression (for both, see Zevit, "Search," 16, 36).

culture which produced such material was itself one "that reified and valued violence."[12]

The prophetic texts of the Hebrew Bible evidence a context of possible and actual defeat at the hands of powerful neighbours, and it can be agued that the images of violence used in texts reflect the confusion and loss of faith which connect with historical instances of invasion and defeat. In this setting violence is no longer used to give shape to Judah/ Israel's relations with other nations, but instead turns in on the home community. The aggression committed by others against the city of Samaria is internalized as valid, for example in Amos 4. Social and economic oppression by the city elite find their balance in the sudden reversal of military fortune by which the city is itself destroyed. Zevit's statement that "Psychically seared, militarily powerless, Israelite aggression was sublimated into...fantastic dreams"[13] can be applied to this context. Here the content of violent images does not arise from a capacity to carry out aggression, but rather from the uncertainty created by the experience of death and destruction at the hands of other societies. Since violence occurs it has to be accounted for, and one way for this is to accept it as retribution to the home community for its aggressive acts which prey upon the urban world in a self-appointed manner. For Zevit, these are dreams of vengeance but they are also the dreams of self-flagellation.[14]

That there are dangerous elements in self-referential violence can be drawn from the manner in which prophetic material has been interpreted by modern readers as expressing justified divine aggression, understood as a form of theodicy.[15] In this perspective, violence can be interpreted as its paradoxical opposite—love. God needs to discipline human violence

---

12. Ibid., 18. The argument is that imagery is used to express historical reality while not creating a timeless value for violence. Hence, divine violence can be said to describe events and thus to allow a meaning for that existential experience, rather than imposing violence as a necessary act.

13. Ibid., 37.

14. Zevit (ibid., 37) addresses the view that in post-exilic texts, Judah, though desirous of vengeance on aggressors, does not seem to nominate itself for that task. Rather, a sense of having been oneself defeated tones down the capacity for action. The present study extends that viewpoint to cover the idea that not only is violence not envisaged as a direct event but also that the community internalizes the aggression carried out against it as its own responsibility.

15. S. Tamar Kamionkowski, "The 'Problem' of Violence in Prophetic Literature: Definitions as the Real Problem," in Klawans and Bernat, eds., *Religion and Violence*, 38–46 (38).

by the use of divine aggression. "God uses violence as a means of judgement and salvation. It is never gratuitous violence."[16] But the effect of this move is potentially to endorse even more acts of human violence, if these are seen to be the expression of such a stern discipline. What started off as an answer to the actual fact of aggression can thus turn into a universal endorsement of violence as inherent in the character of the deity. Hence there can be a paralleling of the role of judge with that of military leadership, for in Amos it is the deity who acts as the leader of armies.

Prophetic violence produces an image of the deity as a violent being. However, this portrait of God reflects a very human perspective on life events and is tied into the entire cultural base of the ancient Near East[17] where such imagery operates in a network of meaning in which issues of power and authority are at stake. This base is one with political questions regarding authentication of a variety of competing power bases in the world of city-state relations and reflects the manner in which religion and secular activity cannot be dealt with except in relation to each other. In relation to *realpolitik*, as Kamionkowski argues, "the prophets were products of their age; cultural violence was embedded in their world."[18] Real violence produces a language of violence which in turn shapes the urban imaginary. The characterization of God is influenced by human experience and icons of the deity thus include the image of a god of wrath as a viable tool for giving religious meaning to civil affairs.

Amos—a Violent Text?

Reflection on the topic of violence in biblical texts has touched on the gap between historical acts of aggression and literature in which images of violence occur. In what follows the stress falls on the literary imagery of violence and the socio-religious message this carries. The first aspect of this study is, then, to investigate how far the theme of violence permeates the book of Amos. It can be shown that it is in fact a key topic

16. Ibid., 39.
17. The argument here is that imaging the deity forms part of human language and that there are broad cultural traditions in this regard within a region. See Bernhard Lang, *The Hebrew God: Portrait of an Ancient Deity* (New Haven: Yale University Press, 2002). Lang, in his Chapter 7, on the Lord of War, asserts the existence of a *deus militans* in Mesopotamian culture, before linking this theme with the God of Israel. As god of a state YHWH has the same responsibility as that of Mesopotamian deities—to secure royal victory in battle—a topic which Lang further develops in his eighth chapter with regard to "apocalyptic drama."
18. Kamionkowski, "The 'Problem' of Violence," 45.

which has three strands—natural violence, human violence, divine violence. The theme of violence in nature is introduced at the start of the book, where the time of the prophet's visions is related to the occurrence of an earthquake.[19] This opens into the image of the deity as roaring, like a lion, connected with the mourning and withering of nature.[20] The theme of the lion reappears in Amos 3:4, where the sound is linked to the animal in search of its prey. By v. 12, this has turned into the imagery of the small body-parts which are all that are left after the predator has eaten his fill. In ch. 5, the imagery is used again, this time in connection with the bear and the serpent—all of them symbols of the sudden, aggressive attack which is part of the natural world.[21]

Between the first part of ch. 1 and the return to nature in ch. 3, the book stresses the nature of human violence. In the Oracles against the Nations the writer describes a variety of social crimes against other human beings perpetrated by named city-states of antiquity.[22] The list describing the retribution which will be enacted on those who initiate such oppressive violence matches the level of the violence to be given back against the measure meted out. To the list of foreign powers who invite violent retribution is added the home states of Israel and Judah,

---

19. The theme of the earthquake can be viewed as one strand of the imagery of a theophanic warrior God. See Paul, *Amos*, 39 n. 43. Paul also links the concept of "roar" with the fear engendered by the noise made by an earthquake. The sudden onset of an earthquake fits into the profile of violence as an unexpected attack, albeit, in this case, that of a natural event and not the result of human act.

20. Paul (ibid., 39) discusses the roaring of the lion as a strategy for intimidating prey and links this with the shattering sound of a warrior deity, which produces cataclysmic sonic reverberation and leads to cosmic upheaval. Wolff, *Joel and Amos*, 124–25, notes that the oracle deals with the devastating force of the divine voice, while a drought which makes whole forests die must be seen as an eschatological theme. Soggin, *Amos*, 29, suggests that v. 2 is reminiscent of the theophanic language of ancient hymns.

21. Paul, *Amos*, 186, suggests that the three predators are those whose attacks are usually ferocious and fatal and thus provide appropriate images of the depth of an unexpected misfortune. Wolff, *Joel and Amos*, 256, notes that the serpent is generally a deadly enemy in Old Testament thought.

22. Paul, *Amos*, 45, notes that the Oracles against the Nations extend the rule of YHWH to foreign nations and indicates that crimes against a common humanity flout divine authority. Zevit, "Search," 17, notes that war is generally regarded as acceptable use of force in the ancient Near East, and would not count as violence. The material in Amos, however, would appear to view war as violent insofar as it represents an excessive amount of force used against civilians, such as would occur in the seizure of city precincts, and the unlawful denial of proper burial to fellow human beings.

whose crimes are not carried out in attacking other societies, but which are rather found in the internal aggression carried out by the elites on the peasant classes of the city.[23] These actions will encounter divine violence, too. In these oracles, the topics of human and divine violence are woven together, as indeed they are in the themes from nature. Imagery of lion, bear and serpent point to the manner in which the deity will be found to have acted in the prophetic understanding of civic affairs. The links between natural and divine violence are made explicit in the vision reports of ch. 7. Here the prophet sees God forming aggressive predation to attack the urban community, in the form of locusts and of fire.[24] Hence the implicit equation of deity and wild beast, both hungrily seeking their prey, is openly endorsed in the later chapter, where God operates directly to inspire nature to attack human habitation and threaten human existence.[25]

This latter perspective, in which God's judicial role in Israelite history is identified with natural destructive forces, is reflected upon theologically in the Doxologies of the book.[26] In these hymns God the creator

23. Paul, *Amos*, 90, points out that the use of second person plurals here creates a sense of urgency with regard to Judah and Israel and results in salvation history being proclaimed as judgment history. Wolff, *Joel and Amos*, 173, argues that the peacetime transgressions against fellow citizens are regarded by Amos as comparable to cruelty carried out in wartime. These acts relate to the *eschaton* and cause the cessation of God's dealings with Israel.

24. Soggin, *Amos*, 73–75, notes that these are Event Visions and regards the image of fire as indicating the effect of drought. Mowvley, *Amos and Hosea*, 114, however, sees the level of attack (*tehom*) as tending towards a mythological level of activity. Wolff, *Joel and Amos*, 299, combines both natural and supernatural levels of meaning. Paul, *Amos*, 230, focuses on the meaning of the verb with regard to fire, suggesting that there is a natural link with the concept of prophetic voice as judgment ("contend" from Hebrew *ryb*). Paul, *Amos*, 227–28, describes the locusts as a classical biblical plague and points out that such an attack would eat not only the late growth, but also the earlier, as yet unharvested crops as well.

25. Cf. the third chapter of Leo Bersani's *The Freudian Body: Psychoanalysis and Art* (New York: Columbia University Press, 1986), where he discusses in detail the friezes depicting the Lion Hunt and the manner in which artistic beauty and violence go hand in hand in this art form. See also Zevit, "Search," 30, who suggests that biblical accounts of warfare may be influenced by what Judah already knew about Assyrian violence, such as that recorded in the palace inscriptions of Sennacherib's campaigns. In the Assyrian material, the political aesthetics is thus driven by the depiction of violence in which the king hunts prey in both human and animal domains.

26. With regard to the Doxologies, Wolff, *Joel and Amos*, 215–17, gives an overview of the genre and the possible layers of composition in the three Amos hymns. He suggests that this is a hymnic style which derives from the general activity of

is praised for his dynamic energy, but all the evidence points to the manifestation of this in destructive power. Thus, in Amos 5:8, the deity darkens the day and sends tidal waves to swamp the land.[27] In Amos 9:5–6, divine power melts the land and once again causes tidal waves.[28] The impact of images of violent destruction is gathered together in two further images. On the one hand, the deity points to the "End," which is mirrored through a basket of fruit,[29] and on the other hand, 8:10 defines the reality for the city as a "bitter" day, faced with a message that sets the teeth on edge.[30] Only in the very last verses of the book does the mood change, the divine acts of destruction being balanced out by urban reconstruction.

God in nature, one which is here re-used from the generic forms of ancient Near Eastern religion, providing one specific formulation. Paul, *Amos*, 152–53, also gives a thorough account of the doxological form with regard to its life-setting. Mowvley, *Amos and Hosea*, 50–51, discusses to what extent these passages may be regarded as the voice of the prophet Amos.

27. Paul, *Amos*, 168, suggests that the power to change day and night expresses divine sovereignty, as found also in Akkadian and Sumerian literature. He also discusses the possibility of waters as indicating seasonal flooding or a unique event (the Flood). God as ruler over nature as well as over history is to be found in Isa 40:22–23, for example. Wolff, *Joel and Amos*, 215–17, reminds the reader of links with Job 9 and 38.

28. Wolff, *Joel and Amos*, 341–42, suggests that the title " Lord of Hosts" is another link with ancient divine theophany imagery, together with references to the world tottering. He makes the comparison with depictions of Ishtar and Shamash enthroned on high. Paul, *Amos*, 279, regards the hymnic doxology of judgment as linked with glorification of the god of the Nile, in Egypt. Mowvley, *Amos and Hosea*, 87, also regards this material as mythological. Paul, *Amos*, 279, suggests that 9:6 should be read as the heavenly vault overhanging the earth, thus bringing the two lines into a parallel meaning.

29. Here the textual meaning turns on a word-play between *qayits* and *qets*. Paul, *Amos*, 253–54, suggests that the key term is not "basket" but "ripe figs" and that this indicates a context of "harvest," a topic suitable for the context of judgment and death. The late harvest prepares for the end of the season. Wolff, *Joel and Amos*, 317, 319, also addresses the nature of the word-play. Soggin, *Amos*, 117–18, echoes Paul's stress on harvest as the key theme, while Mowvley, *Amos and Hosea*, 82, draws this theme also into the setting of the feast of Tabernacles.

30. Commentary on this word links it to the theme of funerary rites. Mowvley, *Amos and Hosea*, 84, suggests that pilgrim feasts turn to sorrow; Soggin, *Amos*, 138, links mourning and lament to the Egyptian cult of the dead, and parallels that with ideas of the death of the sun; Paul, *Amos*, 263–64, also links the death of the sun with funerary cult and aligns this with bitter weeping in Ezek 27:3 and Isa 33:7; Wolff, *Joel and Amos*, 329–30, has the same perspective and relates this to Eccl 7:26.

Images of the natural world and of the cosmic heavenly scene com-
bine in Amos to present an aesthetic of divine violence. This depiction
is justified as a reaction to human violence against other states and to
internal social aggression—as in ch. 4, where elite women consume food
and drink with no thought for anything but their own pleasure, an idea
repeated in ch. 6 with regard to the whole urban elite.[31] This consumption
is founded on taking away the basic necessities of life from the labourers,
as in ch. 5.[32] It is this account of urban existence which draws down
aggression. If the human oppression stops short of murder and ethnic
cleansing within the city walls, it is still viewed as deeply destructive of
civic order and is measured by the wartime context of plundering and
raping armies surging through the city, breaking down its defences. What
emerges here is an aesthetic in which images of violence are woven into
the exploration of political judgment of the city elite. The divine is a
force for terror which brings into the open the hidden horror of a ruling
class which builds its great houses at the expense of a poor labouring
class.[33]

A Violent Text and Its Prophetic Performance

The manner in which violent images are deployed in Amos is designed
to impact strongly on the reader and justifies an exploration of the
text through the tools of performance criticism.[34] William Doan and

31. This material is to be understood as an example of structural violence.
Kamionkowski, "The 'Problem' of Violence," 40–45, notes that the topic of structural violence is concerned with the systematic ways in which a social structure
prevents individuals from achieving their potential. In Amos 4 and 6, the upper
classes of the urban society not only prevent the labourers from gaining proper
economic reward for their work, but threaten the very possibility of survival for
these social groups. Reading the prophetic text as a reflection of social and religious
norms alerts the reader to the way in which cultures may perform violent acts in the
name of a deity.

32. Paul, *Amos*, 172, discusses the use of an extremely rare Hebrew verb in
Amos 5:11, created from Akkadian cognates, to express the idea of a grain tax
envisaged in this verse. Mesopotamian authorities regularly collected taxes from
cultivated land and harvests. Hence oppression is aligned with the exaction of
punishing land tax.

33. Soggin, *Amos*, 29–30, points out that excavation of ancient Samaria has
revealed both some large houses and a number of much poorer dwellings, thus back-
ing up the Amos themes of social stratification. The poor farmer could fall into debt
to the richer city-dwellers and thus enter the state of debt-slavery.

34. Performance criticism is a concept derived from the arena of theatre and
drama, but reapplied to daily life. Hence the term covers a wide range, from all

Terry Giles, in discussing the nature of performance, tease out its social function, asking "whether performance serves to reinforce the primary assumptions and values of a culture or to create new and alternative assumptions."[35] They argue that in fact performance is always open-ended and carries a subversive potential.[36] Fascinatingly, the prophets depicted in the Hebrew Bible are also open-ended, presented without the closure of death and life's ending.[37] In this way the portrayal of named prophets mirrors the importance of prophetic performance, that of helping to re-create social self-identity.

In the book of Amos the scribal author provides a symbolic drama, using the narrative of one man's activity. The prophet-as-character acts out his dramatic role in two parallel ways. In the Oracles against the Nations (OANs) he performs the function of a further actor, namely, the Lord. It is, for instance, Amos who proclaims in the first chapter of the book that God roars from Zion, before going on to announce the content of that roar as oracles of judgment against a number of cultures.[38] His voice becomes one with that of the divine speaker in such a way that the contents of divine utterance strike the hearer as matters of great urgency. In his second role the prophet performs the function of onlooker, in the vision reports. Since it is he alone who can see what God is doing, he reveals the plot sequence to the audience of the text by means of his own sight and his narrative powers of story-telling. In this usage, "prophetic drama draws its potency from the social power of the prophet."[39] It is he who holds the key to evaluating urban culture since it is the prophetic capacity to see and to speak; this is the dramatic medium of unfolding religious meaning—just as at the start of the book it is his ability to hear and to speak truth that is critical.[40]

human behaviour to "restored behaviour" in which existing behavioural patterns are applied to fresh contexts. See, for instance, Marvin Carlson, *Performance: A Critical Introduction* (New York: Routledge, 2003).

35. William Doan and Terry Giles, *Prophets, Performance and Power: Performance Criticism of the Hebrew Bible* (New York: T&T Clark International, 2005), 16.

36. Ibid.

37. Ibid. 23.

38. Ibid., 115.

39. Ibid., 145.

40. Amos 3:7. See Paul, *Amos*, 112–13, which points out that the prophet is understood to stand in the presence of God and hears what the divine council is planning. The term for "counsel" can be set alongside the term *raz* or "secret plan" (in Greek, *musterion*). It is these secret plans which seers have access to.

The power of the text to convey its message is underlined in these reports by the simplicity of the structuring of the prophetic performance. "With all narrative or prosaic distractions removed, the audience is forced to focus upon the essentials required to carry the plot of the drama."[41] The combination of the immediacy of the drama with the social function of the prophet as the sole point of access to divine intention serves to heighten the impact on the hearer of the language of violence. When the prophet announces his own repulsion at the sight of the horrors being planned by the deity, the audience, too, is encouraged to groan and to cry out under the burden of so much suffering.[42] The dramatic enactment of divine violence in Amos strengthens the role of the text as the creator of a changed social understanding. The scribal performance found in the written text concerning the career of Amos (cf. Amos 7:10–17) spells out his role as a subversive at the same time as the story itself deconstructs any certainty a reader might have that traditions of unity between God and state are unchanging in value.

Pile's Urban Vampiric

Violence and subversion can thus be viewed as mutually validating themes within the book of Amos. Prophetic declarations concerning divine control of human aggression—the armies summoned against Samaria—are justified on the grounds of the internal social violence carried out by the Samarian elite.[43] Such pronouncements subvert the authority of the ruler by placing God and king in opposition to one another. It is, therefore, in viewing and hearing of scenes of violent activity that the reader is led to doubt the validity of an urban imaginary in which religious belief and the city-as-nurture run together. Rather, it is

41. Doan and Giles, *Prophets*, 149.

42. See here Stephen Geller, "The Prophetic Roots of Violence in Western Religion," in Klawans and Bernat, eds., *Religion and Violence*, 47–56 (48–51). Geller discusses prophetic violence as a result of internal psychic dissonance. The tension between private vision and the need for public proclamation to an unresponsive audience has the effect of tearing apart the human psyche.

43. Thus the paradox of warfare in which one side resorts to violence to defend itself against violent attack from the other side. Yet violence rarely solves the issues which initiated the response without causing collateral damage, which in turn becomes a cause of war. Cf. Geller, "The Prophetic Roots," 51–52, on the theme of how the written text of the Hebrew Scriptures did not escape older themes of divine violence but gave rise to a new layer of dispute which contested the meaning of the older material.

an image of the city-as-vampire which emerges from this dynamic, as does the characterization of the deity as engaging in justifiable vampire acts.

Pile's book asks questions about what is "real" in cities[44] and finds answers to these questions in Robert Park's viewpoint that the city can have a state of mind[45] and that this can engage with the imaginary and emotional aspects of urban life. Such an approach lends itself to a consideration of phantasmagoria as defined by Walter Benjamin, who suggested "that the many surface appearances of the city give it a dream-like and/or ghost-like quality."[46] The dream-like nature of cities and their populations extends to "the specific sites where this dreaming collective is produced and reproduced."[47] For Pile, the material spaces of the city are created from "the waking dreams of architects, developers, owners,"[48] which he aligns with the production of collective emotional states, stating that he desires "to identify the phantasmagorias of city life, to see the work that goes into reading the dream-like qualities of city life."[49]

The book of Amos can be described as having a dream-like quality insofar as it is constructed from visionary perceptions on the part of the prophet regarding the city of Samaria. Amos 1:1 defines the contents of the book as what the prophet "saw," while chs. 4–9 provide a succession of urban phantasmagorias which come before the eyes of the reader. Here the elite are driven out through the broken walls of their city, the same elite stretched at ease on their couches, consuming luxurious food and drink, as well as locusts who will devour the land and a fire which will consume it. Such images construct an urban profile from the emotional state of the ruling class, in which the key focus is less dreaming generally than experiencing nightmares, the content of the nightmare being the worst disaster which can befall the city and its rulers, and the emotional collective is one of anxiety. Thus, although the elite are presented at their ease, this presentation is deconstructed by the fact that disinheritance is always in the background.

A further dimension of the city-work carried out by urban phantasm-magoria is the examination of the role of the vampire as an urban icon which mediates the urban experience of death.[50] Pile argues that "by

44. Pile, *Body*, 1.
45. Ibid., 2.
46. As cited in ibid., 19.
47. Ibid., 20.
48. Ibid., 48.
49. Ibid., 49.
50. Ibid., 97.

examining the vampire, it is possible to reveal how specific fears and desires are condensed into, or displaced onto, the bloodsucker."[51] In addition, "the vampire scares people because it embodies repressed fears and thereby makes people strange to themselves."[52] The focus here is upon the uncanny aspects of human experience. Social bodies push aside fears for their own continuance while also engaging in underlying concerns with the likelihood of death. The fear of death then manifests itself in the return of the supernatural, an event which both threatens and heals.[53] The vampire nature of violence in Amos is that it makes a populace strange to itself while also bringing into consciousness the view that the return of the deity will lead to destruction for the city. Amos 5:18–20, for example, describes the ambivalence inherent in the "Day of the Lord" motif. The desire for such a day is contrasted with the reality of darkness and not light, flight from danger to a security which is more dangerous than the initial threat. The prophetic voice problematizes both urban desire and the picture of God as protector of urban autonomy. The intention of the prophet appears to be to unsettle the reader's previous religious viewpoint, in which the continuing existence of society is assured by an immanent deity. The endpoint of this unsettlement is to bring into consciousness the reality of death—the death of citizens but, even more, the death of the city-state.

Pile wishes to locate social contexts in which vampires emerge, suggesting that these have a common element, namely, "the fragility of the social settings within which they emerge [such as] the contact zones between Empires or the edges of Empire or in places that are in some sort of crisis."[54] This comment is clearly relevant to the book of Amos, which suggests that there is an inherent instability in a society where the hierarchically powerful use their power to drain the means of subsistence from their laborers. Part of the Samarian vampire is constituted by an attempt to make plain what are the socio-economic predations of the elite. Equally, however, the book can be set against the historical reality of the use of Neo-Assyrian power in the eighth to seventh centuries B.C.E.[55] "Samaria" operates here as the contact zone between independent

51. Ibid.
52. Ibid., 98.
53. Ibid., 101.
54. Ibid., 105.
55. The text clearly expects major military activity to take place against Samaria. Both Paul, *Amos*, 1–2, and Wolff, *Joel and Amos*, 89–90, however, regard the immediate context of the prophecy as a period of peace. In this setting the prophetic voice can be read as one of rumbling unease with the current conduct of the city elite and its capability of effective leadership.

kingdoms and imperial overlord. Finally, the theme of crisis can be extended to cover the possible final date of production of the text of Amos: a post-exilic setting in which a new political regime seeks to establish its local authority as agent of imperial power.[56] In all these three settings the essential urban emotion is worry about power and authority and the complexity of its transfer from one regime to another. The literary use of violent imagery endorses the validity of the actual experience of regime change in this socio-political climate.[57] Its function is in fact to deal with the hopes and fears of the elite class, even while its subject content covers the economic oppression of subordinate citizens.

Establishing Violence

The City
In the prophetic imagination evidenced by the book of Amos there is a love/hate relationship with urban existence. For most of the book, city-states are regarded as inherently predatory beings. The vampire image provides an effective means of embodying, while yet mitigating, the social traumas of urban violence, because it allows the reader to deal with anxieties created by socio-political aggression. The city may be death-dealing, but viewing its own demise both authorizes the topic of death as suitable for public discussion and endorses the anxiety derived from addressing the possible disappearance of a familiar social world. Pile expresses this anxiety, in vampire-related terms, as the product of the city being a site which is "anxious about the human condition of living and dying but also that its life blood will be sucked dry, that it will become vulnerable to a world more ruthless, hungrier than itself."[58] In this reading, the urban fears narrated in violent metaphor in Amos are an example of the inherent emotional instability of city-life as such.

---

56. For one interpretation of the political reshaping involved in the move to a local theocracy funded by a distant imperial centre, see Jon Berquist, *Judaism in Persia's Shadow: A Social and Historical Approach* (Minneapolis: Fortress, 1995).

57. The profile presented in the books of Ezra and Nehemiah is of the difficulties encountered by the returnees and their desire to assert their control of local religion and politics. Thus, Ezra 9 refers to attempts to shape the local cult by denying the validity of cultic officials to function in the light of their choice of wives. Nehemiah 2 describes the reluctance of the local populace to rebuild the walls of Jerusalem and the governor's determination to assert the authority of a temple-state. Insofar as this material genuinely reflects historical tensions, it provides a frame for asserting that the leaders appointed by Persian authority had to work hard to persuade the existing inhabitants of Jerusalem to accept their right to political power.

58. Pile, *Body*, 111.

However strong urban government appears to be, it is in fact subject to sudden collapse. The sense that urban living provides security and nurture for those who succeed in drawing economic wealth to themselves, whose life style allows for leisure and an excess of goods over essential human needs, is problematized in the vampiric reading of urban growth. Furthermore, this vampiric imaginary has within it the shadow of urban cannibalism: it is not wealth for all but wealth for some at the expense of others.

The city emerges as a heartless site, a place where life/lives are not of great value. Pile notes that, like vampires, cities can live beyond their time, but do so at the cost of losing touch with the beating heart of their communal existence and of expressing a "callous indifference for life."[59] With regard to urban societies, such indifference can be both blessing and curse. Non-attachment to a particular political regime is the stance taken by God in Amos and the sufferings of the elite could be described as "callously" portrayed in the imagery of Amos 8:9–10. There is a totality of rejection here, expressed by the repeated use of *qol* and the image of an "only" son. Yet it is through such an indifference to suffering that the deity eventually brings about the collapse of a class which is itself heartless, whose callous indifference parts the poor from their very clothing in Amos 2:8. The determination of the deity to end the ruling class in violent ways manifests the degree of social violence "covertly" occurring in the city. Although the prophetic voice suggests that urban existence does not have to involve economic predation, since God opens the path to conversion from oppression in Amos 4:6–11, nevertheless there has been no return to God and the impression created by the text centres on the cycle of violence which is carried by an urban imaginary. What is set out in this modelling within Amos is a divine retributive which makes the city inherently vampiric.

Taking Pile's initiative seriously, it can be asked about the kind of urban reality which is negotiated by this vampiric imaginary. In both cases it is the powerful elite whose interests are the focus of concern. In chs. 1–2 it is the aggression of a regime towards parallel urban communities which is dealt with, while in chs. 3–6 it is the hostility of rulers towards subjects which is at issue. Although it is the strength of the elite which is viewed as aggressive, the text nevertheless mediates urban fears of its loss of autonomy. For the prophetic voice, such anxiety is justified since the inherent nature of cities as predators destabilizes any given city regime. Why should a city not suffer the same fate as it distributes, at the hands of a state which is stronger than it is? When the violence operates

59. Ibid., 129.

within the city itself, the text suggests that there should be a deep appreciation of how such predation renders a city-state vulnerable to fragmentation.

In this context, the topic of divine violence is a tool for dealing with the morality of urban elite power. If a city is founded on violent aggression, then it will find a match in a religious belief which threatens it with like-minded oppression. Reading Amos 1:11, it appears that the pursuit of violence is an energy which turns back on its instigator: "Because he pursued his brother with the sword and cast off all pity...so I will send a fire upon Teman." Fire will descend also on the Ammonites, for they have ripped open pregnant women (Amos 1:13). A like parallelism emerges within a single society, for in Amos 2:6 the elite sell "the righteous for silver and the needy for a pair of shoes."[60] Hence, in v. 13, Israel will be pressed down without hope of life being saved. It appears that violent acts which destroy the defenceless woman or which are intended to produce gain at the expense of the possessions of others transgress the boundaries of acceptable government. The image of the vampire used in this setting carries the paradox of violence used as a defence against violent treatment. The city-as-vampire is a real and rampant imaginary which defines the city as an actively violent persona.

Two further aspects of Pile's arguments regarding urban imagination are useful here. The first consists in linking urban sites with the production of the urban imaginary. As Pile states about cities, exploring urban space is "almost like walking through the city's web of dreams: at any point, you find places built out of different motivations or contradictory imperatives."[61] This perspective can be used to read the confrontation of Amos and Amaziah in ch. 7. The shrine is, in Pile's term, a place where contradictory elements come together. Amaziah declares it as a place where critique cannot be allowed, for it is a royal site.[62] In this viewpoint, divine vampiric violence is unacceptable if addressed to the home rulers. But Amos' response breaks down the inviolability of the shrine and hence of the city. It is the divine predator who is in control of the sacred site and who declares its managers invalid and subject to death. The fate of Amaziah depicted in v. 17 mirrors the fate of the larger elite. Death is

60. See Paul, *Amos*, 77–79, for a discussion of the suggestions that this refers to bribery of judges or to the selling of debtors into slavery.

61. Pile, *Body*, 51.

62. Paul, *Amos*, 238–39, suggests that Amaziah as a royal official must report all subversive acts at the shrine to the king. Wolff, *Joel and Amos*, 309–10, suggests that Amos' verbal attacks were politically unacceptable and are to be regarded alongside the account of Jehu's revolt in 2 Kgs 9.

all-present here. It is the value implicitly given to the shrine itself through the prophetic indictment of its guardians.

The second point relates to the emergence of the Uncanny as a powerful force in human affairs. For Pile, dream consideration leads into the topic of magic, which, like dreams, lies between worlds.[63] He suggests that tracking magical practices through cities allows us to see the significance of occult relationships for city life.[64] When this idea is applied to the text of Amos, one possible link that can be made is with the flow of divine destructive energy which will pass through the city. The occult moves to inaugurate the desired "Day of the Lord" when God will be visibly present in urban events in Samaria. Yet this energy is repeatedly defined as unpicking the wealthy from their social setting. Thus, in ch. 3, the altar will be broken (v. 14) and houses destroyed (v. 15). In Amos 5:16–17, the God of Hosts declares that the sound of the city will be wailing and mourning. In Amos 9:1–4, the voice of God declares that the entire temple will be destroyed, that it will cave in on the heads of the people so that no one can escape the relentless pursuit of divine hostility. In these examples the flow of energy breaks down the material environment, shattering buildings, so that there is no longer a physical site to give evidence of an urban society.

The Deity

In the end, it is in the characterization of God that the competing strands of life and death, violence and justice, cohere. The book builds on the theme of divine vengeance to produce a growing sense of natural and supernatural menace so that by the time that the reader reaches the vision reports of the later chapters the menace is immediate and life-threatening. The impending plague of locusts and fire are so deeply vampiric that the prophet cries out that all life will be extinguished and begs the deity to cease his predatory acts (Amos 7:5). It is in the event of theophany that the deity will be known as a warrior God, but one whose military might presses down on his own people. The subtext of the graphic images of darkness and gloom drawn from nature is that God is indeed the Other, whose role is adversarial. The expansion of natural imagery into supernatural forms, as with the manner in which the fire consumes the great Deeps (*tehom*) in Amos 7:4, expresses the excessive and transgressive nature of divine power, a feature of vampiric existence. Only if God is envisaged as the cause of foreign invasions and the true

    63. Pile, *Body*, 59.
    64. See Chapter 2 of Pile, *Real Cities* (Thousand Oaks: Sage, 2005), where Pile explores this perspective through a study of urban voodoo and *Feng Shui*.

role of conquest is not to enrich other nations but to draw a deeper humility from the home society can the conclusion be avoided that there is no future and that we are wholly dead, since our world and its imaginary space has disappeared along with the human beings involved. The price of this argument for continuity is the construction of a soulless deity, one who sucks life blood to further a relentless divine demand for urban self discipline.

Thus the vampiric urban imaginary is one that deals with city collapse through the language of divine justice. The central concern is the issue of how to interpret urban events: as indicating the inevitable supremacy of a foreign power and its gods or as the divinely determined collapse of a home society due to its internal, institutional violence. It is this second reality which is promoted in Amos. The god of violence asserts his authority to govern his "own" by whatever means. The deity is not belittled by the movement of political events or subordinated to the gods of a conquering nation.[65] Rather, the local deity emerges as immortal, beautiful and strong, though deeply troubling—as noted above from a reading of the Doxologies of Amos 5. A deity who has immense power is one whose profile can also accommodate vast destruction; thus there is some hope still for the continuity of the city culture.

The profiling of the deity in Amos makes God appear in monstrous form. And yet, as Timothy Beal points out, this profile is not necessarily evil or non-religious; rather, it is "the audacious voice of theodicy."[66] Certainly a vampiric imaginary offers a kind of theodicy, though this is a complex reality in which justice and violence run together. God as a lion who leaps out to kill and consume, in the book of Amos, can thus be described as imaging providence as a bloodsucking event. But that experience mysteriously validates the place of order as the mainstay of existence. Like Pile's vampire, Beal's monster is a character who reveals the deep insecurities hidden in human experience.[67] In Amos, it is in the character of the divine that the pressure of human uncertainties is manifested. Divine violence provides a mechanism for managing the political tensions of a fragmented world in such a way that God is imaged as using political chaos to control urban economic chaos.

---

65. This is a reference to the ancient view that defeat in battle meant not only human subordination to the victor, but also the subjection of the gods of the conquered to the gods of the winning side. In the account of the placing of the Ark of the Lord in the temple of Dagon, the whole point is that it is the home deity who falls prostrate before the Ark of the Lord, a reversal of the norm. Cf. 1 Sam 5.

66. Timothy Beal, *Religion and Its Monsters* (New York: Routledge, 2002), 3.

67. Ibid., 5.

Beal argues that "exploring religion via its monsters presents a challenge to the common conception of religion as exclusively about the establishment of order as against chaos."[68] The chaos monster is a manifestation of the numinous according to Rudolph Otto; it is an encounter with a totally other Being engendering both terror and fascination.[69] Engaging with Beal's viewpoint gives force to the argument that a vampiric imaginary expresses the urban desire for a city's continued existence even in a disordered world. God as chaos monster in the book of Amos terrifies with destructive energy while fascinating with its capacity to manage life at the edge of annihilation. Beal's argument is that the monstrous can be depicted as the voice of disorientation, as "the voice of psychological, political, cosmic horror" and as evocative of an "order falling apart at the seams".[70] This touches on the anxiety and fear carried by the image of the vampire, that existence may continue but only in a disoriented and confusing manner. Insofar as a city may be described as a Subject, its sense of coherent identity thus manages to survive—though only as a pair with cosmic breakdown. The monstrosity of divine violence may thus be summed up as survival through, and in, destruction. For Beal, biblical monsters stand on a threshold between cosmos and abyss and are the "ambiguous edges of a conceptual landscape where the right order of things touches on a wholly other chaos."[71]

It is this concept of excess which is at the heart both of Gothic fiction and of the vampire figure. As Fred Botting notes, Gothic deals with "threats associated with supernatural and natural forces, with religious and human evil, social transgression, mental disintegration."[72] Thus Gothic excess evidences a "fascination with transgression and an anxiety over cultural limits and boundaries."[73] It can be argued that the characterization of the deity in Amos addresses urban excess and transgression of boundaries. Divine violence is shown, in the OANs, to be triggered by the way in which cities have broken across borders of respect for other human beings. Fears for life come to be expressed in the language of death, so that the border between life and death may be re-drawn. In the oracles against Samaria, the reality of excess, of being the object of other kingdoms' aggressive acts, finds expression in the language of transgression of social boundaries on the part of a ruling class. The text slides

68. Ibid., 9.
69. Cited in ibid., 53.
70. Ibid., 29.
71. Ibid., 195.
72. Fred Botting, *Gothic* (New York: Routledge, 1996), 2.
73. Ibid., 2.

between writing out the horror of total annihilation by calling on divine violence as that which provides closure to suffering and writing in almost total annihilation (only bits of bodies survive) in order to fulfil the function of social violence as a reason for urban destruction. As Botting suggests, "Gothic terrors activate a sense of the unknown and project an uncontrollable and overwhelming power which threatens...social order. But such transgression becomes a powerful means to assert the values of society."[74]

Easing the Violence: Cultural and Philosophical Considerations

This essay has so far concentrated on the unmitigated violence of vampiric nature. This profile represents the ultimate vehicle of predatory transgression and excess, especially with regard to sucking life from others in order to continue oneself. The response to contemplation of this reality is a fascinated terror in the face of the wholly other which transcends normal existence. In her book, Molly Williamson notes that the cultural history of the vampire includes a stage in which the vampire comes nearer to us, allowing the reader to experience an empathetic concern for the destiny of the vampire, which drives it to act cruelly even when there is a nascent desire to "return to humanity."[75] Williamson describes the old Dracula as a being of hate/hunger/bitterness and contempt, whereas the modern vampire evidences love/regret/doubt/experience of inner conflict.[76] This profile is found, for instance, in the characterization of the vampire in Anne Rice's *Vampire Chronicles*.[77] Pathos enters into the readerly reaction to the vampire, in line with what Williamson defines as melodrama, "a mode of modern imagination concerned with dilemmas arising out of the struggle for meaning and significance."[78] Thus melodrama expresses the anxiety experienced by living in a frightening new world where old identities and boundaries are no longer valid.[79]

74. Ibid., 7.
75. Williamson, *Lure*, 33–34.
76. Ibid., 31.
77. Williamson (ibid., 36–50) discusses the profile of Louis in *Interview with the Vampire*, for instance, suggesting that the sympathetic attitude to the vampire offers a sense of "moral occult" in which the vampire expresses a human tension between the desire for meaning beyond ourselves and the impossibility of achieving that meaning.
78. Ibid., 40.
79. Ibid., 46.

This critique of cultural issues can be applied to the reading of Amos 7–9, where first the old Dracula and then the new one appears.[80] In Amos 7:1–3, God plans total destruction, as imaged in the locusts which devour the crops that offer humans continuity. At this point the prophet, who has hitherto been the vampiric Other of divine violence, now mediates life; there is a surge of compassion and protest which leads the deity to relent also: "It shall not be" (Amos 7:3).[81] This movement from the old vampire to one who moves back into the realm of a common humanity and shares annihilatory fears, provides a more nuanced approach to divine violence. It is a threat which may not be realized, for its transgressive, death-dealing excess is acknowledged and averted. The same profile is repeated in the formulas of vv. 4–6, with regard to fire: "This also shall not be."[82]

And yet, as with Rice's vampires, there is a swing back to the essential state of predator.[83] By Amos 7:7, God is putting a border in place, a line which God will not cross again.[84] This is not, however, a boundary to keep violence at bay, but the final line which separates God from people. God stands on the far side of that line, rising up with a sword to destroy. By ch. 8 this has moved on to the theme of The End, linked with the theme that God will never pass by the city again. But this absence of the deity is not a helpful cessation of violence; rather, the silence of the vampire is itself a source of great unease. Amos 8:11–12 describes the

---

80.   This comment is linked to the mood swings in the text of Amos between negative and more optimistic messages. It is possible to attach these opposing attitudes to material from separate layers in the editing of the book, although I am reading them synchronically. For a discussion of the possible interpretations of the layers of editing in Amos, see Paul, *Amos*, 288–90.

81.   See ibid., 230, where he argues that compassion and mercy are allowed to emerge here. God accepts prophetic mediation, but there is no sense that there is pardon as such.

82.   See ibid., 233. The prophet does not now ask for pardon but only for cessation of action. Since the first act of intercession did not meet with complete forgiveness, Amos can only fall back on begging the deity simply to stop the violence.

83.   Williamson, *Lure*, 48.

84.   For a discussion of the complexity of meaning of what Amos envisions, see Paul, *Amos*, 233, and Wolff, *Joel and Amos*, 300. Paul argues that the symbolic nature of the imagery should be highlighted. The reference to a wall may be symbolic of the ruler as providing a weak support for the temple and city. At the same time, the idea of a border or line of measurement indicates that this time there will be no cessation of violence. Wolff believes that God judges the guilt to be too great to be passed over. Mowvley, *Amos and Hosea*, 76–77, also regards the wall as relating to a symbol of invincibility. If the sanctuary wall is normally a measure of protection, it is transformed here into an army which is set against Samaria and cannot be defeated.

manner in which the people run to and fro seeking the presence of God, an activity which is only met by an acute silence.[85] This then is the ultimate pathos—a vampire who hides away and cannot be traced even though he still exists.[86]

The ambivalence of this vampiric deity is drawn out in the last chapter of the book of Amos. In the first part of this chapter God wreaks his last great havoc on the living—so that "not one of them shall flee away, not one of them shall escape" (Amos 9:1).[87] Yet, in the second part, the same deity announces that he intends to "raise up...repair...rebuild" (v. 11). The prophetic voice tells of restored fortunes, rebuilt cities, land that is planted by people who are themselves planted forever in their land (vv. 14–15).[88] Here the reader encounters a vampire who can repent of his own violent cruelty and who can produce life beyond death, who can restore boundaries such that the excessive is not outside normal order but within the confines of vineyards and gardens. This brings divine violence back within the human compass for it is now truly controlled, by the concept of The End. The theme of The End is thus an ambiguous sign. It stands for both death and life, for stop and start points to existence. Although there is certainly a death to be found for an urban community, nonetheless there is still hope for a future renewal of urban life. Here is a deity who is not irrevocably set against all human existence, but is recognizable from "the days of old" (v. 11), both in terms of natural order and of civil harmony. Williamson notes that "melodrama dramatises the

85. See Paul, *Amos*, 266. The people now totter, as the earth has done in the case of an earthquake. Wolff, *Joel and Amos*, 330, also addresses the drunken uncertainty of the people roaming as an image connected with the eyes of God. For the origins of food and drink as non-material in the Old Testament, cf. Deut 8:3.

86. See, for example, Pile, *Body*, 128–29, where Pile remarks on the ability of vampires to jump times and spaces. See also p. 112, where he talks of the vampire's ability to lie still for long periods of time.

87. Paul, *Amos*, 275, thinks that the destruction of the shrine indicates a complete collapse of trust in the old royal cult. Wolff, *Joel and Amos*, 339, suggests that the imagery in this passage is founded on the event of an earthquake that physically destroyed the building. The temple smitten by God is at the epicentre of the quake. Mowvley, *Amos and Hosea*, 86, makes a textual link with the image of Samson pulling down the pillars of the shrine in Judg 16.

88. Cf. Mowvley, *Amos and Hosea*, 91, links this imagery to the feast of Tabernacles again. The good fortune here is not as a result of pardon, but as a fact of existence for the generation of the returnees. Wolff, *Joel and Amos*, 355, regards the promised future as relating to the old salvific gifts found in the covenant with David. Paul, *Amos*, 290–95, discusses the unconditional nature of divine promises and the excess of bounty.

impulse to restore the existence of a larger ethical dimension."[89] This larger perspective includes pity and hope as well as aggressive acts, thus indicating that there is a possibility for more conciliatory extensions of the vampiric city profile, in which horror is capable of carrying the concept of the sublime.

In *The Philosophy of Horror*, Noel Carroll explores horror as genre.[90] He notes for instance the non-rational element of religion. He argues that the object of religious experience is the encounter with utter transcendence, causing fear in the subject and a sense of being overpowered.[91] The book of Amos deals with the wholly other via the prophetic voice which describes a series of divine images that threaten the hold that humanity has on a stable identity. The God who fashions extreme material disasters, for instance, is so terrible that it threatens all sense of human life. On one level, such a deity cannot be comprehended by ordinary reason: How can a deity cause his own people such great harm, even though they themselves may be guilty of hurt to others? On another level, the very scope of the chaos intended, to the point of total cosmic collapse, threatens the view that human life has its own inherent viability. Finally, it is non-rational in the sense described by Carroll in that the text implies that it is God who chooses to make known the actuality of divine violence.

The proper response to an encounter with the Other is a stance of awe. That which commands homage and expresses the awesome is surely visible in the Amos doxologies, where the text moves into a poetry which praises God for his powers of darkening the day and thus causing a solar eclipse. The horror of the book of Amos can thus be described as that which "pays homage to the monster,"[92] understanding that phrase to mean acceptance of the overwhelming force of natural energies. Carroll also discusses the human face of horror—which is "invariably the agent of the established order."[93] As such, horror has an ideological function, representing the predatory Other of that which threatens the Establishment.

Two ways of approaching the concept of horror emerge here—a focus on the transcendent and a focus on horror as a tool for the human search for control over life's affairs. Both ways converge with regard to the

89. Williamson, *Lure*, 46.

90. Noel Carroll, *The Philosophy of Horror or Paradoxes of the Heart* (New York: Routledge, 1900).

91. Ibid., 165.

92. Ibid., 166.

93. Ibid., 196.

concept of the Sublime, as this is defined by Philip Shaw. "The sublime marks the limits of human reason and expression, together with a sense of what might be beyond these limits."[94] There is here an element of cognitive failure, "the defeat of the ability to apprehend."[95] Shaw argues that the Sublime "seeks to ravish and intoxicate the audience."[96] Certainly this is true of audience responses to vampire stories as set out in Williamson's study.[97] The use of the sensual imagery of being overpowered to express the impact of the Sublime is paralleled in the capacity of horror to create both fear and desire. The vampire deity pictured in Amos meets the criteria of both Horror and the Sublime in this regard, for the divine is both feared and desired. The divine day of theophany creates enormous fear for those who are the objects of divine warfare, yet a worse fate is the absolute silence of God recorded in Amos 8. Here the vast aimless search for a deity who is no longer to be found represents an existential desire to encounter the other as a means of finding one's own identity.

God as the object of fear and desire in the Samarian vampiric thus unites the themes of sublimity and horror. This move aligns positive with negative, reminiscent of Shaw's comment that the Sublime is "the result of the co-implication of seemingly natural opposites: life/death, unity and fragmentation."[98] Treating the topics of the Sublime and Horror as in some way linked allows for the view that sublimity can be encountered via the contemplation of scenes of violence. It can be argued that the text itself is performative and not just literature that can be performed since a horror story realizes the divine–human encounter, even under the threat of annihilation. This viewpoint brings the reader back to the thought of Pile. In his approach, imaginaries are the means by which cities perform themselves, by managing their spatial existence.

Blood-work, Occult Geography and a Vampiric Imaginary

Pile regards the city-as-phantasmagoria as specifically a place of bodies and blood.[99] Carrying out blood-work, cities manage the reality and

94. Philip Shaw, *The Sublime* (New York: Routledge, 2006), 2.

95. Ibid., 3.

96. Ibid., 14.

97. In the third chapter of his *Lure*, Williamson surveys fans' assessment of the significance of vampire representations in the media, showing that there is often considerable empathy between the fans and the vampires as portrayed in film and television.

98. Shaw, *Sublime*, 25.

99. Pile, *Body*, 169.

morality of death—a topic which carries with it a large emotional charge. For Pile, a vampiric imaginary registers the "efforts of cities to marginalize, deintensify and localize the facts of death and mortality in such a way that the city has a life after death."[100] To survive, a city must "feed on itself," negotiating its mortality through a killing instinct.[101] That is indeed what the divine violence of Amos deals with, matching the aggressive acts of Samaria's elite and their consequences against the intended death-dealing of a warrior deity.

Pile notes that cities are sites where dreams are vital and that these dreams carry out complex emotional tasks on behalf of inhabitants.[102] Urban imaginaries are the tools for performing this work: an idea which can be linked with Williamson's attitude to the place of melodrama as the context for a vampiric profile which is both romantic and destructive. A melodrama involving vampires carries the harsh reality of death and the disappearance of human lives, while also providing a softening light to the inevitability of death, allowing it possibly to have a kind face. The blood-work of the vampire offers strategies for handling death within cities. The blood-work of the book of Amos pushes this issue of strategy in two directions. On the one hand, it engages with the forces of nature and their energies, and on the other, with human activity at the heart of a city community. It is the character of the deity which ultimately performs the task of holding these parallel modes together, thus carrying through the blood-work. The violence of the city is managed by reference to the bloodthirsty image of a theophanic warrior God, promoting the value of the occult as a medium for reflection on matters of life and death.

The setting of the urban prophetic imaginary in Amos is ultimately that of a world torn apart by invasion and then reshaped by the interaction of imperial strategies within a local region. The textual universe which mediates this imaginary in which urban continuity is a dangerous and difficult concept for the living to negotiate is shot through with dark and sombre tones, in which darkness is set above light. The textual universe so engendered is dangerous for the character, God, insofar as violence might appear to be the only viable characterization of the deity. It does, however, carry the burden of a religious world in meltdown, while yet offering the message that there may still be some communal good emanating from a continuing belief in a particular transcendent being.

---

100.   Ibid.
101.   Ibid., 170.
102.   Ibid., 167.

Yet, if the image of inherent violence in Amos provides a dangerous inheritance for the character of the deity, so it is also dangerous for the readers of the book who may embrace such a profile as the major perspective to be had on the person of God, the bottom line of human experience of the divine. It may be better to view the text as providing one, albeit very significant, image of God. Its task is that of social performance in times of particular political need. It is an image which successfully provides the view that when human affairs no longer offer a clear social identity, when meaning turns ambivalent, poised between certainty and loss, the image of a transcendent Other, comforting in that very Otherness, can produce a means for managing grief. Even the association of the origins of that sorrow with the transcendent provides hope that the human being is not totally alone in an impersonal world, lost endlessly in the "bitter day." If the deity can be allowed to be violent, then violence itself can be a boundaried event. But this is a fine line of distinction within the blood-work of cities. Move too far across the line between life and death and death becomes so vast a reality, so cosmic, and so disembodied that it takes over the whole identity of divinity, in an excess of meaning.

In Pile's psychological terms the vampire in the city is an example of how cities cleanse and transform themselves in order to survive. The performance of blood-work is an aspect of the practice of occult geography,[103] and that concept in turn relates to the idea that the city can be perceived as a Subject, a living organism which must deal with its actions, but also with its inner emotional and psychological health. In this context divine violence performs a sanitary function by allowing expression to emotions which simmer below the surface of city life and threaten the fragmentation of the community. Historical events challenge a city's belief in its inherited sense of stability and permanence while also encouraging the social Subject to look directly at the transgressive and excessive aspects of human living. This in turn can produce a fresh and nuanced understanding of urban self-identity. Both the reality of death as the excess for life and the need to find a place for this truth within emotional understanding find expression in the city-as-vampire, as well as in the image of the deity as the vampire in the city.

103. Ibid., 172–76.

INDEXES

INDEX OF REFERENCES

INDEX OF AUTHORS